Why Catholics Can't Sing

Why Catholics Can't Sing

The Culture of Catholicism
and the Triumph of Bad Taste

THOMAS DAY

CROSSROAD • NEW YORK

1992

The Crossroad Publishing Company
370 Lexington Avenue, New York, NY 10017

Printed in the United States of America
Typesetting output: TEXSource, Houston

Library of Congress Cataloging-in-Publication Data

Day, Thomas.
    Why Catholics can't sing : the culture of Catholicism and the
triumph of bad taste / Thomas Day.
        p.   cm.
    Includes bibliographical references.
    ISBN 0-8245-1035-6; 0-8245-1153-0 (pbk.)
    1. Catholics—United States—Religious life. 2. Catholics—United
States—Social life and customs. 3. Catholics—United States—
Attitudes. 4. Church music—Catholic Church. 5. Church music—
United States. 6. Catholic Church—United States—History—20th
century. 7. Catholic Church—History—1965- 8. United States—
Church history—20th century. 9. United States—Popular culture.
I. Title.
BX1406.2.D39 1990
282'.73—dc20
                                                    90-36696
                                                        CIP

Contents

v

Preface

For the insights, anecdotes, suggestions, and inspired outbursts which helped to shape this book, I am indebted to many individuals, especially John Glavin, Theresa Donahue, Thomas Donahue, Brother James Loxham, John Coakley, Peter Fagan, Richard Marquise, Ann Davidson, Mary McFadden, Sister Prudence Croke, Sister Anna Marie Flusche, Reverend David Gallagher, Reverend Michael Barber, S.J., Jane Bethune, Justus George Lawler, and Michael Leach. I am also very grateful to Sister Lucille McKillop and Sister Sheila Megley. Rose Napoli and Reverend George B. McCarthy provided me with the good example which only made the bad example of others more irritating. The Most Reverend Rembert Weakland was kind enough to send me copies of his articles. I am especially grateful to my wife and children for their help, observations, and patience.

A few brief portions of this book appeared in articles I have published: "Meanwhile in Church Music," *America* (December 16, 1972); "Twentieth-Century Church Music: An Elusive Modernity," *Communio: International Catholic Review* (Fall, 1979); "Why Can't Catholics Sing," *America* (May 21, 1983); "The 'Kitsch Revival': When the Congregation Prays Twice," *Commonweal* (March 8, 1985, with responses included in the May 3 issue); "A National Catholic Hymnal," *The American Organist* (October, 1986). I wish to thank these journals for their kind permission to quote from these articles.

All quotations from the *Constitution on the Sacred Liturgy* in this book are taken from *The Documents of Vatican II*, ed. Walter M. Abbott, S.J. and Joseph Gallagher (New York: America Press, 1966).

I have been reprimanded for using old-fashioned terms, such as "celebrant" instead of "presider," "Offertory" instead of "Presentation of the Gifts," "hymnal" instead of "song/service book," "Sanctus" instead of "Holy, holy," and so on. Some Catholics reject these traditional expres-

vii

sions as remnants of a warped theology, but I assure the reader that I use them only for the sake of variety or brevity.

Friends, colleagues, correspondents, and people I hardly know supplied many of the anecdotes related in this book. To protect the privacy of all involved, I have changed the details of these stories. I should also add that inspiration for this book usually came when I was observing things far from home.

The negative reaction to this book will follow a predictable format. The points that I have made — A, B, and C — will be ignored. I shall be excoriated for not mentioning D, E, and F (which do not fit into the limited scope of this book) and for implying G, H, and I (which are nowhere suggested in these pages). I can only request that the enraged reader be patient and see this book as part of a necessary debate — a debate which is not always encouraged.

1

The Opening Theme

Contemplate this very odd situation.

Today, a large number of Roman Catholics in the United States who go to church regularly — perhaps the majority — rarely or barely sing any of the music. (I have heard a congregation of fifty elderly Episcopalians produce more volume than three hundred Roman Catholics.) If you think about it, this stands out as a most curious development in the history of Christianity.

What could possibly cause this odd behavior of American Catholics? The problem is certainly not one of unfamiliarity. The "new music" and the practice of singing during a liturgy were introduced into the American "mainstream" parish over twenty years ago. By now, after all these years of relentless repetition, Catholic congregations must surely know *Praise to the Lord* by heart, and yet, in the typical parish, I would say that two-thirds of the congregation ignores it. Are American Catholics offering some kind of resistance to the liturgical innovations that hit them in the 1960s? If we can judge from all the polls, the answer is no. Most Catholics say they are in favor of "the changes," even though they do not seem to ratify them in song. What is going on here? Why do the polls tell us one thing and why does a visit to almost any parish seem to tell us that a sullen rebellion is taking place? Why won't Catholics sing?

I always ask that question whenever I find myself in conversation with the person-in-charge — the pastor, the parish music director, the chancery official. My question, I find, produces visible uneasiness. I have mentioned the taboo topic. I have brought up the matter of the skeleton in the closet, the drunk in the family, the disability that nobody is supposed

1

to mention. The more polite answers to my query usually circle around the same few issues:

"We need twenty more years." (Twenty more years of *Praise to the Lord*, before it sinks in?) "And, you see, Catholic parishes are a mixed bag of those who are strong in faith and those who are weak." (If the volume of singing measures the strength or weakness of faith, then American Catholicism is spiritually bankrupt.) "You know, many of the smaller Protestant churches don't exactly do a great job either." (Irrelevant and untrue.) "Compared to where they were twenty-five years ago, the people have come a long way." (Accurate, but things seem to have leveled off.) "They're doing wonderful things over there at St. Wilbur's parish. You should visit that place." (The oasis only makes the desert look even more barren.)

For reasons I have never been able to understand, the person-in-charge sometimes responds to my question with downright hostility:

"Get your priorities straight. We are not supposed to go to Mass for the music. Unlike other religions, we Catholics have not made music the center of our worship. Besides, everything is just fine. There is no problem."

Whether hostile or friendly, the person-in-charge invariably manages to maneuver the conversation to the question I dread: "And you, Mr. Day, what line of work are you in?"

"I . . . am a musician."

That does it. A smile comes across the face of the person-in-charge. Yes, the musician. Troublesome people. They can be such perfectionists, and most of them want to bring back the Latin Mass anyway.

"Mr. Day, times have changed. You see, the purpose of the Eucharist is not to provide an occasion for performances of beautiful music and concerts in church. Instead . . . "

I listen respectfully, knowing that I have lost that round. The person-in-charge is now also in charge of this situation. I try not to mention that I am an organist, a member of the American Guild of Organists, a holder of a Ph.D. in musicology from Columbia University, and a college teacher. That would completely discredit me. ("You people are the enemy!" one pious and well-educated Catholic once screamed at me. "Musicians like you ruined the idea of true religious music for centuries." This, I find, is a widely held opinion.)

By now, the person-in-charge is trying very hard to keep a tolerant and superior smile from turning into a grin. "Please do not misunderstand me," I reply. "I am not talking about bringing Beethoven's *Missa Solemnis* into church. And, for the record, I do not consider myself a particularly liberal or conservative Catholic. I'm not even sure that I wear any label, except 'concerned Catholic layman.' I would just like to know why congregational singing in Catholic parishes generally does not seem to have any zest at all. Why are all those other people staring into space, when they're supposed to be singing?"

I win that round. But very soon things take a turn for the worse. The person-in-charge and I start to chat about all kinds of musical matters: hymnals, new music, new publications, what's happening here and there. Then we begin to plan. (Oh, the joys of planning!) We are having a grand time matching this hymn with that Eucharistic Prayer for this feast in that church. Like urban planners letting their imaginations go wild, we dream extravagant dreams about an invigorated American Catholicism of the future, a church alive with liturgical excitement. Our ingenious coordination of liturgical and musical technology thrills us.

Now, at this point in our tête-à-tête, it would be so healthy if a little boy could enter the room and try to interrupt us. We would, of course, ignore the child and perhaps not even realize he was there, so absorbed would we be in our cleverness. But let us imagine that the little boy is insistent. He tugs at my sleeve and says, "Look! The emperor has no clothes!"

The little boy is right. A great many people in Catholic churches do not even open their mouths to sing — ever. Whole families, devout people who go to church every week, do not even pick up the hymnal.

To stand in the middle of a Catholic congregation, surrounded by row after row of people ignoring music they are supposed to sing, can be an unsettling experience; it looks like something from the theater of the absurd. When hundreds of parishioners packed into a church do not even make an attempt to sing *Silent Night* — something I have witnessed — you have a religious, social, and cultural breakdown of astounding proportions.

Over the years, this noncooperation, this malaise, this constant display of failure has caused enormous damage and will continue to do so, yet very little is being done to understand the underlying reasons for this awkward situation. Most of the people-in-charge and the experts still go on at great length about the beauties of the emperor's new clothes. Some books and articles might contain a brief reference to the problem ("Congregational singing is not all that it could be.") and they might propose elaborate schemes to "get the people to sing," but the general policy is to pretend that this congregational silence, this blatant malfunction, does not exist.

But perhaps some believers are not even aware of any failure. The majority of American Catholics, especially the older ones, have an extremely limited experience with the whole idea of congregational singing. They have even come to think of the pale noise they hear on Sunday as the norm, "what you have to expect if you want to be a Catholic." They cannot imagine anything better, because they have never heard anything better. Someone like me impresses them as an elitist and a troublemaker, "who just does not understand," or a cynic who takes pleasure in discovering the imperfections of other people.

In my younger days I worked my way through school as a substitute organist. Sometimes this meant playing for a Protestant service one week and for a Catholic Mass the next. The contrast between these two services — occasionally the different way of singing identical hymns — left me somewhat bewildered. Why, I asked myself, did the small Presbyterian church make such a joyful noise, while the Catholics sounded almost in pain? At another time in my life I lived in Europe. (I was a Fulbright Scholar at the University of Munich in West Germany.) In the German-speaking areas of Europe I heard Catholic congregations sing so powerfully that the floor seemed to shake. In France, at least before the Second Vatican Council, congregations managed to sing old plainchant melodies quite well. I knew a little about the traditions of congregational singing among Slavic Catholics. All of this experience made me ask that obvious question: "Why can they sing well, while we cannot." Only a few American Catholics, I discovered, were asking that same question, because only a few had ever had that opportunity to compare.

I should say right here, very early, that this book is not a "hatchet job." I am not an ex-priest who would like to settle some old scores. I have never even been a seminarian. Furthermore, I am not a crusader who wants to make every Roman Catholic sing like an opera star in church. As I mentioned earlier, I am just a concerned American Catholic layman who has searched for reasons behind the uninspired singing at most (certainly not all) Catholic liturgies. In many respects I have tried to take the position of that little boy who interrupts the pomposities of the two experts; that is, I have tried to approach the whole issue with a certain amount of detachment, objectivity, and even innocence; I have put myself in the role of the outsider. Needless to say, I have failed repeatedly in my efforts to bring a cool detachment to my analysis.

The reader should be warned that this is a personal, somewhat autobiographical book based very much on my own experiences and those of people I know. For this reason, I should explain something about my background and my bias. I was born and raised in the Philadelphia area and attended private Catholic schools there. I have lived in New York, California, New England, and Europe. Sometimes, when I think about my "typical American Catholic experience," I realize that it does not necessarily apply to Catholicism in the Midwest or South. The churches I knew in Philadelphia differed in many ways from, let us say, "ethnic" parishes in Chicago or Milwaukee. My generalizations, therefore, are to be surrounded with many exceptions.

In a sense, this is not a book about music but about a people struggling with their destiny. The uneven singing of the American Catholic congregation is really a symptom, not the disease itself. It is the result of a human history that stretches across the centuries, not the result of some recent artistic or musical development. These historical realities intrude into every Catholic parish and every Mass. Because the Catholic past is so important, many parts of this book seem to start in remote corners of history and (logically, I hope) somehow lead to the parish congregation which politely resists *Praise to the Lord*.

In writing this book I have had to presume that the reader is familiar with the Second Vatican Council and its consequences. When I talk with people in their twenties or younger, I realize that I can no longer presume that everybody knows what I mean when I say "Latin Mass" or liturgies with virtually no verbal or musical participation from the congregation. A large number of American Catholics, I have to report, do not know what is meant by such terms as "good, standard hymns, vigorously sung," "Gregorian chant," "pipe organ," or "sung Mass." Some bewildered readers may have to visit various churches of different denominations and listen to recordings to become familiar with music once considered the common inheritance of all Roman Catholics.

2

The People without Music

"That Shit"

In the early 1970s a friend of mine attended Mass in one of Philadelphia's grand old parishes, an immense pile of stone built to last for eternity. In the same pew, right next to him, was an elderly lady who energetically fingered her rosary beads all during Mass. She stood, sat, and knelt with everyone else, but her thoughts seemed to be far removed from the activity around her.

The time came for the Handshake of Peace, one of those "new things" which made everyone feel a bit silly. My friend turned to the elderly lady at this point and, holding out his hand in friendship, said, "May the peace of the Lord be with you." The old lady scowled. She looked at the proffered hand as if it were diseased. "I don't believe in that shit," she replied and, without missing a breath, went back to the quiet mumbling of her rosary.

Before we start imagining that the old lady must have been some charming fossil from another eon, let us remember that as late as 1963 nearly every Roman Catholic bishop in the United States would have agreed with her. They did not believe in "that shit," and neither did the majority of the faithful. Something called Liturgical Renewal, in some form or other, had been building for more than a century, but the American bishops and nearly all the lower clergy kept their distance, especially in the case of congregational singing. And as far as the average Catholic layperson was concerned, Liturgical Renewal before the Second Vatican Council generally came down to one thing: about once a year a sermon would contain a sentence or two on the usefulness of following the celebrant's actions with a missal. Very few American Catholics — clergy or

6

laity — saw a need for anything beyond that optional use of a missal; certainly it was hard to find anyone who suggested that people in the congregation should do anything *required*, such as shake hands.

The elderly lady with the rosary knew, as I did, a religion that approached worship in a way which seemed perfectly logical, at the time, and which seemed to need no improvement. In the front of the church a man, who kept his back to the congregation most of the time, whispered his way through prescribed prayers in Latin. Behind him, in the pews, a kind of laissez-faire spirituality prevailed. Some people, like the elderly lady, said the rosary. Some paged through battered prayerbooks stuffed with holy cards. (The prayers in these books usually had little to do with the actual liturgy taking place.) A number of people, but certainly not the majority, followed the priest's actions with their own missals. Many, many people just stared into space, lost in "their thoughts."

In 1960, if someone had asked that lady or her bishop why things were done that way, the answer might have circled around many ideas, but all of them could have been reduced to just one point: "This was the way things were done because this was the logical expression of what Catholics believed." The Latin Mass and the silent congregation were the inevitable consequence of faith. Tampering with the received forms of worship really meant tampering with the faith.

The logic of this argument was implicitly or tacitly accepted by most American Catholics, but what everyone forgot was that faith must be filtered through culture. Just as my ideas come to the reader through the vocabulary and grammar of the English language (plus the whole outlook on life inherent in that language), so too religious ideas always have to be "translated" into a cultural language before people can approach them. Between faith, on one side, and a representation of that faith, on the other, is culture.

"Culture," unfortunately, brings up the image of dowagers in diamonds at the opera house; it now often implies artistic masterpieces reserved only for the elite. Mention this word to some pious Catholics and they will immediately slice you down. For them, "culture" (Renaissance popes contemplating madonnas by Raphael) represents something degenerate and a betrayal of the church's mission to preach the gospel. "The church wasn't founded in order to transmit Western culture!" and "The church is not a museum!" are statements heard in today's most indignant sermons.

Perhaps I can soften the impact of the word and rid it of its unfortunate connotations by pointing out the following: "Culture," in its original sense, means cultivation of the land. (You will find the word on a set of directions describing how to grow a plant or a bush.) From this image of tilling the soil the meaning of the word expanded to include the breeding of animals, keeping of livestock, the building of dwellings, the establishment of laws, the development of customs, and indeed the whole ordering of society — all the things necessary to keep control over the land and nature. People who identify themselves with a particular culture have, in effect, made choices that help them to find a sense and an order in the chaos of the universe. Their culture is what they choose to remember and cherish. Culture, then, is a way of life, a system of signs and symbols which people call their own. Individuals communicate with one another through the culture's symbols (language, dress, manners, etc.). Christianity and all other religions of the world did not just announce their messages in mathematically neutral formulas; instead, they "acted out" these messages, they "translated" them into the signs and symbols of culture.

The elderly lady with the rosary did not spend her spare time reading liturgical treatises and she certainly did not know much about the theological complexities of her faith. Nevertheless, the signs and symbols of the old liturgy — conducted in Latin and watched by everyone in silence — very powerfully communicated the essence of her faith in a way that she and her culture understood perfectly. The church had given her a style of worship which harmonized beautifully with all of her cultural values. She was perfectly content. In those days, the majority of American Catholics were secure in the knowledge that the tomblike silence of the parish Mass was the best of all possible liturgical worlds.

American Catholics justifiably took pride in belonging to the "one true church" located in the "greatest country on earth." There were other nations, but, according to popular mythology, these countries had inadequate plumbing and were civilized only to the degree to which they had adopted the American Way of Life. If Catholics did things a little differently in other countries, it was because they were backward, or simply wrong.

My memory stirs. I can recall the case of a particular priest who went into culture shock when he celebrated Mass once in a parish for Polish Catholics. (This was years ago.) "Those people sing all during Mass!" he fumed. The quaint peasant hymns brought over from the old country were, as far as he was concerned, just that: musical intrusions into the silent Mass by backward people from an old (backward) country. The colorful fiestas in Italy and the gaudy processions in Latin America embarrassed Catholic tourists. I was raised to believe that, on the continent of Europe, Catholicism was almost extinct. The flashy organ playing in French churches or thunderous hymns in the churches of Bavaria (not to mention the orchestras for High Mass) were unmistakable signs of decadence. And then there was that elegant, haughty monsignor in New York. "French Catholic congregations," I innocently informed him, "actually sing parts of the High Mass, and perhaps this practice will catch on in the United States." (This was in the early 1960s.) "Ah yes," he said, lowering his eyelids slightly, "They have such...*flair*. But who needs that?"

Catholics in most of the rest of the world may have had *flair*, but it was highly suspect, my teachers informed me. The church supposedly acknowledged the weakness of the faith among these foreigners when it tolerated all manner of bizarre religious practices; there was the hope that, with prayer and good example, foreigners would come to their senses, abandon their strange ways, and realize the truth: genuine Catholicism expressed itself most profoundly — and correctly — in the silent Mass, a liturgy untouched by the human noise of music.

American Catholics not only accepted the idea of the Mass without a note of music, they boasted about it. This was their mark of distinction. It set them apart from their Protestant neighbors who went to church "only for the music" and who had made music "the center of their worship." To a largely working-class Catholicism, music was the religion of the employers. The special attention paid to it in other denominations was a sign of their spiritual corruption. American Catholics, in contrast, had a higher and purer form of worship with a message so awesome that it could only be watched in silence and communicated through the most exalted symbols. When we recall this aspect of Catholic liturgical life in the United States, we have to keep in mind that Catholics in Germany, Austria, and Eastern Europe had a long history of participating in the liturgy (at least the Low Mass) by singing hymns, chorales, and pieces that paraphrased or approximated the Latin that the priest said quietly at the altar. We also have to remind ourselves that the Vatican, especially during the reign of Pius XII, had enthusiastically approved of this phenomenon called "congregational participation" (which included the "Dialog Mass," the High Mass sung in part by the congregation, lectors who read the Epistle and Gospel of the Mass in the vernacular, and commentators). But with rare, oddball exceptions, parishes in the United States spurned these attempts to take away their beloved silent Mass.

"Waste Not" and "Control"

If the silent Mass, unblemished by music or any response from the congregation, seemed bland and even absurd from a theological point of view, it was at least accepted in this country because it resonated with the cultural values that many people cherished. And what were those values? Probably four words can sum them up: *Waste not. Control thyself.*

The Catholicism of my youth had lost its love of Baroque ostentation and had become obsessive about "waste." By the 1950s the religion which had defied the laws of gravity with Chartres cathedral and had lovingly adorned parish churches with great artworks was now constructing grim warehouses for worship. It was almost as if someone had decreed that the people who used these structures would be punished by the banality of the architecture. The bishops and pastors who made the architectural decisions quite rightly wanted to avoid the mistakes of their predecessors. The old stone basilicas in the cities were losing parishioners rapidly and not paying for themselves; all of that effort, all of those nickels and dimes from hard-working parishioners, had gone into erecting monumental edifices that were almost empty now. Nobody wanted to be accused of wasting the church's resources and taking funds away from parochial schools. Those yearnings to express one's religious fervor in some kind of physical statement (monumental or modest) would not be permitted to come out in such wasteful forms as art and architecture.

Of course, just what constituted waste could be subject to the most peculiar interpretations.

In 1964 I was shown a college chapel donated by a wealthy Catholic businessman in the 1950s. My host pointed out that the structure had a quality and a solidity found only in older buildings. No expense had been spared. The thickness of the walls was called to my attention. The finest workmanship had gone into everything, from stained-glass window to pew. (The chapel was large enough to seat a few hundred people.)

"Where is the organ?" I asked.

My host showed me a miserable Hammond electronic organ — the "burp box" as some musicians call it, the kind of instrument one might find in a sleazy cocktail lounge. It was stuck in a corner. In this chapel, built only a few years before the Second Vatican Council met, no place had been set aside for either a pipe organ or a choir. On a per-square-foot basis this was the most expensive kind of church that could be constructed in the mid-twentieth century, and it contained the cheapest kind of organ, an electronic fuzz-maker.

Stonework, marble, gold, and stained glass were all considered the things that made a church a church. They had a high priority. Liturgical music was tolerated as a nicety or a ritual requirement, but anything beyond the minimum was scorned as a waste, especially in the decade before Vatican II and in the northeast corner of the United States. Here and there, a clever pastor realized that, with an emphasis on simplicity, a parish could have a perfectly respectable form of liturgical music without spending much money. But the majority of pastors and their parishioners seemed to think that the ability to endure musical pain in church was the mark of the devout Catholic who, unlike his non-Catholic neighbors, did not believe in wasting money on music. Besides, the parish that spent money on a new pipe organ or a qualified music director quickly got the reputation for being presumptuous and for putting on airs.

The philosophy of "Waste not" really grew out of American Catholicism's other cherished cultural ideal: "Control thyself." What was so remarkable about Catholic worship in this country before the 1960s was not the silence or the absence of music (most of the time) but the control over the emotions, the curious suppression of enthusiasm.

This word "enthusiasm," I realize, carries with it unflattering connotations of people dancing in the aisles or shouting spontaneous exclamations of joy. Certainly, in the eighteenth century "enthusiasm" was an insulting term used by Anglicans to describe the disorderly services of Methodists. Even today, "enthusiasm" can suggest a certain excess, eccentricity, and, above all, "losing control." Yet, in spite of all this, enthusiasm has always been an essential ingredient of Christianity and Christian worship. To be a Christian one must be, in some way or other, "enthusiastic," and worship without "enthusiasm" is not Christian. I hasten to add that this enthusiasm can take many different forms, including some that look perfectly calm. Whatever form it comes in and no matter how we analyze it (physical release, psychological defect, the working of the Holy Spirit, etc.), we can say this much about enthusiasm in religion: on the eve of the Second Vatican Council, American Catholicism went out of its way to hide all manifestations of this troubling aspect of Christianity.

Divine Lunacy

Perhaps, before we analyze this "missing" enthusiasm in worship, we should first look at the various shapes that Christian enthusiasm can assume. We must begin with the Acts of the Apostles, where we read that the disciples of Jesus rushed out of a house on Pentecost and began to "speak in tongues." They were "filled with the Holy Spirit" — with a wild enthusiasm which some onlookers mistook for drunkenness. The Pauline epistles make it clear that this glossolalia (the gift of "speaking in tongues") had an important place in the early church; at the same time, they also reveal that Paul was uneasy about the whole thing. He found that he had to patch up misunderstandings between Christians who had the gift (*charisma*) of "speaking in tongues" and those who did not. He had to remind his flock that the most impressive demonstration of Spirit-filled glossolalia meant nothing if the "speaker" lacked charity.

Speaking in tongues flourished as long as Christians worshiped in small communities and in private homes. It did not, however, survive for long, probably because, as Christian worship became more structured, the believer who began to babble ecstatically only created a disturbance. And yet, speaking in tongues, this outburst of enthusiasm in worship, never disappeared entirely; it only changed into more manageable forms, adapted for Christianity's needs under different circumstances:

Anyone who has ever attended a Latin High Mass in an old-fashioned Benedictine monastery has really attended a charismatic event. This style of worship makes us realize that the early Christian church had taken the wild fires of charismatic zeal and compressed them into the intense flame of monastic chant. The monks do not simply move from one place to another in the sanctuary; they really dance. They do not speak their religious sentiments; instead, they utter them in this strange singing, unlike any other singing on earth. Through the medium of music, the monks become "filled with the Spirit." They are madmen, breaking out in a focused, unified, musical glossolalia.

The early Christians at, let us say, Corinth watched and listened as one of them burst forth in a spectacular glossolalia; this individual's personal religious "performance" ("virtuoso performance?") inspired others, emotionally and spiritually. In eighteenth-century Austria peasants watched and listened as a choir, soloists, and orchestra performed a rollicking *Gloria* by Haydn. Inwardly, the peasants danced and their hearts leapt with joy. By the eighteenth century the gifted "speaker in tongues" had become a musical setting of a Mass text.

The "Hallelujah Chorus" from Handel's *Messiah* is one of the most enthusiastic and charismatic pieces of music ever written. While one part of the choir tries to proceed with a conventional Baroque work, another group in the choir appears to break things up with "spontaneous" shouts of "Hallelujah!" or "Forever." This piece is glossolalia in a form that Handel's audience could grasp. The same thing could be said about thousands of religious compositions by Bach, Beethoven, Palestrina, and many others. The choir is ecstatically "speaking in tongues" and the enthusiasm it creates is infectious.

In Protestant churches and in the Catholic churches of Europe where the congregation speaks German or a Slavic language, a hymn begins with a surge of power, "the rushing mighty wind" that worshipers can almost feel. The joy and energy released here, regardless of the particular style of the music, are examples of pure, charismatic enthusiasm.

And that elderly lady mumbling contentedly over her rosary — if that was not "speaking in tongues," what is? She was enthusiastic about her religion and she wanted everyone to see it. The liturgist might have complained that her form of witness was too private, too personal. But because of her culture, this was the proper way her inner joy could come (almost) to the surface. This was her glossolalia, her Gregorian chant, her hymn, her "Hallelujah Chorus." She probably strengthened the faith of many people who just watched her in church. She was as inspiring as the most dazzling charismatic performers in Paul's day.

The Christian Pentecost has never really stopped. Christians will always be lunatics who confound the crowd with their preposterous expressions of enthusiasm. The dignified High Anglican service, the monastic ritual, the backwoods Baptist tent revival, the rosary, elaborate cathedrals, hymns, and so on are all the work of "lunatics" who have become "drunk on the new wine" of the Christian message. The brand of enthusiasm depends on the cultural values. One person will practice a particular variety of charismatic enthusiasm which looks somewhat odd to a person who practices another.

After this long detour, let us return to the problem we encountered earlier in this chapter: "Where was this necessary Christian enthusiasm in the American Catholicism that existed just before the Second Vatican Council?" The answer is, "Underneath the surface." Catholics in the United States had become more and more reluctant to display enthusiasm, of any sort, in church. A subdued faith, one that burned intensely but quietly in private, had emerged as the ideal for mainstream American Catholics.

"Waste not" and "Control thyself" doomed American Catholic church music. If the Second Vatican Council had not met, music would have virtually disappeared from the majority of churches, except for pastel background music during communion and wedding marches; the decorously enthusiastic High Mass would have survived only in seminaries and some convents. By the year 2000 the almost total absence of music in a particular parish would have been widely interpreted as a sign of a well-managed institution, where money was not wasted and where the parishioners, completely in control of their emotions, did not need such stimulants to devotion. In other words, the Catholic population would have congratulated itself for being "the people without music," without new church buildings of artistic merit, without joyful liturgies — in short, without many ways to express religious enthusiasm as a community.

There was, to be sure, a reaction to (one might even say alarm about) this trend. Various papal statements and Vatican decrees in the first part of this century consistently encouraged some form of "participation" from the congregation. At one time, forward-looking parishes used to teach Gregorian chant to the children in the parochial school so that the youngsters could sing at Mass. A few Catholics prepared for the wave of the future: the High Mass sung in part by the congregation. All of this and much more came under the strange heading of Liturgical Renewal. From today's perspective it would appear that this renewal (this healthy reaction) was on the way to inevitable triumph, a victory only hastened by the Second Vatican Council. But this perspective is a mirage. Without the council, Liturgical Renewal did not have a chance in the United States. Slowly but effectively that American Catholic culture would have suffocated it. Renewal, of any sort, implied enthusiasm and the understanding that things could be better. The assimilated, thoroughly Americanized Catholic (ca. 1960) thanked heaven repeatedly that he or she was *not* enthusiastic (like Holy Rollers, Protestant hymn shouters, Catholic foreigners, and others who needed to display their piety in public); thanks were also offered for belonging to a perfect church that did not need renewal.

Here is one fact which illustrates perfectly the character of this culture developed by "the people without music." In the year 1963, when the Second Vatican Council promulgated the *Constitution on the Sacred Liturgy*, very few Catholic congregations in the United States sang Christmas carols at a Mass on Christmas day. I doubt if there were, in the Northeast, more than a dozen parishes where the congregation was asked to sing *O Come, All Ye Faithful* or *Silent Night*. The church did not allow the singing of vernacular music during the High Mass but song in the local language was permitted during the Low Mass. A Polish or Austrian Catholic congregation took it for granted that one sang beloved old hymns on Christmas but, incredibly, most American Catholics sang nothing at all on this great feast.

In the early 1960s, a publisher in the United States issued a "Mass Card" which contained Christmas carols and the congregation's parts for the Latin Mass. These cards allowed a congregation to "participate,"

well within the strictest interpretation of church law. I remember showing the Christmas "Mass Card" to saintly Father H and watching him
turn pale. "The Mass does not *need* music," he muttered. I remember
showing the card to my relatives. "But we are not Protestants," was
their reaction to the idea that a Catholic congregation would sing hymns
(which happened to be Roman Catholic in origin). I clearly remember
one of my Jesuit teachers deploring and belittling the notion that people
might want to sing carols in church on Christmas day. "Why, that would
take away from the importance of the consecration. . . . It's like gilding
the lily. . . . It's against canon law. . . . "

A congregation singing *O Come, All Ye Faithful* at a Christmas liturgy — this looks like a natural, obvious, logical, and perhaps inevitable
consequence of Christian enthusiasm. A good choir singing a Latin work
so beautifully that a congregation, although silent, feels an intimacy with
the music — that too appears to be natural, obvious, logical, and perhaps inevitable. But, by the 1950s most Catholics in the United States
had convinced themselves that such forms of Christian exuberance were
somehow immoral, or at least not for ordinary laypeople. To maintain
this control over enthusiasm took an enormous amount of repression.
By this, I do not mean "suppression," a sinister clerical plot to keep
the faithful silent and docile. Instead, I mean a self-imposed control, a
check on the emotions, a determination not to show what was hidden
underneath the surface. The Catholic hierarchy and pastors who had
steadfastly ignored Liturgical Renewal for as long as possible knew their
flock and served it well. The clergy correctly sensed that "mainstream"
Catholics in this country were inordinately proud of their self-control,
their "repression."

Behind this scorn for displays of enthusiasm, behind this deliberate
"self-repression" was a genuine sense of reverence. American Catholic
respect for the sacredness of the Mass and the holiness of the church
building went to the point where any music-making in church had to
be done with fear and trembling. When the congregation sang — at
Benediction, at private devotions, and sometimes even at Mass — the
repertory or the style of the music always suggested extreme caution. If
hymnbooks, back then, had contained specific performance instructions
for the organist, the wording would have gone something like this: "To
be played meekly, with a sense of blushing shame." *Holy God, We Praise
Thy Name* is a fine rousing hymn, but before the 1960s any Catholic
who belted it out — enthusiastically — would have been grabbed by
the ushers, taken to the church door, and thrown bodily onto the sidewalk. Singing in church came pretty close to presumption, but singing
energetically was outright blasphemy. (Exceptions were made during the

Second World War, when Catholic congregations sang patriotic songs in church quite powerfully.)

Many Europeans who came to the United States before the 1960s were stunned by the coldness of the liturgies in this country. The French expected glorious fountains of sound to come from the organ and, instead, heard only hushed performances of novena hymns. The Germans waited for the mighty chorales and, instead, heard only silence. The Austrians went to the cathedral or the biggest church in town and asked when there was a High Mass; they were told there was none. What all of these visitors were looking for was not necessarily grand music performed grandly but some signs of group enthusiasm. American Catholics, they discovered, boasted that they had no need for enthusiasm, especially as expressed in music. The streamlined American church was quietly stripping away these useless, wasteful affectations left over from the past (except in special places, such as seminaries). The Liturgical Renewal reformers were losing ground every day.

Oddly enough, one person who was not entirely pleased with this Waste-not, Control-thyself Catholicism was our elderly lady with the rosary. She grew up in the days when the building of the massive stone parishes was a communal effort, a proud sign of enthusiasm for all the world to see. She remembered High Masses with fifty altar boys, and each one in a spotless surplice. (She "participated" by ironing some of those white vestments and was proud that she could contribute to this liturgy in her own way.) But, alas, long before the Second Vatican Council, her church had begun to withdraw the cherished symbols of her old-fashioned enthusiasm. The new parishes looked so cheap, so temporary. Two quick Low Masses replaced the big High Mass that used to involve so many youngsters. The boys' choir disappeared years ago. (Catholic parishes in the United States probably got rid of or downgraded more choirs during the 1940s and 1950s than during the puritan purges of the 1960s.) Vespers was discontinued about the same time that the trolley cars were replaced by buses. The efficient Catholic culture of the 1950s had very little room for the kind of religious enthusiasm she had known in her earlier days.

... And then — was it in 1964? 1968? — the priest in the front of the church announced to the congregation that all the old cultural values would have to go. Everyone was to become vocally and outwardly enthusiastic, immediately.

A number of authors have written about this complex phenomenon called American Catholic culture. James Hennessey, S.J., provides a very useful survey of the facts and statistics in *American Catholicism: A History of the Roman Catholic Community in the United States* (1981). John Cogley, John Tracy Ellis, Thomas T. McAvoy, Theodore Maynard, John L. McKenzie, and Gary Wills also tell this same story, but each author sees it from a different perspective. J. F. Powers, although a writer of fiction, has produced the most fascinating, entertaining, and accurate description of American Catholicism's "mood" in the decades just before Vatican II. These writers and others describe a religion with a culture all its own, a culture that puzzled even Roman Catholics from other countries. Most historians and observers would agree that no one could even begin to understand the idea of American Catholic culture and its music without first encountering its most important feature, and that is Irish Catholicism.

3

The Irish Way

The Green Mainstream

While my friend was recounting the story of the lady who snubbed his offer of a handshake, I just knew that he would eventually add one essential detail: "And I suspect that she was as Irish as they come," he said.

If she had been an Italian and in Italy, she would have dressed in black and spent hours groaning in the back of the church. A devout Mexican woman of her age would have made pilgrimages to basilicas on her knees. A Methodist lady would have poured out her religious emotions in the singing of hymns, and she would have known dozens of them. But the lady with the rosary — and her culture — would have nothing to do with "displaying" devotion. Consequently, all her spiritual energies stayed within her and were released only in the quiet whispering of the rosary. I am in no way ridiculing her as an example of backwardness. I am only reminding the reader that, not long ago, she represented the norm among Catholics in the United States. Normal Catholics kept their piety bottled up, at least for the duration of the Mass, and this religious enthusiasm was seldom permitted to escape elsewhere — even, for example, in a choir acting on behalf of the congregation. This "normal" behavior was learned not from the Spanish or the French or the Austrians but from the Irish.

American Catholicism derives a great part of its character from Irish Catholicism. All one has to do is pick up the latest edition of the *Official Catholic Directory* and look at the lists of the bishops, heads of seminaries, and pastors who have shaped the American church. Irish names are conspicuously represented. Here and there, notably in the Midwest, other

18

ethnic groups have managed to hold on to distinctly non-Irish interpretations of Catholicism, but Irish Catholicism and the values of the Irish are considered the norm. Everything else — the Portuguese parish with its lavish festivals, the German parish with its powerful choral music — falls into the category of "exception" which will, it is hoped, eventually become assimilated into the American (i.e., Irish) style. This explains why you might meet a priest with a sonorous Polish last name and a mind that might as well have come from County Cork. This also explains why an American of Italian extraction (two generations removed from Ellis Island) will visit Italy and be scandalized by "the way those people behave in church" but will visit Ireland and feel very much at home in the churches there.

Any discussion of a particular group of human beings can easily turn into a mindless retelling of ethnic myths and stereotypes ("All Jews are..." "All Italians..."). In the case of the Irish the situation can be summed up in the apocryphal story of the corrupt political boss who ran into a bit of trouble with a grand jury. On the steps of the courthouse, this gentleman of Irish extraction was met by a swarm of reporters. "I just want you all to know," he announced indignantly, "that half the lies told about me are untrue." Half the lies told about the "Irish character" are indeed untrue; we can be somewhat skeptical of the other half, too. If we want to find out how the Irish have shaped American Catholicism, we must search for answers not in the vague territory of "ethnic character" but in history.

To be Irish is to be ever conscious of a history of tears and oppression. From the sixteenth century to the nineteenth, the Catholic Irish were the most systematically and ruthlessly suppressed people in all of Western Europe. English misrule over that unfortunate island will long stand out as one of the most miserable episodes in human history. The story of persecution and famine remains vivid to this day, even among "Irish-Americans" (to use a clumsy expression) who have never set foot on the Old Sod. Throughout the worst years of English oppression, the one institution which preserved a separate Irish identity was the outlawed Roman Catholic church. During that period, a priest, someone who had the same status as a criminal, would go down to the hedge in the fields or perhaps set up a makeshift altar in a barn and celebrate an illegal Mass. The faithful would come from miles around to attend. Their presence at this religious ceremony represented both an act of genuine devotion and also political defiance. Under the circumstances, singing was risky.

The image of a crowd silently standing in the drizzle to watch the Mass is a powerful one. A people could form a whole set of cultural values just from this. The ironic thing here is that this image goes back

even farther in history, to the centuries long before the English dominated Ireland. A rural and even nomadic people who lived in tribes
and clans, the Irish did not settle down in villages with parish churches
until relatively late in their history. The earliest Christian chapels in Ireland were tiny stone huts that could accommodate a priest or two. The
Mass took place within the little oratory and the people stood outside,
presumably in silence.

During the worst years of British domination, the Catholic Irish were,
for the most part, reduced to abject poverty, taxed heavily, and given
no room for private initiative. They were also cut off from artistic and
cultural developments in the Roman Catholic parts of Europe. A Bavar-
ian farmer saw nothing unusual about worshiping in an ornate Rococo
church; he thought it perfectly normal that the choir would sing a Mozart
Mass occasionally. In the eighteenth century, the Italian priest quietly
celebrated the Low Mass, while the town string players performed a
reverent concerto grosso in the choir loft. The Spanish added all kinds
of explosive Baroque decoration to their churches. The Catholic Irish,
in contrast, did not have any of these luxuries. Their worship had to be
discreet, even secret. The local landlords might have looked the other
way when their tenants watched a Mass being said in a barn, in the
fields down by the hedge, or in a hidden chapel (which everyone knew
about), but hymn singing, processions, or other conspicuous displays of
devotion would have provoked reprisals. The result of this situation was
the "secret Mass," with all enthusiasm hushed, a religious act touched
by fear and danger, a clandestine meeting of believers who dared not
call attention to their activities, a style of worship stripped of the forms
of artistic expression familiar to Catholics on the Continent.

One small fact will give us a good insight into the whole evolution of
Catholic Ireland's set of values on this matter of liturgy. After the Reformation, the Catholics of Dublin did not hear a bell ring from one of their
churches until 1815. From the sixteenth century until the nineteenth,
whenever they heard a bell, it was a sound coming from a Protestant
church. Church bells were something they associated with Protestants.
And also, when they heard hymns, pipe organs, and choral anthems,
they heard them coming from behind the doors of Protestant churches.
What must have sustained the Catholic Irish through these years of persecution was the knowledge that they did not need these things (bells,
hymns, etc.). Their faith was precisely that — faith, unadulterated by
amusements. Their belief, after all, brought them hardships. In their
opinion, the courageous and the strong kept the faith, while the weak,
lured away by music and other niceties, became apostates.

"The Mass does not *need* music." I heard this sentence many times in my youth; it was the standard response to any suggestion that the music of the Roman Catholic church in the United States could use some improvement. The theological point of view in those words rests on solid orthodoxy. But this statement was not meant to be theological. It was, instead, an expression of honest cultural preference and it followed logically from a history of the Irish associating religious music with the oppressors. The Catholic Irish farmer, during the years of persecution, heard the sound of the bell and the hymn coming from the Protestant church, but, as far as he was concerned, these things were not beautiful; they were a provocation, a slap in the face. The enthusiasm and jubilation of the music only rubbed in the bitter fact of *their* triumph and *his* defeat.

In the early nineteenth century, when they could worship freely and build their own churches, the Catholic Irish emerged, like Rip Van Winkle, from a long slumber (or nightmare) and suffered immediate "reentry" shock. After centuries of associating liturgy with suffering and silence, they now encountered new and strange music added to their silent Mass. Here was the painful Irish dilemma: How could they reconcile this lovely music with a culture built on the proud knowledge that they did not *need* such things?

There were exceptions — exceptional parishes, bishops, and choral conductors — but, before the Second Vatican Council, the Irish and their cousins in the United States acquired the reputation for being people who were frigidly indifferent to liturgical music, if not hostile. They did not *need* such things.

History, economics, and even geography might help to explain, in a very abstract way, the reasons why liturgy and liturgical music did not have what could be called a "normal" development among Irish Catholics on both sides of the Atlantic. But these explanations, perfectly adequate for the historian, somehow leave us unsatisfied. They seem to be missing the "human element." If we want to discover the human and the personal dynamics at work here, we have to look at human beings, and perhaps we can learn a great deal by listening to the story of my acquaintance Conrad (not his real name).

Intense, humorless Conrad. What a character! A passionately conservative Catholic and molded in the old "Irish-American" tradition, Conrad found himself one Sunday in Corpus Christi Church, near Columbia University in Manhattan. This is a charming building with white classical details and crystal chandeliers; it looks like a chapel in an Austrian palace, only much simpler. Thomas Merton was received into the church at Corpus Christi. I was married in that happy, sunny place.

Back in the early 1960s, when Conrad decided to attend High Mass at Corpus Christi, this was one of the rare American Catholic parishes which encouraged congregational participation. (We shall hear more about this later.) It was also one of a handful of Catholic parishes in the New York archdiocese with excellent music.

"I shall never set foot in that place again," Conrad vowed. "Never!" He was stiff with rage.

Dumbfounded, I asked him to describe the nature of his complaint.

"It's too Protestant," he snapped.

Too Protestant? In those days, the High Mass was in Latin almost from beginning to end. At Corpus Christi the choir sang the ornate Gregorian chant Propers. The congregation sang, with gusto, all of the chant responses and sometimes the chant versions of the Ordinary (Kyrie, Gloria, etc.). They did everything that Pius XII had recommended. Here was a church that had preserved, in the most conservative and sensitive way, the greatest traditions of Catholic worship — and conservative, traditionalist Conrad was furious. What did he want? The place was more Catholic than the pope. It took a little questioning, but eventually Conrad acknowledged the source of his irritation. As far as he was concerned, the whole liturgy was "too Anglican, too English."

Conrad's loathing of things English was founded on the notion that anything of quality, anything that exhibits "the best" in art or music is somehow English. He was not unique in believing that, to be a real Catholic, one must despise all music which sounds "English." In Conrad's mind — American, but formed centuries ago in the bogs of Ireland — ritual decorum, pomp and circumstance, and, above all, noble church music are the property of the queen of England. The very thought of noble religious music infuriated him. Nobility meant pretension; nobility was English.

The "Foreigners"

In the nineteenth and early twentieth centuries, wave after wave of immigrants came to the United States and most of them soon discovered that the "ethnic character" they had brought with them would get very little room to grow in the new land. Many of the Catholic immigrants from the Continent suffered the worst kind of culture shock when they went to their local church and discovered there, not the familiar old folk customs and festivals, but the Immense Irish Silence. This was the start of a most unedifying feud. From a safe distance we, today, can say that it was all a very complex and inevitable clash of cultures, a natural struggle over style and turf. To those who did not have the advantage of distance (i.e., the immigrants directly involved), the battle seemed to be a very simple matter: the Irish against everyone else.

In the 1870s my great-grandfather emigrated to the United States from Ireland when he was a young boy. Somehow, even after more than fifty years of living in his new homeland, he managed to keep his tight brogue. Without the slightest trace of malice, he always referred to his Jewish, Italian, Greek, and Polish neighbors as the "foreigners." (It never occurred to him that he was one, too.) This pleasant man, who played the bagpipes and fiddle and who spent much of his spare time performing Irish folk music, considered himself a total American patriot. He would shake his head in disgust at a plate of spaghetti on his table; those "foreign entanglements," as he called them, were simply un-American.

I am certain that his first-generation Irish pastor and his bishop shared his world view. Non-Irish Catholic immigrants, no matter how much cultural memory they had brought with them, were still "foreigners" whose misguided ideas about liturgy had to be corrected at once. (When Italian parishioners clapped as the bishop processed into the church, "Irish-Americans" would almost go into cardiac arrest.) These "foreigners," for their part, did not think much of the quiet decorum that the Irish preferred. For them, Catholic worship was sometimes a matter of "soaring" in ornate liturgies or gaudy processions and sometimes a matter of "tunneling" into the deep personal world of private devotion. As these "foreigners" soon found out, the "Irish-Americans," products of a church that had survived underground for centuries, knew a lot about "tunneling" but they were not famous for liturgies which were grand, public, soaring events.

The snarling animosity between Irish and non-Irish Roman Catholics in the United States has faded somewhat in recent years but, at one time, tensions were so great that large-scale defections of the non-Irish seemed like a distinct possibility. Part of the trouble stemmed just from the matter of liturgical "style." Fortunately, the church managed to keep most of the feuding "ethnics" together thanks, in part, to the Latin Mass and the establishment of national parishes. The Latin language seemed to put everyone on an equal footing and ethnic parishes allowed congregations to indulge in their old-world customs. The "Slovak parish" or the "Italian parish" was the officially designated enclave where ethnic peculiarities could survive. The other parish down the street — Irish in history, outlook, personnel, and liturgical "style" — was not an ethnic enclave; it was the "American" church. *The Official Catholic Directory* may have "Slovak" or "Italian" in parentheses after the name of a parish, but not the word "Irish."

One group that sometimes bumped heads with the Irish in the nineteenth century was the substantial number of Catholics from parts of Europe where German was spoken. When they came to the United States, the German-speakers brought with them a thriving tradition of congregational singing and a love of hefty choral music. (The quality of this music was another matter.) American Benedictine congregations which traced their origins to the German-speaking parts of Europe quickly became leaders of Liturgical Renewal. Back in my youth, the weary, discouraged church musicians on the East Coast used to bewail their fate but they would console themselves with the comforting thought (or myth) that "things are better out there in the Midwest, where some pastors have German last names."

Those pastors and parishioners with German last names and the Catholics with Irish last names did not always "think alike" on the matter of music for the church. A good example of this cultural disagreement can be seen in the persons of George William Cardinal Mundelein (1872–1939), archbishop of Chicago (1915–39), and Francis Cardinal Spellman (1889–1967), archbishop of New York (1939–67).

Cardinal Mundelein let it be known that, when he processed into Holy Name Cathedral in Chicago, he wanted an orchestra in the choir loft and the kind of Great Master music that one could hear in the big churches of Europe. He sent talented priests to France, so they could study chant and teach it in his seminary. It has been said that, in spite of his last name, Cardinal Mundelein's managerial style was pure Irish, but in musical matters he revealed his German tastes.

When Cardinal Spellman processed into St. Patrick's Cathedral, he probably did not care what music was used, as long as it was unmemorable. During his years as archbishop of New York, visitors from Continental Europe were shocked by the paleness of the vocal music in St. Patrick's, a building located in the cultural capital of the United States. (The organists, I should add, have always been tops.)

The famous conductor Joseph Krips was one of many foreign visitors who could not comprehend the timid, second-rate vocal music he heard at St. Patrick's nor could he understand why a tremendous potential was not being realized. Krips resolved to do something about this, he told me in a letter.[1] During lunch with Cardinal Spellman in 1959, Krips made a bold suggestion: he (Krips) would conduct a suitable Mass by Palestrina or Mozart or Bruckner in the cathedral, free of charge; after all, this kind of music, Krips explained, could be heard at the High Mass in many of Europe's great Catholic cathedrals. Firmly, the cardinal declined the maestro's offer, and I suspect that the suggestion of using robust, confident choral music at a Mass horrified him. Such things were done in St. Patrick's years ago, but not during his efficient administration.

Cardinal Spellman's line of reasoning for rejecting Maestro Krips's offer was probably based on a whole set of assumptions that every "Irish-American" Catholic (including most of my educators) took for granted: "Contraception had ruined France; the decadent French just collapsed in two world wars; the church in that country only survived in Lourdes.... The Italians were anticlerical and pagan.... Slavic Catholics got carried away with their emotions.... The Spanish shot their bishops and priests during revolutions.... The Germans and the Austrians started two world wars...." The list continued in similar fashion until you reached the conclusion that only the Irish and their American relatives had maintained Catholic orthodoxy in faith and music. Did the Irish in Ireland ever ask a prominent conductor to amuse them with great music during Mass? Of course not, and their churches were full.

Who would win this controversy over musical style: "New York" or "Chicago"? (Congregational singing would have grown naturally out of the "Chicago" style.) On the eve of Vatican II, it looked as if Cardinal Spellman's tastes had prevailed. The Mundelein ideal of exuberant, splashy, Great Master music, with orchestra, was considered a scandalous aberration. St. Patrick's Cathedral on Fifth Avenue, under Cardinal Spellman and even earlier, would serve as the prestigious model and would shape the musical tastes of American Catholicism. In the decades just before Vatican II, perhaps the most widely performed composer in Catholic parishes was not Palestrina or Mozart but Pietro Yon (1886–1943), an organist at St. Patrick's.[2] Without the association with that cathedral, Yon's competent but excessively cautious music would have been ignored. (Today, his compositions, except for the popular Christmas song *Gesu Bambino*, are forgotten.)

The Beloved Repertory

"Are there any requests?" asks the folksinger in a Dublin pub, just after he has sung a selection of hauntingly beautiful songs from the folk repertory.

"Yes," responds an annoyed American tourist sitting at a nearby table. "Don't you know any real Irish songs like *Too-ra-loo-ra-loo-ral* and *My Wild Irish Rose*?" (The audience groans.)

"No," the folksinger replies. He and most people in Ireland do not know these "real Irish songs" or, for that matter, *I'll Take You Home Again Kathleen*, *Sweet Rosie O'Grady*, *Galway Bay*, and all the other St. Patrick's Day favorites that Americans associate with the Irish.

Until the musical group the Chieftains became very popular in the 1970s, Ireland's genuine folk music, vocal and instrumental, did not have a large popular following in the United States, even among people who were proud of their Irish ancestry. My great-grandfather, about whom we have heard already, used to get together with his cronies in the parlor of a Sunday afternoon and all of them would play or sing their way through one Irish folk piece after another. His children and grandchildren, however, could not tolerate this noise. They would get out of the house; they wanted to hear ragtime, then the Charleston, and then swing; their idea of a "real Irish song" was *Clancy Lowered the Boom*. My great-grandfather simply could not understand why his children would reject his real Irish songs and, at the same time, want to remind themselves of their Irishness with a whole assortment of fake "real Irish songs," like *My Wild Irish Rose, Down Went McGinty, Sweet Rosie O'Grady, Throw Him Down, McClosky, Who Threw the Overalls in Mistress Murphy's Chowder?*, and *When Irish Eyes Are Smiling.*[3]

What accounts for the popularity and endurance of these stage-Irish songs is their nostalgic description of the Golden Age of "Irish-American" culture. Back then (perhaps 1890–1930) "Irish-Americans" were still Irish and proud of it. (George M. Cohan's Harrigan, in the song of the same name, swaggers down the street "proud of all the Irish blood" that's in him.) They had real power then. They controlled the political machines in the big cities. Back then, they did not run the police departments; they *were* the police departments. And, of course, the Roman Catholic church in the United States was their wholly-owned subsidiary. Behind the cockiness and the swagger, there was, let us not forget, a sense of uneasiness and insecurity about measuring up to the colossal WASP culture that threatened them on all sides. But in moments of anxiety, when it looked as if Protestants and Jews were getting more than their fair share, when blacks were moving into the comfortable old neighborhood, one could always slide into those "real Irish songs," with their reassuring message that everything was "all right." The Irish, as the songs suggest, are wonderful people who can steal your heart away.

No other ethnic group in the United States has at its disposal anything like that assortment of "real Irish songs" paraded out every St. Patrick's Day. No other ethnic group has needed to advertise its ethnic characteristics (mostly mythical) in so many songs. I know people who dismiss this whole repertory as an example of crude ethnic stereotyping, but the fact is that many Americans have a truly affectionate feeling for these lilting tunes written in the days when every cop had a brogue. Sometimes, at a party, it seems that everybody — black, white, oriental, Jewish — likes to pretend to be Irish, for the duration of a song or two.

After this immense digression, I must come back to the topic of this book and the point I am trying to make, which is this: *I'll Take You Home Again, Kathleen, Galway Bay*, and all the rest in that repertory of "Irish-American" songs were, and in some ways still are, the foundation of Roman Catholic church music in the United States. I know that sounds bizarre, but just allow me a few paragraphs to explain.

When the great waves of Irish immigrants arrived at the docks during the nineteenth century, they came with very little baggage. The only enduring religious tune they managed to bring with them and transplant in the New World was *Holy God, We Praise Thy Name*, an excellent hymn with a melody that originated in Austria and was later published in a Dublin hymnal. These immigrants soon needed songs for their novenas, sodality meetings, and various private devotions, but they had in their "racial memory" almost nothing. To fill this vacuum, they and their descendants composed hundreds of hymns and published numerous hymnals, mostly for local use in a particular diocese or in the schools of a religious order. The research of J. Vincent Higginson and others clearly proves that, in the nineteenth century, "Irish-American" Catholics — priests, nuns, and laypeople — were industriously producing all kinds of "contemporary" congregational hymns.[4] The size of the output is remarkable. And where did the style of this music come from? What was the "sound" that inspired the composers? From what kind of egg did this music hatch? The answer is simple: "real Irish songs." There is a little bit of *Galway Bay* and *My Wild Irish Rose* in all the mawkish, drippy, sentimental songs that were once considered examples of "real American Catholic hymns."

To see what I mean, the reader should page through the Catholic section of *The Hymnal: Army and Navy* (copyright 1941), the official hymnal of the United States military for many years and a book that, at one time, was as close as one could get to a national Catholic hymnal for a congregation (as opposed to a hymnal used mostly by choirs). It gives us a very clear picture of what a Catholic congregation thought of as "their own music," ca. 1940. We can find in the Catholic section of the hymnal the grand old benediction hymns and a few tunes with origins in the German-speaking parts of Europe, but most of the music is pure "Irish-American": *O Lord, I Am Not Worthy, On This Day, O Beautiful Mother, Bring Flowers of the Fairest, To Jesus' Heart All Burning, Like a Strong and Raging Fire, O What Could My Jesus Do More*, and *All Praise to St. Patrick*.

The reader should carefully study the Catholic music in *The Hymnal: Army and Navy* and then think of a St. Patrick's Day medley of tunes. Start with *My Wild Irish Rose, The Sidewalks of New York*, and *Sweet Rosie O'Grady*; then glide right into *Mother Dearest* and *Bring Flowers of the Fairest.* Switch now into a more serious mood with *Galway Bay* and then immediately slip into *On This Day, To Jesus' Heart All Burning,* and *Mother, at Your Feet Is Kneeling.* (The last piece was not in the hymnal, but was accepted nearly everywhere in the United States as a canonized Catholic hymn.) You will find that your medley is a seamless bolt of the same cloth. You cannot tell where St. Patrick's Day ends and the novena hymn begins. Up until the 1960s, "real Catholic hymns" duplicated the mood, the manner, and the style of "real Irish songs," with the tempo slowed up slightly.

What distinguishes this music from Protestant hymns or the kind of chorales that Catholics sang east of the Rhine is the perverse "un-singability" of the music. *To Jesus' Heart All Burning, Bring Flowers of the Fairest,* and most of the other products of "Irish-Americans" were confoundedly difficult for a congregation to sing. Maybe the problem is just an awkward leap or a tortured melodic line that is pushed all over the place. Whatever the cause, nearly all of these "Irish-American" hymns were simply too "tight," too chromatic, too twisted in their melodic line for a congregation.

The classic Christian hymn is big and broad and essentially simple in its construction; it can hold a group of people in its large motions. The German-speakers, the Poles, the Slovaks, and other ethnic groups carried this broad "sound" in their memories when they arrived in America, but the Irish had nothing like this in their culture — except the music they associated with landlords and bigots. What the "Irish-Americans" did was to rebel against tradition, break away from the mainstream of European music for congregation, and create a kind of congregational antimusic: songs for the soloist but not really for an assembly of the faithful. "Real Catholic hymns" were not supposed to sound like big, clumsy music for a big, clumsy congregation. They were supposed to go in the opposite direction and sound exquisitely sweet and beautiful, too beautiful for a congregation to blemish.

The Last Sung Hurrah

On September 12, 1953, Jacqueline Bouvier and Senator John F. Kennedy were married. The music for this sumptuous society event had to be nothing but the best. A tenor, up in the choir loft, sang *Mother, at Your Feet Is Kneeling, To Jesus' Heart All Burning, O Lord, I Am Not Worthy* (with the barbershop-quartet tune by Burns), and Schubert's *Ave Maria.*[5]

Ten years later, President John F. Kennedy was assassinated. A grief-stricken nation watched the President's funeral on television, and many non-Catholic viewers wondered what type of ceremony this would be.

Here was a great religion with an impressive legacy of religious music; here was the funeral of the first Roman Catholic president of the United States, and heads of state from all over the world would be in the congregation. The music had to be nothing but the best. While Cardinal Cushing barked his way through the Low Mass, up in the choir loft the same tenor from President Kennedy's wedding sang the same old parlor ballads heard at the 1953 Nuptial Mass.[6]

In 1953 the American Catholic church had at its disposal the *St. Gregory Hymnal*. By 1963 the *Pius X Hymnal* was also in most choir lofts. Yet, for the Kennedy wedding and funeral, the tenor did not sing any music at all from these two excellent volumes. As far as most parishes were concerned, religious music began and ended with *Mother, at Your Feet Is Kneeling, To Jesus' Heart All Burning, O Lord, I Am Not Worthy*, and (the only gem) Schubert's *Ave Maria*. Organists who were around at the time will remember that it was almost impossible to break the "tyranny" of those pieces. You could not easily convince laity or clergy (even those with Polish or Italian last names) that other vernacular religious music existed. Three old Victorian saloon ballads (I refer to the music only) — with Schubert's elegant *Ave Maria* added to this shabby trio — were held up as genuine, traditional examples of "real Catholic music." All other liturgical music had to be adjusted to sound like it. Even Schubert's immortal song had to be "liturgically corrected" to make it sound more like its musical partners — which meant that the glittering accompaniment he had composed to offset the simple melody of the *Ave Maria* was routinely omitted and replaced with throbbing, vibrato chords.

If you look at the words of these maudlin songs which were associated for so long with "Irish-American" Catholicism (for example, the vernacular hymns sung at President Kennedy's wedding and funeral), you will notice that a few basic ideas keep returning: the congregation as a gathering of poor children, Mary as a source of consolation for the poor children, Jesus as the private savior for *me* alone, frailty, and weakness. This kind of music may have served well for private devotions, such as novenas, but using it at Mass is a little like studying yourself in a mirror while everyone else is standing at attention for the national anthem. Nevertheless, by the 1960s those three "real Catholic hymns" were setting the standards for what was considered to be the right kind of "tone" for all liturgical services, including nuptials *and* funerals.

On January 19, 1964, Richard Cardinal Cushing celebrated a Solemn Pontifical Mass for the late President Kennedy in Boston's Holy Cross Cathedral. This was to be a Mass for the repose of the president's soul and a civic occasion, where the people of Boston could express their condolences. Across the United States people tuned in their television sets to watch this liturgy. Non-Catholics were curious. (What do these Catholics do in church?) American Roman Catholics, however, knew exactly what to expect. The Mass began predictably enough. Cardinal Cushing processed into the huge barn of a church. The organ played. A schola cantorum, made up of seminarians, was there to take care of some of the choral chanting. It would all be very old and very familiar.

And then came the shock. Near the front of the cathedral, Maestro Erich Leinsdorf (and him not even Catholic!) lifted his hands and began to conduct an ensemble consisting of musicians from the Boston Symphony and singers from Harvard, Radcliffe, and the New England Conservatory of Music. (No one was paid. All the musicians, including the conductor, volunteered their services.) The music was Mozart's *Requiem*. As soon as Mozart's deeply moving music for the words *Requiem aeternam* was carried across the airways, strange things began to happen from one end of the United States to the other. In rectory parlors, convents, and Catholic households, eyes widened; jaws dropped; some members of the Catholic community watched their television sets with sputtering incomprehension. Wasn't the religious music of Mozart officially banned in some church document somewhere? Wasn't it against canon law to have any instrument in church except the organ? That Introit! The energetic drive in that Kyrie! That majestic Dies Irae! Wasn't church music supposed to sound frail and debilitated, like *Mother, at Your Feet Is Kneeling*? Everybody knew that the Second Vatican Council had loosened things up a bit, but, really, Cardinal Cushing was going too far.[7]

This Requiem Mass in Boston was indeed shocking to many American Catholics; it represented the beginning of a new era. After that singing of the Mozart *Requiem* in Holy Cross Cathedral, I never heard *Mother, at Your Feet Is Kneeling* in a Catholic church again (although I am told that it is not dead yet). Of course I never heard Mozart's *Requiem* again either.

In 1964 it took courage for Cardinal Cushing to break ranks with his American colleagues. At that time, nearly all the bishops in the United States would have rejected outright the suggestion that a great outpouring of public grief could be expressed in the singing of Mozart's *Requiem* at a Mass. (Most of their nineteenth-century predecessors, however, and certainly their colleagues on the European Continent would have had no problem at all with this kind of music, for unusual occasions.) By allowing Mozart's *Requiem* in his cathedral, Cardinal Cushing was, as it were, opening up the doors of the bombshelter and letting the sunlight pour in; he was also letting everyone know that Roman Catholicism in

Boston was now ready to take on everything in this wide world of ours, even the liturgical music that belonged to his church.

For the sake of completeness, we should move ahead four years to 1968 and yet another tragedy in the Kennedy family: the assassination of Senator Robert Kennedy. This time the method of expressing sorrow and hope took a form that would have been considered absolute madness just a few years earlier. Hosannas, hallelujahs, and hymns shook the pillars of St. Patrick's Cathedral in New York. Members of the New York Philharmonic, conducted by Leonard Bernstein, played an excerpt from a symphony by Mahler. Richard Tucker, a famous opera star and also a Jewish cantor, sang Franck's *Panis Angelicus*. It was quite an event — and the congregation did not hear any of the old Gay Nineties sob songs that were, just four years earlier, thought to be essential for the Catholic wedding and funeral.

The New Beloved Repertory

That strange noise, which the reader can probably hear in the distance, is nothing to be alarmed about; it is only the sound of my Irish ancestors rolling in their graves.

I know from unpleasant experience that this ethnic aspect of why Catholics can't sing does not always produce the most calm and reasoned sort of discussion. Sometimes, while defending myself against the charge of spreading unfounded ethnic slurs, I cannot even make the point that "times have changed." This chapter was written largely in the past tense. Everything in Roman Catholicism, including its "Irish-American" manifestations, has had the dust knocked out of it in recent years. And yet, in spite of all the upheavals and changes in the church, history has not gone away; it still lingers.

I saw history lingering back in the 1960s, when parishes were frantically trying to put together some kind of repertory of congregational music. I remember the committee meetings where we would flip through missalettes and homemade hymnals. Nobody liked this old German Catholic chorale. (It sounded too Protestant.) That confident, chest-thumping Methodist hymn frightened some people. Sublimely tasteful hymns by Vaughan Williams disgusted people who mistrust anything sublimely tasteful. ("Too English.") We were all very frustrated, very discouraged — until somebody came across *Kumbaya, Michael, Row the Boat Ashore, Take Our Bread, Let There Be Peace on Earth, Sons of God,* and other pieces loosely called "folk music." A sense of relief came over the committee; there were smiles all around (except from me). The words might have been quite different and the guitar accompaniment something new, but what everybody called "folk music" brought back memories of *Mother, at Your Feet Is Kneeling* and *To Jesus' Heart All Burning*. With a continuity that is stunning in its logic, the music of the parish folk Mass and later the gentle songs of the "groups" like the St. Louis Jesuits would pick up where *Mother Dearest* and *Galway Bay* left off. (*Dwelling Place*, one of the honored works in the folk, "contemporary" repertory, begins, "I fall on my knees." The music for these initial five words is identical to the beginning of *My Wild Irish Rose*.)

"Outrageous! Nonsense! A total misreading of the facts! The words are *biblical* in the newer folk songs. The 'contemporary' church music of our time avoids the mushy sentimentality of the older hymns. And, besides, you are making the Irish into scapegoats."

Let me defend myself.

Look closely at what is called the "contemporary music scene" in the Catholic church. Notice how those biblical words are lolling in the soft, quilted sentimentality of the music. Talk to the performers and listen to them tell you how they have nothing but disdain for ("English") notions about musical taste. Study the mannerisms of the "contemporary" performers and their affectations about being poor folk-children with guitars. All of this goes back to the late nineteenth century when many "Irish-Americans" revolted against the traditions of European music for congregation and replaced them with something more "popular" but also much more difficult to sing: the *sweet song*.

When it comes to church music, the enduring legacy of the Irish in the United States may be the idea that religious music culminates in the sweet song, preferably sung by a soloist with a light voice. Authentic congregational music is always a little dumpy and lumpy but strong. The sweet song, however, strives to create the impression of a drooping weakness and delicacy, which a congregation will only muss up by singing. The sweet song, which has now evolved into the "contemporary" religious song, is the antimatter of congregational singing. The sweet song is killing congregational singing in Catholic parishes.

One day I am going to put together a book entitled *Believe It or Not: Bizarre Moments in Catholic Liturgy Since Vatican II*. I certainly have collected enough material, an assortment of grotesque and sometimes hilarious stories about attempts to make liturgy "relevant" and "meaningful" (for example, the "Basketball Mass," during which the local basketball team dribbled basketballs, and the many "Children's Masses," for which the celebrants dressed themselves as clowns). I thought that I had reached the point where nothing would surprise me until I began to hear about a new addition to the repertory of Catholic music for congregation: *When Irish Eyes Are Smiling*. This "real Irish song" now shows up at weddings and funerals. An organist I know tells me she must include this sweet song in the prelude for the St. Patrick's Day Mass — performed by congregation, choir, and organ — or risk the wrath of influential members of the parish.

When Irish Eyes Are Smiling sung during a Mass confirms the suspicions of those who say that, at the very center of Irish and "Irish-American" Catholicism (in the midst of the rising incense, behind the golden doors of the tabernacle, as it were), you will find not Jesus or the Gospels but the map of Ireland. *When Irish Eyes Are Smiling* sung in church only reinforces the accusation that religion is merely an attic for storing the nationalistic and ethnic values of the tribe.

Why did St. Patrick insist on worship in Latin and not Gaelic? (He was miles from Rome and the pope did not send him to convert the Irish.) In J. F. Powers' short story "Prince of Darkness," the old pastor put on green vestments for the St. Patrick's Day Mass, instead of the Lenten purple required by the rubrics. Why did the bishop get annoyed about this and summon the man to his office? As late as 1963, the organist who played *O Danny Boy*, discreetly and quietly during the communion part of the St. Patrick's Day Mass, would have been fired on the spot. Why? In all of these cases, the answer is that, throughout the centuries, Roman Catholicism feared the Mass would merely become a specimen of the local ethnic folklore or pep-rally for nationalism. The church, in its collective wisdom, kept its eyes ever fixed on the job of fulfilling the commands of the Jewish Jesus. It certainly did not always succeed, but at least it fanatically tried to preserve the idea that the Mass was not an occasion for ethnic and nationalistic boosterism.

The priest who thinks it is very cute for a congregation to sing *When Irish Eyes* is probably not concerned at all about the words. His primary and exclusive intention, he says, is "to get the congregation to sing," anything. It is only a matter of time before an "Italian-American" priest will come up with the same bright idea and ask his congregation to sing *O Sole Mio* at Mass, because that is the way you "get the congregation to sing."

Perhaps a Catholic university should call together a scholarly conference to discuss the emergence of *When Irish Eyes* as music for congregation. What does it all mean? One seminar could perhaps analyze the matter of "taste." Another could concentrate on "the sacred." The results of these discussions would be intellectually stimulating, but I think that most of the real insights would come from the seminar on ritual. Over the centuries, the Catholic church presented congregations with rituals; the words of those ceremonies were artistically elevated in music. In the more "contemporary" approach to liturgy, ritual is something that happens between the sweet songs; any kind of irrelevant music, no matter how trashy, is acceptable, as long as somebody thinks that this is what it takes to "get the congregation to sing."

Singing sweet "contemporary" songs *at* a ritual rather than singing the ritual — we cannot blame "Irish-Americans" for this development. Everybody, as we shall see, is doing it.

4

De-ritualization

Good Morning!

"As we all know, ritualistic behavior is a sign of a sick mind."

"We must get away from this absurd notion that sacraments are rituals."

"Someone filled with the Spirit has no need of rituals."

Statements like this turn up occasionally in conversations with people who direct the Catholic church's liturgical life. The ideas behind these words are valid, up to a point, but the tone of voice with which they are spoken reveals a nervousness about this thing known as ritual. Many Catholics today — after encountering the formidable writings of Sigmund Freud — have become downright uncomfortable about the whole idea of ritual. Some think of it as a fossil from Catholicism's medieval past or as a bothersome requirement which gets in the way of pure Christianity. Others are embarrassed by its formality, in this the era of rehearsed informality. Whatever the reason, they are united in their distrust of ritual. This, of course, leads to something that the psychologists call cognitive dissonance: How does one stay a faithful member of a church which constantly uses rituals, if one sees them as somehow sick?

The only way out of the dilemma is to take the ritual out of ritual or (a less drastic solution) to let everyone know that you are not being completely fooled by ritual. We can call this "de-ritualization" and we can find it in many places where the priest, the musicians, and lay assistants have stayed up late devising ways to remove the ritual from ritual; that is, they try very hard to send this signal to the congregation: "What you are witnessing is a ritual, but it is not a ritual."

35

Many readers are probably familiar with one very blatant form of de-ritualization. The scene is a parish church. A congregation has assembled for Sunday Mass. The opening hymn begins with a grand flourish. The celebrant processes into church amid alleluias and mighty blasts from the organ. We reach a mini-climax. The music ends. Then, there is a moment of silence while the celebrant adjusts his microphone. He smiles. And what are the first words out of his mouth? "Good morning, everybody." THUD! You can almost hear something collapsing. Later on, just for symmetry, the celebrant will conclude the liturgy with a cheerful "Havernice day."

We can be reasonably sure that the Last Supper did not begin with the words, "Good evening, apostles." Intuition tells us that John the Baptist did not cry in the wilderness, "Repent, sin no more, and havernice day." Common sense tells us that there is something so immensely wrong and contradictory about starting off a ritual with "Good morning." We might even say that the laity in the pews "short circuits" when greeted this way at Mass. The church building, the music, and the celebrant in flowing robes all seem to say, "This is a ritual," an event out of the ordinary. Then, the "Good morning" intrudes itself and indicates that this is really a business meeting and not a liturgy, after all. Every time I hear "Good morning" and "Havernice day" at a liturgy I am reminded of that famous painting by René Magritte, "The Treachery of Images." This painting shows a smoker's pipe and underneath the pipe are the French words for "This is not a pipe." This is a ritual, but it is not a ritual.

"Good morning" at the beginning of a ritual quickly and effectively de-ritualizes. The congregation, standing there bewildered, has to make sense out of the messages that go in opposite directions at the same time: the man who is clothed in an unusual costume, who is positioned in a "dramatic" setting . . . and who then starts off with the most pedestrian, twit greeting in the English language.

De-ritualization is not something new. It goes back in history, to the days long before Vatican II.

Polishing the Chalice

"Father O'Fogarty is such a fine man, and he says such a *beautiful* Mass."

Before the vernacular Mass, Catholics would come across that phrase "beautiful Mass" now and then (I remember overhearing it on the steps of the church, as the women were putting on their gloves after Mass). It was a tribute to that special priest, with the odor of sanctity all over him, who would go through the Latin Mass reverently and, yes, beautifully. But there was also another side of the coin, an unspoken continuation of that observation about beauty: "Father So-and-so, on the other hand, says an absolutely ugly Mass."

Younger readers might have to be informed that in the days of the Latin Mass there were many Father So-and-sos who did their best to make sure that nobody would ever accuse them of saying a "beautiful Mass." I can still see Father M dashing through the Latin Mass with all the solemnity of a tobacco auctioneer in a hurry; he was part of that breed of priest who included liturgical speed and a clickety-clack recitation of Latin among the cardinal virtues. Father K seemed to be operated by springs and gears when he celebrated Mass; all of his abrupt gestures reminded me of a wind-up toy. The late Cardinal Cushing of Boston confounded many non-Catholics when they watched him honk his way through a ceremony; this fine, saintly man always sounded like someone selling peanuts and popcorn at a baseball game.

When I was a young boy, I used to think that there was an important part of the Latin Mass — right before the consecration — where the celebrant polished the chalice. Father A used to swing his right arm vigorously. Father B used to push back his sleeves just before he attacked the job with swift fury. When I began to use a missal, I discovered that the priest was not putting a shine on anything; those rapid gestures were supposed to be ritual signs of the cross made over the bread and wine. A beautiful act of reverence — something resembling a gesture from a ballet — had been de-ritualized, transformed into movements more appropriate for a garage mechanic at work.

Complaints about de-ritualization were probably discussed at the staff meetings of the apostles; certainly at the time of the Reformation the situation was catastrophic. (Priests had to be reminded not to spit on the floor when they were saying Mass.) Nevertheless, de-ritualization, in the form of a sincere and calculated disrespect for the beauty of the liturgical forms, somehow became an accepted part of Catholic liturgy: not the exception, but the rule. Indeed, some Catholics *looked* for it; they expected it in their parishes.

Wasted Motions

Ritual has been around since the first days of homo sapiens and is a universal phenomenon found in the activities of African witch doctors, Freemasons, Benedictine monks, Southern Baptists, and college fraternities. Ritual is everywhere and in every culture. All of it is perfectly "useless" and yet an essential part of our humanity. When Jesus cured a blind man (John 9: 1–7), he rubbed mud on the man's eyes and told him to wash in the pool at Siloe. These wasted motions — the mud, the staggering walk to the pool, the washing — were all part of a ritual which turned this occasion into something colossal, something which allowed the onlookers to become "participants," just by watching.

But what *is* ritual, this thing which is "useless" and yet so important? Language? Communication? A way of acting out subconscious anxieties and society's need for ritual murder? A meaningless custom which gives life a bit of color? No one has the answer. We must content ourselves with mere insights, and some of the most profound ones come from the great historian and scholar Jan Huizinga. Ritual, he tells us, is a game — a sublime game, to be sure, but a game nevertheless. This somewhat disturbing idea (ritual put in the same category with tennis and Scrabble) is at the center of his book *Homo Ludens* (English edition, 1950).[1]

Huizinga begins his classic study by analyzing the idea of play — the seemingly meaningless play of young children and animals; the love of "fun" in society; play that is serious; and civilization itself, which is a highly elaborate game. Play, he observes, shows up in the nursery, in clubs, in courtship rituals, in the theater, and in everyday social contacts. The normal development of a child, in fact, is helped along by this playing of games; the child deprived of play (in the broadest sense of that word) will not be able to function in society, which is built on a whole series of interlocking games. Huizinga sums up the formal characteristics of play by describing it as a "free activity" which "promotes the formation of social groupings" and yet stands "quite consciously outside 'ordinary' life as being 'not serious,' but at the same time absorbing the player intensely and utterly." He constantly stresses his respect for this cultural activity called play and he points out that the tendency to organize elaborate social "games" is one of the things that makes man-the-animal man-the-human-being.

The author's awe of the human ability to "play games" can be seen in his treatment of ritual in advanced cultures or civilizations. In these societies, play goes beyond the wordless play of children or sports; it begins to represent something and assumes a poetic form; it becomes the supreme teacher of inexpressible truths. "In the form and function of play, itself an independent entity which is senseless and irrational, man's consciousness that he is embedded in a sacred order of things finds its first, highest, and holiest expression." When, in the case of higher civilizations, play begins to represent something, gradually "the significance of a sacred act permeates the playing. Ritual grafts itself upon it; but the primary thing is and remains play." Ritual "is seriousness at its highest and holiest," and yet a form of play; play is fun; true ritual is supremely serious, solemn, earnest fun. In religious ritual the beautiful and the sacred can come together. Ritual (the medium) can become the divine game and from it people can become conscious of their role in the divine order of things (the message).

Huizinga candidly admits that his analysis of ritual does not yield some absolute truth or scientific fact. This whole idea of ritual as a form of serious play, he concedes, hovers "over spheres of thought barely accessible either to psychology or to philosophy." When we study this enigma of ritual, "we plumb the depths of our consciousness."

An archbishop going through the elaborate motions of a Solemn High Mass during the Middle Ages knew instinctively all about ritual as a "game" or "fun." So did the poorest peasant standing in the nave of the cathedral during that same ceremony. You will find the same "game" in a simple Baptist church or a mosque. But by the 1940s and perhaps even earlier, most American Catholic churches were beginning to lose any sense of their ritual as something which was "fun." Ritual was becoming a chore, a requirement, a respected cultural habit, a decorated iron box which merely encased something more important. The sense of ritual as the sublime game which involved the efforts of the whole community survived only in relatively few places where the High Mass and its music were taken seriously: monasteries, nunneries, and those rare parishes that had discovered this new phenomenon called Liturgical Renewal.

Farewell, High Church

To see just how far American Catholicism has moved away from its heritage of liturgy as "fun" (or how far it has gone with de-ritualization), all we have to do is perform a little experiment. Ask someone to lie down on a couch, relax, and describe the things that come into his or her head when you mention a certain expression. Perhaps start with "trees" and "yellow." Then, after a few minutes of this free association, try this expression: "High Church."

A few people will probably get it right, historically speaking. They will think aloud and describe how "high" refers to a "high voice," that is, a singing voice; in the days before microphones, the "high" service made it possible for the congregation to be aware of the sacred words; the chanting in the "high" voice also represented Christian "enthusiasm," this Pentecostal zeal barely under control. ("Low" referred to the spoken voice.) Most people, however, regardless of their religious background, will hear the term "High Church" and start talking about those Anglican and Episcopalian establishments that are "higher than the Himalayas." Only a few, very few, will associate the expression "High Church" with the American branch of Roman Catholicism, which (at least since the

1940s and in the parishes) sometimes has given the impression of being militantly anti-High Church.

The odd thing about "High Church Christianity" is its historic association with the needs of workers and peasants. Protestant observers, atheists, and implacable enemies of the church have sometimes conceded that Roman Catholicism's historic rituals, "when really done up right," have a way of bringing a sense of relief and assurance to a troubled humanity, especially the "lower classes." In the nineteenth century, when the leaders of the Oxford Movement tried to restore pre-Reformation practices in the Church of England, one justification for the chanting, the incense, and the gorgeous choral music was that such things would convey a feeling of hope to the workers oppressed in dark satanic mills and mines. The popish ceremonies and music were supposed to help the common people feel like important participants in an important act.

"High Church Christianity" can easily serve the purpose of bolstering monarchical pretensions. It can degenerate into entertainment for the rich and eccentric. And, let us be frank, it can, at times, become a tad too precious for words. But in its origins, the High Mass — Latin or the vernacular, with cherubic choral music or austere chanting, with imperial ceremonial or humble simplicity — was supposed to be liberation theology in action and slightly subversive. Far from being one form of "opium for the people," the old High Mass was meant to be a kind of medicine that invigorated people, reminded them of their uniqueness, and sent them refreshed but determined into a hostile world.

Modern Catholics have sometimes forgotten that, as late as 1964, the "fun" High Mass with good choral music and maybe some congregational singing was considered "liberal" and "progressive." "Liberal Catholics" loved chant and lamented that they never heard it done properly or done at all in their parishes. "Liberal Catholics" were somewhat High Church in their preferences. A great example of this High Church "liberalism" was Father George Barry Ford, the controversial pastor of Corpus Christi Church in Manhattan.[2] (This was the church which, the reader will remember, had so offended my acquaintance Conrad.) Father Ford constantly infuriated his superiors down in the "powerhouse" behind St. Patrick's (then the location of the diocesan chancery) because of his liberal notions on ecumenism and his open exchange of ideas with the atheists at nearby Columbia University. It was considered only natural that someone with his dangerously liberal leanings would be in charge of the only parish for miles around which treated the church's liturgical heritage as if it were "serious fun." The bedrock, faith-of-our-fathers conservatives in the archdiocese did not know what was worse about this radical Father Ford: his too-friendly relations with Protestant ministers, university professors, and other dangerous types or his church, where the choir energetically sang Masses by Mozart and where the congregation sang . . . *Gregorian chant!*

For decades before Vatican II, most of the promoters of renewal through liturgy had always looked to the sung Mass (the old-fashioned High Church ceremony) as the most thorough liturgical expression of faith in action. The future, they predicted, belonged to the High Mass — not necessarily the Baroque spectacle but a liturgy so intense that emotions could only "come out" in song. For me, the predicted future arrived in 1961. In June of that year I attended a Baccalaureate Mass at a Jesuit preparatory school. For this event, the graduating seniors did something new and a little shocking: they, not the choir, sang the various choral parts of the Ordinary of the Mass (Kyrie, Gloria, Credo, Sanctus, Agnus Dei), as well as all the responses. The chandeliers rattled from the glorious noise of their singing. The language was ancient Latin and the music Gregorian chant, but for everyone there this High Mass with the singing congregation was the liturgical equivalent of the latest nuclear technology. "This is the future," I said to myself, "and it works." Latin and English will share space in this future, but more liturgies will be High Masses, sung by congregation and choir from beginning to end, just like this one.

The future, as often happens, decided to take some unexpected turns before arriving. A few years later, the music for the Baccalaureate Mass at this same school was something in the folk manner and striking only for its juvenile banality. Most of the graduates did not sing. The future now belonged to the Johnnys-come-lately who had hitherto shown no interest at all in Liturgical Renewal; they demanded that the High Mass, even in English, would have to go.

In the early 1960s only a handful of Catholic parishes in any diocese had weekly High Masses which seemed to sum up and reaffirm the spiritual aspirations of the parish. Today, only a few parishes — a tiny minority — attempt anything that even vaguely resembles a sung liturgy. The typical parish liturgy is the old spoken Mass (the Low Mass, but in English) with a few songs pasted on, in order to keep the congregation occupied. Things have reached the point where that typical parish no longer fits into that category of "Catholic" when it comes to worship. To put it another way, the majority of Roman Catholic parishes in the United States do not share with the Eastern Rites, the Orthodox churches, and Anglicanism a common understanding of the sung ritual as a symbol of a burning faith. Most Roman Catholic parishes are no longer part of the "Catholic" liturgical family; maybe they left this family long before the Second Vatican Council.

The Trauma

All I did was just casually mention to a very clearheaded priest that, since the introduction of the vernacular Mass, I have never heard a priest begin Sunday Mass in a parish by singing "In the name of the Father..." and never heard the congregation respond to him, in song, "Amen." The sung liturgy, the goal of Liturgical Renewal for so long, seems to be a nearly extinct species, I said. The priest interrupted me angrily. "But we can't turn back the clock!" he snapped.

This same man celebrates Mass in vestments designed in ancient Roman times and he puts candles on the altar, more than a century after the invention of the light bulb. He has no difficulty about using the "new" Mass, the Rite of Paul VI, which is based on archeological research, antiquarian restoration, and nostalgia for a long-lost, utopian Christian worship of the fourth century, A.D. When he shudders about "turning back the clock," perhaps he really does not mean the Middle Ages or Renaissance but a more recent time that is still very fresh and very unpleasant in his memory. Two anecdotes illustrate what I mean:

Sometime back in the 1940s, when I was a little boy, I can remember sitting in church one Sunday and waiting for Mass to begin. I noticed that, up in the front of this stone basilica, there was a slight commotion when the pastor, dressed in a suit, appeared at the altar railing and looked as if he had something important to say. "I have an announcement," he shouted. (This was the era before the multiple microphones in the sanctuary.) "The next Mass will not be a Low Mass. Because of a schedule change, it will be a High Mass. The next Low Mass will be at 12:15."

All the members of my family looked at one another in terror. You would have thought the pastor had just announced that there was a bomb hidden somewhere in the church. My family did not need any discussion. We all got up at once and headed for the exits, as did three-fourths of the congregation. I was young at the time but I can remember the relief we all felt when we stepped into the sunshine. It was like escaping from a dangerous coal mine, just before the roof collapsed. Even at that tender age I knew that in our relatively prosperous parish (which claimed to have "one of the finest adult choirs in the archdiocese") only the deaf willingly attended High Mass.

My second anecdote takes us to London in the 1970s. A middle-aged couple I know was visiting this city and on the recommendation of a hotel clerk they decided to attend Mass in the Roman Catholic cathedral. After waiting quietly for a few minutes in that great church, the couple sensed that things were about to begin. Lights went on. Majestic music from the organ thundered through the cathedral. Then, all of a sudden, they realized what was happening. "Let's get out of here!" the gentleman whispered loudly. "It's the High Mass!" In panic, they tried to escape by the center aisle, but that exit was blocked by the procession earnestly marching up the middle of the church. They could not escape via the side aisle either, because that route was blocked, too. (I forget what the obstruction was.) They were doomed, these two devout Catholics thought. They would have to endure the torture of the High Mass, Purgatory on earth.

A few minutes after they had resigned themselves to their fate, it gradually began to dawn on them that this event would not be so horrible, after all. Indeed, for the first time in their lives these pious Catholics encountered a sung Mass which was "fun" and which seemed to draw them into the ritual. They loved every minute of it.

As these two anecdotes nicely illustrate, many older Catholics, those who can remember the days of the Latin High Mass, were burned and embittered by painful experiences. Some of them recall abominations perpetrated by yodeling sadists up in the choir loft. Some recall the lovely voices of the girls in the sixth grade who sweetly chirped their way through the *Missa de Angelis* every Sunday — but how much sweet chirping can one take? Besides, the majority of American Catholics never had the experience of playing the game (i.e., singing part of the service or just feeling they were immersing themselves in the beautiful ceremony); for them, the High Mass remained a remote and fragile *object d'art*. This is why any mention of "sung liturgy" still makes many Catholics in this country break out into a cold sweat. If you describe the virtues of the sung or Solemn Mass to them, they get that what-planet-does-he-come-from expression on their faces. If you point out that the "new" Mass actually moves Roman Catholicism closer to the ideal of the "continuously sung" liturgies used in the Eastern churches, the reaction will be, "But we can't turn back the clock."

The "High" liturgy in any language was once the symbol of a faith so intense and filled with joy that it had to burst forth in almost continuous song. Today, among many Roman Catholics, it has become a symbol of a distorted eucharistic theology which focused too much on adoration and mystification. Therefore (so the conclusion goes), the genuine sung liturgy, as well as any "artistic" music which could go with it, is discredited.

While working as a substitute organist for various denominations, I began to realize that the little, unpretentious Lutheran parish and the lowest of the Low Church Episcopalian establishments are often much more liturgically High Church than the Roman Catholic parish down the block. I have even attended Methodist and Presbyterian services that came closer to the ideal of an old-fashioned High Mass than anything I have ever encountered in most Roman Catholic parishes since the 1960s. My point is not a matter of incense density or beautiful choral singing. I am only saying that at perhaps a dour Calvinist service you sense that the singing (congregational and choral) is "fun" and an integral part of the whole "game." In the American Catholic tradition, the people in the sanctuary play the "game" called ritual; the singing congregation and the choir play a completely separate "game" called musical participation.

One fact will make this clear. According to the ancient traditions of Christian worship, the Eucharist should include a Penitential Rite near the beginning of the ceremony. In the Orthodox churches the walls vibrate from the resounding "Lord, have mercy," over and over again. In a Rococo church somewhere in rural Austria, a Mozart Kyrie makes perfect sense. In a Lutheran or Episcopalian church the congregation might sing a setting of the "Lord, have mercy" from the hymnbook. In the American Catholic parish, however, the sung Penitential Rite, in any form, is a rarity today. Surely, one would think that it would be sung at least once on Sunday, but this is not the norm. In the typical parish there might be end-to-end music provided by cantors, singers, guitarists, and congregation, but this declaration of sinfulness remains spoken and rarely lasts more than twenty seconds.

The defect here is not the absence of pretty music or singing to keep the congregation active. What is missing is *ritual*. Someone makes the decision that the Penitential Rite, like all ritual, embarrasses us or wastes time. And yet, at the same time, a great deal of attention might be given over to the sung Communion Meditation, something added on to the ritual. The game called ritual becomes smaller and smaller; the game called music takes on an independent life of its own and compensates for the vacant spaces left by a retreating ritual.

Objectivity and "Me"

"Roman Catholic ritual just isn't what it used to be. . . . The Mass has lost its sense of mystery and transcendence. . . . We have taken too much of the sacred out of liturgy. . . . Our sense of reverence is gone."

These grumblings confuse matters. If "something" went down the drain when Roman Catholicism switched from Latin to the vernacular, it was not necessarily a feeling of mystery or transcendence or the sacred but the sense of ritual as *communal action*. In real ritual — ritual in the universal sense, ritual recognized as such throughout history — individuals cease to act as individuals and, instead, surrender themselves to a collective consciousness, an idea, something bigger than one person.

The "I" ceases and becomes "we." The participants give up at least a part of their individuality and become anonymous performers of the rite.

Think for a moment of this worldwide practice of making the leaders at the center of a ritual put on unusual costumes and perhaps use a special, noncolloquial form of speech. This sort of thing is done in an effort to "hide" these ritual leaders (and their "I"). Once they have become safely "hidden," they can act as the representatives of everybody ("we"). What we call an act of reverence is, more often than we realize, an act of conformity — someone denying his or her independence for a moment and surrendering to tribal custom. What we call "mystery" and the "sense of the sacred" may really be what we experience when we "hide" our individual personalities and try to become part of something that is larger than any individual. What we call de-ritualization is simply a matter of individuals refusing to "hide" in the collective action.

Liturgists used to give a name to this "hiding," this denial of the self: *objectivity*. The Mass, they reminded us, was a "common prayer" for everyone who walked in the door, not a special meeting of the club or a show. Objective was the natural character of a liturgy that tried to be a public undertaking.

Objectivity is a term that wins few friends today. It suggests the image of a bloodless, fastidious Anglican prelate intoning prayers at evensong. It might even suggest something sinister, such as prisoners lugging stone from a quarry. Modern Catholics, we are told, want liturgy that is *alive* and presided over by clergymen who do everything with conviction, warmth, sincerity, and vigor. Objectivity, confused with aloofness, is dismissed as a leftover style of behavior from the days of monarchy and etiquette books — something fine for coronations and diplomatic protocol, but not for Mr. and Mrs. U.S.A.

A good example of objectivity in place or removed for purposes of de-ritualization can be found in the manner of proclaiming scripture aloud at a liturgy. According to the traditional method, someone chants the words from the Bible or reads them in a neutral tone of voice; that is, objectively. The words themselves might tell of something joyful or horrible or ecstatic, but the voice of the reader remains steady and objective. According to the latest de-ritualizing technique, the reader dispenses with all efforts to remain objective and, instead, colors the story with little, personal touches: dramatic pauses, emphasis on certain words, quotations spoken "in character," and so on. The reading takes on the style of one of those novels or children's stories on tape; everything is all very vivid, to be sure, but, without the objectivity, those words of scripture disappear behind the display of personality. We do not hear the words of Genesis or Matthew or Paul; we hear (and watch) Bob or

Suzy or Joe give us a personal interpretation of scripture. Bob, Suzy, and Joe do not want to be participants in a collective action; they want us to remain aware that, above all, even above and beyond the words of scripture, they are Bob, Suzy, and Joe.

The backwoods, hillbilly folksinger knows all about objectivity. When he sings the tragic ballad *Barbara Allen*, he maintains the same tone of voice and stays detached from the story. He is, after all, acting as the voice of the whole tribe; he represents the collective memory. As soon as he begins to color the ballad with his personal feelings (i.e., as soon as he ceases to be objective), he becomes Jethro or Zeek or Clyde.

"Liturgy," we should keep in mind, comes from two Greek words: *laos*, meaning people or multitude, and *ergon*, meaning work. When Christianity emerged from persecution, the Eucharist and other ceremonies of the church became public projects, a work of the populace. The theology behind "liturgy" may have assigned different roles to different individuals, but the etymology of the word itself implies everybody, the public.

Part of the "sacred atmosphere" and the "mystery" once so strongly associated with liturgy used to come from the congregation knowing that clergy in the front were "cut down to size" and even made to look somewhat pitiful by the ritualistic burdens placed upon them; the laity sensed that, although bishops and priests were members of a special class, the ceremony and the confining language had the odd effect of harnessing the clergy in a public endeavor and making them public servants — servants who gave up their identity, their personality, and their personal preferences during a liturgy, in order to become "we" and serve the public good. With personalities minimized (and all the possible hostility or uneasiness that comes with trying to adjust to another personality), the laity could join the clergy in this objective, collective action, which took everyone to matters beyond the commonplace: perhaps to the mysterious, the transcendent, and the sacred.

A Poem Should...

All of this talk about the mysterious, the transcendent, and the sacred — the natural results of a communal action, rather than a personal show — can give the impression that this whole discussion of ritual leads only to the realms of serene philosophical speculation, somewhere above the ozone layer. Perhaps for this reason we should come down to earth, as it were, to a source of wisdom noted for his impatience with philosophical flights of fancy; I refer, of course, to H. L. Mencken, journalist, curmudgeon, iconoclast, and shrewd observer of the human condition.

Mencken's contribution to this issue is the brief essay "Holy Writ," from the journal *Smart Set* (October, 1923). It remains one of the most perceptive studies of liturgy ever written.[3]

Mencken begins by declaring that the person who translated the Bible into clear, excellent French prose "is chiefly responsible for the collapse of Christianity in France." But the translators who put the Bible "into archaic, sonorous and often unintelligible English" (i.e., the King James Version) "gave Christianity a new lease of [sic] life wherever English is spoken." This translation "was so beautiful that the great majority of men, in the face of it, could not fix their minds upon the ideas in it. To this day it has enchanted the English-speaking peoples so effectively that, in the main, they remain Christians, at least sentimentally."

Perhaps as a way of infuriating his fundamentalist adversaries, Mencken proceeded from this discussion of the Bible to Roman Catholicism, which he found himself admiring, "despite its frequent astounding imbecilities." Unlike the Protestant sects which were forever trying to explain scripture, "the Latin Church," Mencken observed, "has always kept clearly before it the fact that religion is not a syllogism but a poem" and leaves theological argumentation to a few harmless theologians who stay far away from the faithful.

Rome, indeed, has not only preserved the original poetry in Christianity; it has also made capital additions to that poetry — for example, the poetry of the saints, of Mary, and of the liturgy itself. A solemn high mass must be a thousand times as impressive, to a man with any genuine religious sense in him, as the most powerful sermon ever roared under the big-top.... In the face of such overwhelming beauty it is not necessary to belabor the faithful with logic; they are better convinced by letting them alone.

Mencken saw clearly that the poetry of religion — the special language of scripture, liturgy, and all the rest — provided a mask which hid the weaknesses of individual clergymen. "A bishop in his robes, playing his part in the solemn ceremonial of the mass, is a dignified spectacle, even though he may sweat freely." Without the masks, Mencken observes, we find ourselves confronted not by poetry but by personality: "the same bishop, bawling against Darwin half an hour later, is seen to be simply an elderly Irishman with a bald head, the son of a respectable saloon-keeper in South Bend, Ind."

Please note that behind the know-it-all cynicism, behind the you-can't-fool-me posturing, there is respect for the idea of the exalted Roman liturgy, which in Mencken's day was done in Latin. Mencken recognized that the Latin Mass and the King James Bible derived their strength from their unashamed, frank use of "poetry." This almost offhand observation is the insight of insights: the "human side" of liturgy is indeed poetry, maybe epic poetry.

Poetry is not simply a matter of rhyme, meter, and form, although these can be important in a poem. Rather, poetry begins with the poet transforming the ordinary into the extraordinary, something which goes beyond the practical and the necessary. In some way those who write poetry and those who read it "leave the everyday world" and enter another form of thinking. The odd language of poetry — perhaps heightened by rhyme and meter — helps to carry the listener to this different mental state.

There is poetry of the poems but there are also social gestures which can only be described as poetic. In courtship rituals, a gentleman might give flowers to his beloved as a token of his love; in church, Catholics genuflect before the tabernacle as a sign of their faith. Both gestures are completely unnecessary (perhaps some would call them artificial) but, like poetry, they are attempts to transcend the ordinary. The male suitor could have sent his beloved a note to the effect that certain biological and socially conditioned responses had produced in him a feeling that might be classified as affection; the Catholic could have quite simply stated that he believed in a divine presence and walked past the tabernacle. But in both cases the emotions spill over; ordinary language and actions cannot contain the feelings; there is a need to break the restraints of the practical, to lose control, and the result is an irrational, out-of-the-ordinary poetic gesture.

Mencken was right. Liturgy is a theological and sacramental matter expressed not as a syllogism but as a poem. What "carries us away" when hearing a poem is not so much the meaning (and that might not occur to us on the first hearing) but the mysterious power of the poetic tone of voice. What draws us into the collective spirit of liturgy is not a logical and scientific presentation of its meaning but the "poetry" — which is the way of saying that the meaning of it all will constantly elude our mere human understanding. This does not imply that theological matters must remain untouchable and forever shrouded in mystery. The only point being made here is that human elaborations of sacramental acts are poetry, and poetry must be treated as poetry, not everyday prose. Perhaps it might help to read Archibald MacLeish's poem *Ars Poetica* and substitute the word "liturgy" where he uses "poem." The last lines of the poem provide an especially valuable insight:

> A poem should not mean
> But be.

You can explain what a genuflection tries to convey, you can explain its history, but you cannot explain a genuflection, a poetic gesture. Just let it be.

The left brain, scientists tell us, controls the right side of the body and specializes in the logical aspects of life: mathematics, language, analysis, and so on. A few inches away, the right brain controls the left side of the body; an incurable romantic, it deals with the poetry in life: art, music, love, nonverbal insights, and so on. Ritual makes a very direct appeal to the right brain, that territory of our mind that deals with the irrational, the emotional, and the poetic. During the more austere moments of the old Latin Mass, the right brain sometimes had to work overtime. During the more de-ritualized examples of the vernacular Mass, the right brain — that miniature Homer or Shakespeare in all of us — is smothered to death.

I cannot say when it happened, but sometime in the recent past (perhaps the 1940s) many Roman Catholic clergymen became uncomfortable about the poetic aspects of ritual. In a very real sense, they initiated a quiet revolution at the parish level. Liturgical "poetry" (like the High Mass), if not eliminated, was gradually translated into "prose." The Second Vatican Council and the changes that followed it only brought out into the open this revolt of the left brain against the embarrassing poet in the right brain.[4]

De-ritualization means taking a poem and forcing it into a syllogism. A poem will flow easily to song. A syllogism, on the other hand, repels song. Nobody wants to sing a syllogism.

5

Ego Renewal

Presenting Father Hank and Friends

It is Holy Thursday and we are at the solemn evening Mass in a midwestern parish. The moment comes for the celebrant of the Mass, the pastor, to wash the feet of twelve parishioners, just as Christ washed the feet of the apostles at the Last Supper. During this deeply moving ceremony, the choir sings motets and alternates with the congregation, which sings hymns. Finally, this part of the liturgy comes to a close with the washing of the last foot. The music ends; you can almost sense that the congregation wants to weep for joy. Then, Father Hank (this is what the pastor wishes to be called) walks over to a microphone, smiles, and says, "Boy, that was great! Let's give these twelve parishioners a hand."

A stunned and somewhat reluctant congregation applauds weakly. Father Hank continues.

"Now, you take Mrs. Smith here, the first parishioner to get her foot washed. She has four young kids at home, but she managed to find the time to come here tonight. Let's give the little lady a hand."

He leads the congregation in applause and resumes his speech.

"Mr. John Jones, our next parishioner, works at the plant down the road all day and he is probably a pretty tired guy by now. So, take a bow, John, and let's all give him a round of applause."

One by one, Father Hank goes down the row of twelve parishioners; each one gets a little testimonial and applause. With that job out of the way, Father Hank, visibly pleased with himself, resumes the liturgy, while the congregation, visibly annoyed, contemplates various methods of strangulation.

50

One scratches one's head. This is the kind of strange episode that cries out for anthropological analysis, but where does one even begin?

Perhaps the best way to start is by noting that Father Hank's idea of Holy Thursday solemnity, while a little warped, is by no means unusual. Similar things have happened everywhere. We can classify this manner of behavior under the heading of Ego Renewal, the use of liturgy as an opportunity to display, for all the world to see, the greatness of "me." Put bluntly, Father Hank's primary reason for interrupting the Holy Thursday ritual was not to thank the twelve parishioners, not to inject a little warmth into the ceremony, but to show everybody what a grateful, warm person *he* was.

Ego Renewal, this tendency to put "me" in the center of the liturgical landscape, is the single most influential thing to happen to the way Catholics have worshiped since the Second Vatican Council. Nothing else comes close to it in size and influence. From Ego Renewal flows everything that is annoying about liturgy in the Catholic church today. It even helps to explain, as we shall see, why Catholics can't sing.

To witness Ego Renewal at its worst, select ten parishes at random. The chances are very good that Ego Renewal will be flourishing, in various forms, at perhaps nine of them. American Catholics are familiar with one of the most irritating and most common possessors of the renewed ego, the parish songleader, whom we shall call Mr. Caruso.

"Good morning," Mr. Caruso says to us. A few people in the pews mumble a "Good morning" back at him.

"Let us all sing hymn number one hundred," he cheerfully announces.

Then, for the next couple of minutes, Mr. Caruso roars into the microphone at the top of his voice and performs a duet with the organist, while most of the assembled worshipers watch him in stupefied silence. Sometimes the congregation tries to project its singing, sometimes the organ tries to assert its presence but, whatever happens, Mr. Caruso makes sure that his voice, his immensely amplified voice, will be the loudest thing there and will crest *over* the sound made by everyone else.

Sometimes it appears that Mr. Caruso, his wife, and his children have installed themselves nearly everywhere. In stately basilicas and in little parishes you will find one of the Carusos — with a mouth only inches from a microphone. In fact, the Caruso clan has taken over in so many places that they have created what amounts to "the new Catholic sound," the official music of the church, what you expect to hear on Sundays if you call yourself a practicing Catholic: that is, the big am-

plified voice of the soloist belting out *Be Not Afraid* into a microphone.
The congregation is inaudible.

"But, Mr. Caruso has such a lovely voice." He does indeed, and
it repeatedly discourages people from singing. That lovely and elec-
tronically enlarged voice guarantees disaster. One loud voice, magnified
to unnatural proportions, produces what could be called a "command
sound." Instead of conveying the message "Join me," this type of amplified singing orders the congregation to listen and declares, "I am in
charge. Admire me." The parishioner has no choice but to cringe in the
face of this overwhelming show of musical force.

The average Catholic will, without any embarrassment, join a group
that produces a musical sound. There is, after all, safety in numbers and
a certain sense of security when one person blends his or her voice with
a group sound. Mr. Caruso, however, completely destroys that feeling
of being safe in the crowd. When he lets loose the full volume of his
amplified voice, the parishioner finds that the group disappears and he
or she must now perform a duet with the songleader. In other words,
five hundred people could be standing in a church and every last one
of them could be singing, but it does not sound as if all are singing together; instead, the amplification creates the feeling that each and every
member of the congregation is absolutely isolated and is singing a duo
with the powerful Mr. Caruso. Another difficulty is a sound "feedback"
that would confound even the most skilled musician in the pews. The
brain, as experiments have shown, becomes extremely confused when
one single voice anticipates or echoes everything a person tries to say or
sing. The amplified songleader, never quite synchronized with everyone
else, seems to be "stealing" the sounds that the congregation and choir
are trying to get out.

A few of these leaders of song do their job competently and actually
encourage the congregation's singing. The secret of their success is their
restrained use of amplification (and, by extension, their refusal to indulge
in ego ballooning). They start the congregation off and then step back,
away from the microphone. They let the congregation hear itself. In
some cases they do sing out with full force and, to some extent, show off
a lovely voice, but without amplification; they become one of the crowd.

An amplified soloist belting out *Praise to the Lord* in front of a silent
congregation produces one of the most unappealing sounds in Christen-
dom. Why, then, do parishes and cathedrals put up with it and punish
themselves with that massive load of Carusoian sound? Why do people
submit themselves to musical masochism and intimidation, week after
week? (You can almost see that huge amplified voice hovering menac-
ingly over the congregation, like the face of the Wizard of Oz in the movie

of the same name.) The various explanations for this range from simple human weakness to the more complex levels of psychiatric disorder:

Naiveté. Many Catholics have become so accustomed to the commanding voice of Mr. Caruso and the organ that they now presume "congregational singing" means one person's voice, amplified to the maximum degree, and everyone else watching in respectful silence.

Pretending. When parishes began to implement the reforms outlined by the Second Vatican Council, they soon discovered that congregations would not cooperate by singing robustly. To compensate for this failure, church authorities put up a cardboard façade: Mr. Caruso, the congregation's proxy. Thus began what one observer has called American Catholicism's "pretend music."[1] Everyone *pretends* that the congregation sings when, in reality, Mr. Caruso supplies nearly all of the noise.

Authoritarianism. The Roman Catholic church, according to this explanation, remains an authoritarian institution and unregenerate. Authoritarian types, so the reasoning goes, feel threatened by the sound of a singing congregation. They prefer to hear one authoritative voice at a time. To wreck everything, they bring in Mr. Caruso, the Big Brother of church music.

It could be that naiveté, pretending, or authoritarianism are somewhat harsh explanations for why Catholic congregations bravely endure these amplified soloists who are neither inspirational nor helpful. Many parishes have just overextended themselves with unrealistic programs of five or even seven "sung liturgies" every weekend, and the choir (the original "songleader") only sings at one of them; these parishes have to rely on an assortment of failed opera stars who get their thrills from bullying people with their voices. Sometimes a pastor and his music director are just too respectful of the People of God, who are considered infallible; for diplomatic reasons, one does not correct or even offer polite suggestions to the lay volunteers.

If the reader is searching for one technical reason why Catholics can't sing, just observe how Mr. or Ms. Caruso, week after week, forces down the lid on everything. Just watch how that amplified voice (lashing the congregation with sound) beats back the voice of the assembled faithful. And yet, it is amazing how many in a congregation react favorably to this punishment. "My, doesn't he have a lovely voice!" they say. These are the people who never sing.

You're Lookin' Great, Narcissus

The opening hymn has finished — or, to put it correctly, Mr. Caruso has just finished yelling the opening hymn into a microphone — and then comes that moment of supreme emptiness, that massive liturgical klunk: the celebrant's "Good morning." What is so subconsciously jarring about this greeting is its blatant display of the ego. "Good morning" really means, "*I* wish *you* a good morning. *I* [the person, the individual called Father Hank, Father Chuck, Father Bob] deign to wish *you* a pleasant continuation of the morning. *I*, the center of your attention and probably the reason you have come, *I*, the one and only *me*, welcome you to *my* show and it will be a good show with a good performance by *me*, and for this reason you will be fortunate to have a good morning."

"Good morning" — a greeting in the English language reserved for cold situations where the greeter wants to distance himself or herself from the greeted, the sort of hello we toss at the janitor or a shopkeeper we do not particularly like — is all that is needed to turn the spotlight on Father Hank or Father Chuck or Father Bob. ("Good morning" at a Mass also has the odd effect of demolishing the effectiveness of any music used before or after it is uttered.)

Catholics occasionally encounter the priest, the atypical priest, who begins Mass with, "May the Lord be with you." You can almost sense a sigh of relief as the congregation responds, "And also with you." The reason why that dialog is so much more powerful than "[I wish you a] good morning" is a little-noticed secret in its construction: the priest does not use "I" and the congregation does not answer with "we." Immediately, right at the outset of proceedings, the priest signals that he is renouncing his ego so that he can democratically lead the assembly — and the grateful congregation imitates his renunciation of ego.

Alas, this type of priest may not be around much longer. According to the latest theory, the liturgical presider must avoid a "sterile" and "impersonal" manner. Instead, he must say everything "as if he really means it." He must radiate warmth, measurable in BTUs. In short, he must become an actor.

The priest of the future will probably resemble Father Histrionicus, a person that most Catholic laypeople have come to know and dread. "Gooooood morning!!!" he almost sings at the congregation. (Does he rub his hands in gleeful anticipation at this point or does that gesture come later in the script?) "It's great to be here today," he continues, giving us his biography, his feelings at the moment, his observations on the weather, and so on. During the next forty minutes or so, the whole congregation watches apprehensively as he waves his arms in one broad liturgical gesture after another. (Will this man someday let his arms swing just a bit too energetically and knock over a vase or perhaps give a black eye to one of the acolytes? What is this man going to do next?)

As Father Histrionicus goes through his performance, he sets up this proposition in the brain of everyone watching him: "Do I like this liturgy because I like Father Histrionicus or do I dislike this liturgy because I dislike the man?" In other words, the whole matter of "liking" liturgy depends on "liking" the celebrant and his style. He forces the worshipers to choose. In most cases he loses.

Some bishops have even adopted a version of the Histrionicus style. I am thinking of the much-in-the-news archbishop who processed into his cathedral for his inaugural Mass and then, during his homily, cracked jokes, put on funny hats, and made everyone feel that this would be a very relaxed event. What can you say about this sort of thing? What can you say about a bishop who is all seriousness one minute in a liturgy and then a stand-up comic the next? Maybe, "What a great guy, a real *mensch*!" Or maybe, "What an ego!" He knows perfectly well that the little frivolities he adds to the liturgy will change the focus of the whole liturgical event: from a communal act of worship to a one-man show.

A "Good morning" placed at the beginning of a liturgy and the thousands of other stunts which say, "Notice my great personality," will not cause the pillars of Christianity to collapse. But, at the same time, it is important to recognize that all of the "little sins" of Ego Renewal are not just temporary lapses in taste, minor difficulties that will disappear one of these days. Rather, they must be seen as symptoms of a disease which is progressing rapidly. This disease is narcissism. Somehow in an era that has given new meaning to the pronoun "me," it is only fitting that the Roman Rite should also be transformed into a series of episodes during which the "me" has an opportunity to display itself in front of a congregation — for approval, if not adoration.

The Icon

The Catholic church has been fighting a running battle with narcissism in worship ever since apostolic times. There has never been a shortage of people who want to take over public worship for their own purposes. In this battle — really a tug-of-war — two powerful forces struggle for supremacy. On the one side there is "me": the personal dimension of religion. The faith of Christianity must involve the personal, private relationship of the individual ("me") to the personal Jesus, who will always listen to every prayer. On the other side of this tug-of-war is the *job* of faith. Christians come together to worship as a community. The

Mass is a public, communal effort, in which individuals act and pray as a group. Tension between the private and public sectors is inevitable.

We can see this tension in two thousand years of Christian art for a liturgical setting. The painters of the Byzantine icon, for example, were ready to burst with emotional religious fervor and yet at every stage of artistic creation they pulled this zeal back; they held the reins tightly, as it were. They would not permit themselves the luxury of painting their own version of what they felt. Instead, they submitted to a canon of taste that belonged to something larger than themselves: the highest expectations of the community, the culture, or, if you wish, the tribe. The painters of the icon put their private, inner faith into the painted image but they did so according to strict conventions and traditional formulas; in this way they communicated to the beholder the message that the image went beyond the mere feelings of the artist and beyond the commonplace.

The great mosaics of the churches in Ravenna or St. Mark's in Venice, the stained glass of the Gothic cathedrals, the serene Renaissance madonnas, Michelangelo's Last Judgment, and the highly theatrical painting that Rubens intended for a church all show off the brilliant ego of the master artist — the "me" side of art. These artworks are very open celebrations of the human spirit and human accomplishment. Yet, at the same time, we can also sense a restraining objectivity. Feeling and emotion are quite visible but, as in the icon, the artist sends out dozens of signals which say, "This is not really *me* in complete control of this work. I am only the instrument of a much larger ideal of faith."

For centuries, this tug-of-war between the "me" (subjective) and the "we" (objective) usually resulted in a compromise, at least when it came to the official, public worship of the church. The Mass would slowly proceed with all its objective, communal, iconic splendor in the front of the church; the ordinary people in the nave would follow the ritual or go about the business of their own subjective, personal devotions, whichever they preferred. We must not imagine, however, that the price for the iconic objectivity in the sanctuary was a kind of artistic stiffness that put an end to creativity and personal expression in liturgical art. The fact is that, throughout much of its history, Roman Catholicism had been surprisingly liberal, experimental, and even radical when it comes to the matter of the liturgical arts. For example, the ancient Jews and the early Christians considered statues to be a pagan abomination. (The Eastern Rites and the Orthodox churches still ban all statues.) But Roman Catholicism eventually permitted statues in its churches — a revolutionary departure from tradition — and even boldly displayed them. The Roman Church broke with the long-standing Christian tradition of allowing only vocal music in church when it permitted the organ and other instruments to play during divine services. A hundred years ago, worshipers in an Austrian cathedral could hear a "modern" Mass by Bruckner (with its daring Wagnerian harmonies). When Franck or Fauré or Messiaen improvised organ music for Mass in a French church, when Gounod composed a setting of a Mass, they all used a modern, even progressive style, with archaic moments. The list of examples could go on for pages and the conclusion is not all that surprising: the church which nurtured an exploring, dynamic Western civilization frequently allowed artists and composers a great deal of freedom to create art that was exploring and dynamic.

This freedom, however, was not entirely unrestricted. The church insisted on obedience to a great Unwritten Law which went something like this: "As a creative artist you may follow your own instincts but your art or music for the church must not clash with the liturgical function; it must take its place in the objective liturgical setting and not seem like an intrusion. Your creation must display a degree of quality and craftsmanship which will be agreeable to prince and peasant, male and female, young and old. Everyone who sees the artwork or hears the music must sense a group endeavor, a group prayer: maybe something performed by the assembly or by a choir acting in the name of the assembly, maybe a painting that seems to sum up the highest religious aspirations of a whole people. In the past, the icon painters prayed and fasted as they struggled to put the holy images into the exacting forms prescribed by tradition. You must try to do something similar."

It was once thought that Beethoven, the titan who "liberated music," pretty much ignored the text of the Mass when he composed his *Missa Solemnis*, but historical research has shown that he too was haunted, even obsessed by this Unwritten Law.[2] When composing the *Missa Solemnis* he carefully studied precedents in the Masses of other composers, to see how they had handled certain situations; he even made sure that the type of music he wrote for certain words would conform to the theology behind those words. To put it another way, Beethoven — totally deaf by this time, a famous composer who could do whatever he wanted, somewhat paranoid, fiercely independent, difficult to get along with — submitted to the accumulated wisdom of the culture; his ego is on every page of the *Missa Solemnis*, but so is the restraining humility of the Unwritten Law.

We should not conclude that this Unwritten Law was exclusively reserved for great masters laboring over great art for the church. Long before the 1960s, German-speaking and Slavic Catholics sang a very plain form of religious "folk music" which blended with liturgical rites.

(*Silent Night*, for example, sounds like an Austrian peasant dance or song.) Also, we have to remember that the Unwritten Law was probably broken as often as it was observed. Beethoven may have behaved himself when he wrote his self-effacing *Mass in C*, but his *Missa Solemnis*, despite the best of intentions, is so colossal that it will blow the priest and acolytes right out of the church. It is not easy to write music which (1) expresses the noblest aspirations of the communal, cultural, tribal consciousness and (2) seems to submit to the higher purposes of the rite itself. Underneath the skull of every composer there is always going to be an alluring, tempting voice which whispers, "Forget the collective and the iconic. Write what you *feel*."

The Reformed-folk Style

Paul fretted about the charismatics who could impress everyone with a gift of tongues that was more theatrical than spiritual. In the Middle Ages, the liturgical cantors "stopped the show" with their thrilling virtuosity (which included a sparkling version of a hiccup!).[3] Mr. Caruso and the ego-renewed bishops and priests of today may just be one more episode in this continuing saga of people who treat worship as a theater stage for their solo performances.

A few of my Catholic friends assure me that the sacerdotal actor may be around for centuries to come but Mr. Caruso and family are on their way out; the Carusos have invested all their efforts in an exhausted traditional form of church music and that stuff will soon find its way to the museum or the trash can. The future, these people tell me, belongs to music that comes not from the elitists but from the heart and soul of the people, from our time, from our own culture. They call it "folk music" or "contemporary music." I know it well.

I can remember attending those first parish "folk Masses" back in the 1960s, when the liturgy was partly in Latin and partly in English. Most of the people there seemed to be having a grand time. At the entrance they sang *Michael, Row the Boat Ashore*. At the Offertory there was *Kumbaya*. Communion featured *Sons of God* (with the happy-go-lucky refrain, "Eat His body, drink His blood. Allelu!"). Hands clapped. Guitars twanged. A somewhat nervous clergy, not quite sure of what it should do with the folk believers, often put them "downstairs" in the basement church. The "upstairs" church would be reserved for the "regular" liturgy. Back in those days (the 1960s) all the signs indicated that nothing would stop the "downstairs" revolution — not even its own excesses, its very own innocent blasphemies. Who could ever forget those three-chord guitarists! They certainly gave another dimension of meaning to the word "monotonous." Communion meditations became interminable exercises in self-pity. Members of the folk group would sometimes tell little stories or jokes before each song; sometimes they would have arguments about the music while the priest and congregation watched and waited. It was considered so very natural, so very much in the folk style when a mother and father, two singers in a folk group, changed their baby's fully loaded diaper right in front of the congregation (So help me!). If someone ever gives a prize for conspicuous vulgarity, above and beyond the call of duty, I would like to nominate one especially inept parish folk group in Connecticut. While the congregation tried to follow the actions of the Mass, the women in this ensemble — they wore tight clam-digger pants — would writhe in a kind of heated agitation, directly in front of the congregation, and slap tambourines against their ample buttocks, in time with the music.

And congregations willingly took this kind of abuse. As bad as the folk group was, it at least showed signs of life. The "downstairs" liturgy with all its shortcomings was, in many cases, immeasurably preferable to what the "upstairs" church passed off as standard music for the church: that is, an incompetent organist accompanying Mr. Caruso, a perfunctory stanza of *Praise to the Lord*, an Amen here, a response there, and other stale musical crumbs. Traditional music, no matter how you define it, died in the "upstairs" church long before the 1960s and left a huge void where the musical enthusiasm was supposed to be.[4] Everything good or bad rushed in to fill that void: every trite, halfbaked musical idea found its way into the repertory of the "downstairs" folk group, and all of it was above criticism because it was *Spiritguided*.

I like to think that this early phase of the folk music phenomenon culminated in 1967 with the publication of a piece called *Glory* by Joe Wise. (It later appeared in *The People's Mass Book*, a hugely successful hymnal.) The tempo of the work is marked "Walking Blues," in order to insure the right type of interpretation from the kind of people who would perform this music — white, suburbanite Catholic folk groups which would have to pretend that they were but poor, southern sharecroppers. The composer and the editors, sensing that the performers really had no instinctive "feel" for this music, had to specify that the word "Glory" was to be sung "Glo (*ho-ho*)-ry, (*hee*)." When I first beheld this printed text which directed me to coordinate my spontaneous "Walking Blues" with the syllables "Glo (*ho-ho*)-ry, (*hee*)," I wanted to throw up, intellectually speaking. The whole thing, the whole folk craze, was a fraud, and this fact was now out in the open where everyone could see it. This fad would soon fizzle out, I predicted.

I erred. I had neglected to take certain realities into consideration. First of all, there was the microphoned Mr. Caruso "upstairs"; his version of traditional church music made any monstrosity look brilliant by comparison. Then there was about a century of sweet-song hymns which American Catholics called their own (e.g., the music that a tenor sang at John F. Kennedy's wedding and funeral). The parish that had once placed *Mother, at Your Feet Is Kneeling* at the pinnacle of religious music would now be the parish with the thriving folk group and a musical life heavily weighted to favor the so-called folk repertory. Finally, I did not count on a self-correcting reaction within the folk movement itself. Some of the folk enthusiasts, starting in the 1970s, began to clean up their act. Their new philosophy went something like this: "We, the practitioners of the *reformed-folk* style, are not like those misguided hootenanny Catholics of the 1960s. Heavens, no! Today, we follow the example set by the St. Louis Jesuits, the Dameans, the Weston Monks, and the others who have given us a form of religious music which, for the first time in history, reveals the depths of scripture's meaning."

The composers of this reformed folk music have created a large repertory of songs with mild harmonies, comforting words, and a sort of "easy listening" sound; it is all so very undisturbed and appealing, the musical equivalent of the warm bubblebath. The whole enterprise has been resoundingly successful and some publications sell in the millions. A cathedral music director I know estimates that 65 percent of the religious music heard in the archdiocese where he works is folk/"contemporary," reformed and unreformed. Often the remaining 35 percent is accompanied in a way that makes it sound folk.

For the time being, the reformed-folk repertory (also known as "contemporary" church music) occupies the high ground; it has the advantage of appearing to possess a musical and a moral superiority. It enjoys the reputation for being "new" and "what the people want." The "upstairs" liturgies seem to be stuck with Mr. Caruso and a few recycled Protestant hymns.

The victory of the folk style, reformed or otherwise, is so great and so blinding that many people cannot see beyond that apparent success to what could mildly be called the *problem* with this music: simply put, nearly all of it — no matter how sincere, no matter how many scriptural texts it contains — oozes with an indecent narcissism. The folk style, as it has developed since the 1960s, is Ego Renewal put to music. Here is a sampling of some of the most egotistical and narcissistic folk songs introduced in the 1960s, songs which would set the tone for countless imitations:

Gonna Sing, My Lord by Joe Wise. In this song the constantly re-peated message is that "I" sing "for all I'm worth."

All That I Am by Sebastian Temple. The word "I" appears fifteen times on two small printed pages. The implication of the text is that in the Mass the congregation offers "I," something truly wonderful, a spotless oblation lifted up to the Father.

When I Sing by Jack Miffleton. With repeats, the words "I" and "me" are sung twenty-one times each — a record for a piece of music which takes up only one small printed page.

Make Me a Channel of Your Peace (Prayer of St. Francis) by Sebas-tian Temple. The founder of the Franciscans intended this deeply moving prayer to be recited privately. The same words, when mag-nified in song and proclaimed in public, sound like an obnoxious form of boasting, an inventory of *my* spiritual greatness.

Let There Be Peace on Earth by Sy Miller and Jill Jackson. For a mo-ment, forget the melody which, as someone put it, sounds like the kind of waltz you would hear at an ice-skating rink. Concentrate on the words and the climax of the melody: " . . . and let it [peace] begin with me." There is not a syllable referring to God's saving grace or the peace that flows from Christ. "I" bring peace on earth by myself; God merely watches on, approvingly.

Sometimes the "I" and "me" are expanded to "us" — not the uni-versal church, not the struggling Christian faithful, but the "us" who are the special people at this folk liturgy, the selected few who tower above all others in saintly virtue.

They'll Know We Are Christians by Our Love by Peter Scholtes. This song canonizes every member of the perfect, sinless congregation.

We Are Your Bread by Joe Wise. "We are your bread now; the bread of love are we." The garbled theology implies that the congregation is the eucharistic victim offered in the Mass, or at least the most important aspect of the whole event.

We Are the Light of the World by Jean A. Greif. By about the third verse, the worshipers get the implied message that they have lived up to the standards of the Beatitudes, without faltering once and without a speck of sin. As a result of this perfect record, they are now the light of the world.

"I" and "me" songs or sung versions of intense personal "conversations" with God can be found in the psalms and in almost two millennia
of Christian worship, but great care was taken to make sure that the music would not sound like a presentation of *individual* "I-me" emotions.
The words of the psalm might say "I" and "me," but the music, intended
for public worship, said "we." A good example of this can be seen in the
various settings of Psalm 90/91, a song of comfort and a reminder of
God's abiding protection. In the Middle Ages, the words of this psalm
were lifted out of the commonplace and uttered in the Latin language
(*Qui habitat in adjutorio Altissimi* ...); the sentiments in the text were
then twisted in the unusually shaped melodies of chant, the musical
equivalent of the icon. These two "artificial" steps (the Latin language
and the odd melodies) reminded everyone that this particular text, as
sung, was not the personal property of the singer but an integral part
of a public act of worship.

The early Protestant reformers translated that same psalm into the
vernacular so that the congregation could sing it, but they too kept this
important element of distance and "artificiality"; that is, they preserved
the ideal of the "icon in music." The words of the psalm were jammed
into the pattern of a strict poetic meter with rhyme. ("O God, our help in
ages past, / Our hope for years to come ... ") Melodies were foursquare
and totally without a sense of private intimacy. Sometimes the melodies
were so "neutral" and generic that a tune could be used for any kind of
psalm: one with a joyous text or one with more mournful words. Today,
in modern psalm settings by Deiss, Gelineau, Somerville, and others,
we can see this same concern about keeping the sung structure of the
psalm as "artificial" and as iconic as possible.

Now, with the above versions of Psalm 90/91 in mind, analyze the
same text as found in the song *On Eagle's Wings* by Michael Joncas.
Note the enormous difference. The Joncas work, an example of the
reformed-folk style at its most gushing, does not proclaim the psalm
publicly; it embraces the text — lovingly, warmly, and even romantically. That moaning and self-caressing quality of the music, so common
in the reformed-folk style, indicates that the real topic of the words is
not the comforting Lord but "me" and the comforts of my personal
faith.

One composer of "contemporary" church music described perfectly
what is going on in this type of music. He said that in his own compositions he tried to bring out the "felt meanings" of the sung words. There
is indeed something quite tactile about the way this music manipulates
the words; the meaning of the text has to be molded, shaped — felt. As
a result, the performance of reformed-folk music depends heavily on

a dramatic realism, on the ability of soloists to communicate personal feelings, *felt* meanings, to a congregation.

Publishers never tire of calling the reformed folk style a "revolutionary" innovation, and the adjective is, for once, not a commercial exaggeration. The music of the St. Louis Jesuits, the Dameans, the Weston Monks, Michael Joncas, and all the others is, without any doubt, a revolutionary addition to the Roman Rite. These composers have, as it were, smashed the icon, an exceedingly revolutionary act. The singers, especially the soloists, are not really proclaiming the word of God; instead, they are *feeling* the drama in the text and acting out cozy tableaux, charming theatrical episodes, in which "I" — regardless of the text — play the leading role; God belongs in the supporting cast.

In the song *On Eagle's Wings* and similar compositions, the icon or the mosaic of Christ in Majesty is replaced with the glossy poster of the male Hollywood heartthrob, the latest take-your-breath-away movie star. Perhaps *On Eagle's Wings, Be Not Afraid*, and countless other "contemporary" sweet songs are just another product of the Great Hollywood Factory of Dreams and Romance. Certainly, this kind of music tries very hard to imitate the sound track of a three-hanky romantic film starring Greta Garbo or Bette Davis. You know the scene:

HE: I love you forever, Samantha.

SHE: We can't go on like this, Rodney. [The melody rises in the background. Violins soar.]

HE: You are beautiful by moonlight. [Waves crash against the cliffs below.]

SHE: Oh, Rodney! [Globs of sound from the orchestra. Fadeout.]

And the music sounds like *On Eagle's Wings*.

When St. Teresa of Avila levitated, she may have heard music that sounded like *On Eagle's Wings* or *Be Not Afraid*. But when she went into the chancel to sing with the other nuns, she was just "one of the gang." She shared the liturgical work with everyone else. Her private rapture remained private. She did not presume to turn liturgy into a session where everyone would admire everyone else's romantic rapture, accompanied by the romantically rapturous sounds of a Hollywood sound track.

Whenever I point out this obvious Hollywood connection with the folk style — especially in its reformed moments — I always get the same reaction: "You are just a cynic who is ridiculing the heartfelt faith of simple people."

This is untrue. What I am ridiculing is their astounding egotism, their mischievous habit of making God, through the medium of song, bless their spiritual superiority.

"Besides being a cynic, you are forgetting that God is our friend."

Christianity was founded on the principle that God is indeed our friend, but those casual, la-dee-da melodies, the easy familiarity of the music, and the let-me-show-you-how-sincere-I-am expressiveness all indicate that God is our *little* friend and very much under our control, on the end of a leash. As one music critic put it, the music seems to say (to our little friend), "Have a nice day, God."

True cynicism is to be found among those who have taken a religious act (or interaction between God and humanity) and turned it into group therapy; the music always seems to be assuring everybody that the good news of the New Testament goes something like this: "I'm OK, you're OK, God's OK" — in that order.

I Am the Voice of God

A good deal of what I have presented so far concerning the folk phenomenon in church could be dismissed as a matter of taste: an elitist musician's taste versus the taste of the Spirit-guided Catholic laity, ordinary people. If we are discussing taste, then dispute is out of the question. But is the folk phenomenon just a matter of taste? Is the narcissism just a figment of my imagination and this whole issue a mere quarrel over preferences? There is one innovation of the folk phenomenon which takes the discussion out of the area of "mere taste," and that is the tendency of this music to let the congregation become the "Voice of God." (Shall we call it the *Vox Dei*?) In other words, the composer sets the text so that the congregation sings God's words, usually without quotation marks, in a somewhat bored, relaxed, almost casual style. This is startling and unprecedented in the history of Christianity.[5] The following is just a partial list of these religious songs which require the congregation to play the role of God, and a very laid-back God at that:

> *All Who Drink the Water* by J. H. Miffleton
>
> *Be Not Afraid* by Bob Dufford
>
> *Come to Me, All You Who Are Weary* by Dan Schutte
>
> *Come to Me, All Who Labor* by Gregory Norbet
>
> *Come unto Me: I Will Make You a Jewel* by Bob Hurd
>
> *Come with Me to the Fields* by Dan Schutte

Hosea: Come Back to Me by Gregory Norbet

I Am the Bread of Life by Susanne Toolan

I Am the Resurrection by Jim Anderson

I Am the Vine by Bob Hurd

I Am the Vine by J. H. Miffleton

I Am the Way by Charles Blankenship

I Have Loved You with an Everlasting Love by Michael Joncas

I, the Lord by Tom Kendzia

If I Be Lifted Up by Gregory Norbet

If You Belong to Me by Bob Hurd

In My Name by Willard Francis Jabusch

Isaiah 49: I Will Never Forget You by Carey Landry

Lord of the Dance by Sydney Carter

My Friends, I Bless You by Gregory Norbet

Peace I Leave with You by Gregory Norbet

Peace to All Who Come to Me by Angel Tuciarone

Return to Me by Bob Hurd

This Is My Body (anonymous)

This Is My Body by John Foley

Whatsoever You Do by Willard Francis Jabusch

When You Seek Me by Carey Landry

Here is the revolution. Here is where the folk phenomenon has completely changed the very idea of worship. In all of the above religious songs, "I" and "me" do not mean the individual worshiper but God Himself. Through the miracle of "contemporary" music, the congregation (and each individual in it) becomes the Voice of God. The words sung by this God/congregation always seem to be reassuring everyone that they live lives of unfailing, heroic saintliness and that they have purchased their own salvation through their good works. (The way the congregation divinely and repeatedly congratulates itself in *Whatsoever You Do* is especially crass.) And then there is this added complication: since God is our friend who loves us and since the congregation so effortlessly becomes Him when singing His words from scripture, it would appear that the congregation is really in love with itself.

In *Here I Am, Lord*, this "Voice of God" self-love leads to comic complications. In the verses of this song, the worshipers become God. They, the plural God, sing about how grand They are, how They divinely command the earth and sky, how They hear the supplications of those in distress. Then, in a miraculous transformation, the worshipers become human beings during the refrain ("Here I Am, Lord"). In the same song, the congregation is the loving God and the loved individual. Simultaneously, the congregation divinely offers and humanly gives love to itself.

If there is a theological underpinning for the "Voice of God" song, it perhaps can be found in Thomas Sheehan's book *The First Coming: How the Kingdom of God Became Christianity* (1986). The author of this challenging study tries to prove that Jesus, in his teaching, destroyed the idea of God-in-Himself and replaced it with the experience of God-with-mankind. In Jesus' revolutionary message "God threw in his lot irrevocably with human beings and chose relatedness to them as the only definition of himself. From now on, God was one with mankind." The current disarray in Christianity is, Sheehan suggests, a hopeful sign that the false ecclesiastical institution called the church is crumbling and will be replaced with the kingdom that Jesus actually promised — and the doctrine of the kingdom meant "that henceforth and forever God was present only in and as one's neighbor."

A visit to any parish where the reformed-folk repertory dominates and where the "Voice of God" song is a great favorite will provide enough evidence to suggest that the beginnings of Sheehan's kingdom may have already come.

In the past, a very sensitive Catholicism (Roman, Byzantine, Orthodox, and even Anglican) hesitated to let divine words come from the lips of anyone, in just any commonplace way. The monks in a cloister, for example, wanted to begin the Easter Mass by singing the words "I arose." To avoid the presumption of "playing God," they sang the text in Latin (*Resurrexi*) and in a musical style reserved exclusively for the church. Roman Catholicism has now gone from this type of extreme caution to a situation where the congregation, without giving it a second thought, "plays God" in song and makes Him into a dreamy, slow-moving divinity, that endearing mascot of the believers at the folk liturgy.

The Softer Image

"Why are we singing all of this 'contemporary' music?" an acquaintance of mine asked a parish liturgy committee. "Why can't we make some room for other types of music?"

She received a stern answer: "Because we're getting away from all of this *adoration* nonsense: adoring the communion bread in a gold monstrance, adoring God as if He were some oriental potentate who demanded offerings of art. The Mass is people. The Mass needs people-music, not adoration-music. The People of God are beginning to realize that God has a softer image."

There is nothing new under the sun. This "softer image" has been around for some time.

Roman Catholicism has a long history of defending the "hard" image of God — such as the Trinity, the Incarnation, Calvary, the Lamb of God slain for sins, and the intricate dogmas of the Mass. These are all exceedingly "hard" and demanding concepts, wild theological propositions that refuse to be tamed by reason; they cannot be simplified, prettied up, and placed on the corner of the coffee table. They defy domestication. But constantly insisting on dogmatic "hardness" — that is no way to run a business, especially a universal religion. This is why Catholicism also has a long history of directing the believer to the "softer," more approachable aspects of the faith, like the Sacred Heart, the Virgin Mary, the saints. The church has even provided opportunities for experiencing slightly bizarre forms of "softness," on quite a different level, in the Infant Jesus of Prague and in the veneration of that ghastly kitsch religious art which comes so close to the comic.

The "hard" and the "soft" peacefully coexisted in Roman Catholicism for centuries. The priest at the altar tended to the "hard" business of the faith; behind him, many members of the congregation indulged themselves in the more personal dimension of this same faith. While this priest read off the dogmatic certainties compressed in the unyielding Latin language, a soprano soloist softened things up by singing *To Jesus' Heart All Burning* in the choir loft. Her song did not seem to make any difference to the "hard," iconic ritual going on down below, since she was as far away from the altar as possible, and yet still inside the church.

When the Latin Mass virtually disappeared, the dam broke. Catholic worship in the United States was flooded with wave after wave of softness. The soprano soloist now sings *Be Not Afraid* and *On Eagle's Wings* from the front of the church. In many cases, the sanctuary has been remodeled (with wall-to-wall carpets over marble floors and with philodendron plants here and there) to make this place of theological "hardness" look more like a living room. Softness has moved in from the periphery; it now threatens to take over the center. Roman Catholicism in the United States is rapidly becoming the church of abundant niceness, of sweetness and light, of feather-pillow softness. This does not necessarily refer to a theological or doctrinal softness, a weakening of the articles of faith. Rather, it means a growing tendency to make Catholic worship a soft, personal experience, an occasion during which the warm feeling of the music and the priest is radiated to the believer in the pews. In this kind of a church, there is little room for any gesture or music or activity which goes beyond the personal, anything which is "hard" or profound, anything which is not "nice."

The "hard" God of the past was described as "holy" in scripture. Rudolf Otto, in his book *The Idea of the Holy*, put special emphasis on the ability of religion to bring the individual to the edge of this immense concept of the "holy God." He points out that the holy or "numinous" (to use his term) is not just a matter of ethics or piety. In its original sense, "holy" implied an indefinable force, a mystery, something completely beyond the usual, something unintelligible and unfamiliar. Human beings have a primitive, instinctive feeling about this holiness, this *mysterium tremendum*, and they sense its enormous power, over which they have no control. This feeling of awe in the believer produces a "peculiar dread," which is, at the same time, somewhat appealing. God's holiness, far from being something sweet and "soft," is terrifying and yet fascinating. According to Otto, this experience of the holy as something overpowering but also enticing arouses a feeling of religious humility and unworthiness in the believer.

The psalmist knew all about this human awe of God's holiness, an awe which elicits feelings of dread and, simultaneously, longing. In Psalm 65/66 we read, "Say unto God, How terrible art thou in thy works!" Elsewhere in the Old Testament God is referred to as mighty and "terrible." In Genesis 28, God speaks to Jacob in a dream. When Jacob awakes, he is "afraid" and says, "Surely the Lord is in this place. . . . How dreadful is this place! this is none other but the house of God, and this is the gate of heaven." The same words are used in the Introit of a Mass for the dedication of a church (*"Terribilis est locus iste"*). The medieval architects who built the great cathedrals understood perfectly that a "dreadful," "terrible" God needed to be worshiped in an appropriately "dreadful," "terrible" house. So did the architects of those charming Rococo chapels in Germany and so did the New England Calvinists who built those severely plain wooden churches.

Somewhere in their brains, modern Christians might respond favorably to this concept of the "holy," "terrible" God and yet still not quite accept it in their deepest emotions. To put it crudely, they have ceased to be impressed. The "dreadful" God, after all, no longer controls lightning or storms; that sort of thing now belongs to the weatherman on television. The "terrible" God who visits plagues on the wickedness of His people can now be outsmarted by a vaccine or wonder drug. Human beings, with all kinds of new power at their disposal, now become the ones who are truly dreadful and terrible. Stripped of His awesome majesty, God becomes merely a "soft," endearing old distributor of love.

The musician who works for the Catholic church sometimes has to make sense out of a liturgical system that has wires dangerously crossed. The "softer image" music does not seem to go with the "harder image" ritual and its dogmas. The concept of "the People of God" has degenerated into "the people are God," at least during the "Voice of God" songs. Collective, corporate worship must begin with the renunciation of ego and this will invariably lead to liturgy and music with an objective character, but such things are denounced as "adoration" today. The modern church inherits the theology of the "hard," "holy" God but it should not adore Him, because He is friendly and "soft." When the music director of a parish tries to put all of this together, the result is a crazy quilt of musical impressions. The great majority of Catholic laypeople sense that the theology behind the music is confused, at best, and to protect the orthodoxy of the church they frequently refrain from singing.

Glory and Praise

Ego Renewal, the "softer image," and people-music (as opposed to adoration-music) are somewhat abstract concepts. To make these ideas come to life, the reader should page through a songbook entitled *Glory and Praise*. This collection, published by North American Liturgy Resources (NALR), started out in the 1970s as a book for the folk group, for that special folk liturgy once a week. By the mid-1980s, however, *Glory and Praise* had received a new format to make it look like a regular hymnal. Some Catholics now insist that *Glory and Praise* is exactly the sort of thing that the laity and religious communities have been yearning for: a collection of religious music devoted almost exclusively to the works of the St. Louis Jesuits, the Weston Monks (i.e., Gregory Norbet), Michael Joncas, Carey Landry, and other big names in the folk-contemporary genre. The book is a best seller. Indeed, this publication or something derived from it might eventually become *the* "national Catholic hymnal."

I have used the term "revolutionary" to describe the kind of music found in *Glory and Praise*. A perusal of this publication (1984 edition) will show why this adjective applies not only to the musical style but also to the whole agenda of those who promote that style:

1. *Glory and Praise* (1984) makes almost a complete break with the past. Except for a few Christmas carols, *Amazing Grace*, and *Peace Is Flowing Like a River*, there is no old music in this collection, nothing written before the 1960s. The past is repudiated.

2. Music for liturgical texts, such as "Lord, have mercy" or "Lamb of God," is scarce. The pew edition rarely refers to the liturgical year; finding specific songs for Advent, Lent, Pentecost, or Marian feasts is difficult.

3. The priest (the celebrant, the presider) has no musical voice in *Glory and Praise*. The editors have silenced him. There is no music at all for a dialog between priest and people.

4. Most of the music is quite difficult to sing and not really intended for the congregation.

In order to make room for *Glory and Praise*, countless Catholic institutions have tossed most of the great hymns (Catholic and Protestant), organ music, chant, and choral music into a trash can called "churchy music." The whole "churchy" repertory, no matter how beautiful or appropriate, makes many Catholics angry. They hate every moment of it. These angry ones are not necessarily radicals on the fringes. In some plain, "typical" parishes the congregation and choir sing very little music written before 1970, because the pastors, the liturgical committees, and the musicians, with righteous anger, have gone out of their way to avoid anything that sounds too "churchy," too much like the standard music associated with Catholicism and Protestantism.

As we have already discovered, there is good reason for this anger. In a large number of Catholic parishes, "churchy" music has come to mean failure, something which does not work as it should and never did, even back in the days just before the Second Vatican Council. Millions of good, practicing Catholics are alienated from their church's ritual, partly because of the indifferent performances of the sort of "churchy" music associated with that ritual. Some of these people have just taken a leave of absence. Others have seceded and established a parallel denomination, the pietistic church of *Glory and Praise*.

The emergence of the secessionists and *Glory and Praise* as major forces in Catholic church music is usually explained as just one of those normal shifts in taste which happen from time to time. One era of taste supposedly has ended. A new one is beginning. *Glory and Praise*, according to this theory, is but the first example of what the musical future will be like for all Roman Catholics in the United States. "Churchy" music has had its day. Now the folk-contemporary style will have its turn.

This assessment of the situation may indeed be correct concerning future trends, but the reasons for those trends are another matter. What has shifted is not aesthetic preference but theology.

"Churchy" music evolved from a Catholic theology which saw the assembly as people who have come together in order to offer thankful praise to the "holy," "terrible" God for the redemption brought by His Son; in the eucharistic liturgy Christ Himself continues His redemptive death for each new generation. There may be bishops, acolytes, virtuoso musicians, and distinguished laity at the Mass but all must leave their egos at the door and humbly surrender, because this is a communal act. The assembly, overwhelmed by gratitude and awe, thanks God, with deep humility, as members of the Mystical Body of Christ. Because of this, nobody is a star, not even the priest who stands *in persona Christi*.

The theology which produced *Glory and Praise* rearranges the spotlights, as it were. The lighting is now directed away from the sanctuary and pointed to what is considered the central aspect of liturgy: the individuals in the congregation, graced by the presence of the Risen Lord. The congregation, in song, boasts of its special status and its supreme confidence; it comes very close to worshiping itself in the "Voice of God" songs. Humility, either joyous or abject, is not encouraged at the folk liturgy because humility means adoration and adoration means worship directed away from people.

NALR must have realized that the narrowness of the repertory in *Glory and Praise*, no matter how popular, does not make sense in a church which calls itself universal. Moreover, for financial reasons the publishers had to take into consideration the large number of Catholics — a substantial market — who do not willingly attend the select "folk liturgy." This may explain why the 1984 edition of *Glory and Praise*, for the first time, included Christmas carols and some useful compositions by Lucien Deiss (with their "churchy" moments). In 1986 NALR went even further and issued a missalette-booklet entitled *Assemblybook* which contains "churchy" hymns scattered among the many works in the reformed-folk manner.[6]

Assemblybook, with its mixing of "contemporary" and "traditional" styles, is an example of a process called blending. Supposedly, this mixing of a bit of the old and the new, a chief characteristic of the missalettes, is a way of recognizing the diversity of the Catholic population. The "blended liturgy" might begin with a classic hymn; a favorite by the

St. Louis Jesuits might make an appearance after the first reading, Deiss at communion time, and then another classic hymn to send people home. It sounds like an astute compromise, but blending does not really work. The folk enthusiasts hate this arrangement because "churchy" music, presented well, always makes their reformed-folk repertory look anemic by comparison.

One example will illustrate why the folk believers would prefer to keep their music segregated. Let us suppose a congregation sings the Penitential Rite in chant. Perhaps they sing an old Gregorian Kyrie or perhaps the cantor sings (without amplification) invocations in English which are followed by a chantlike "Lord, have mercy." The music, with light organ accompaniment, is supremely objective and "ultrachurchy," but right from a standard hymnal. Then, a minute later guitars twang and the congregation has to sing *All I Ask of You* by Gregory Norbet (No. 250 in *Glory and Praise*, 1984 edition). This is a "Voice of God" song (at the refrain only, I think) with the following words at stanza 4: "Oooooooooo./Laughter, joy and presence: the only gifts you are!/Have you time? I'd like to be with you." The refrain goes back to the words of Jesus ("All I ask of you is forever to remember Me as loving you") and then the singing proceeds to the final stanza: "Ooooooooooo./Persons come into the fiber of our lives/And then their shadow fades and disappears."

The tune is pleasant; by itself or in the context of other reformed-folk songs *All I Ask of You* sounds harmless enough. But as soon as it is placed anywhere in the vicinity of "churchy" music, trouble begins. This contrast forces everyone to compare, to ponder, and to evaluate. First of all, the congregation will begin to wonder who is saying those words about "laughter" and "gifts" and "fiber" in the *Glory and Praise* song. Jesus? The congregation? And what do they mean? Are these words complete babytalk? How do they fit into this liturgy? Who is this "you"? (The pronoun seems to have one meaning in the refrain and another in the stanza.) Who is addressing whom about the "only gifts you are"?

To put it briefly, "churchy" music will make *All I Ask of You* and every piece of music like it sound so muddled, so adolescent by comparison. The depth simply is not there. Comparisons can be devastating to the reformed-folk style. The folk repertory can only survive where "churchy" music is (1) excluded or (2) kept within very narrow confines or (3) rearranged so that it will sound folksy. Like bad money that drives out good money in Gresham's Law, the reformed-folk items in the blended liturgy will gradually force out the "churchy sound," even though some old-fashioned items might remain.

Perhaps the most dangerous aspect of "churchy" music, as far as the promoters of *Glory and Praise* are concerned, is its unmistakable character as *work* music, *toil* music. The composers of "churchy" music tried very hard to produce a "sound" which seems to give the impression that everyone (priest, congregation, choir, organist) is working hard to build something. In its very etymology, "liturgy" contains the Greek word for "work." "Liturgical music" is essentially "work music." It is hard work for the congregation to sing a "churchy" Kyrie and it is also hard work to listen to a choir singing one gloriously.[7]

The Kingdom and the Power

The Roman Catholic church in the United States is right in the beginning stages of the Great Churchy Controversy. When and if this controversy ever reaches the point of turning into an ugly full-scale war, the central issue will not be a matter of High Church versus Low Church or restraint versus emotion or professional taste versus popular taste. The root of the matter will be power.

In the old Latin liturgy (or, for that matter, the liturgies of the Eastern churches) everybody had power, and yet nobody had power. The priest, it was said, monopolized everything; he supposedly had all the power. Yet the tight rubrics and the Latin language kept him in a "powerless" state. The congregation had the power to do whatever it wanted during a liturgy: pray, meditate, read devotions, follow the Mass, ignore the Mass, sleep. Yet, here too, that same power was lost whenever the congregation submitted to the customs of standing, kneeling, sitting, making the Sign of the Cross, genuflecting, remaining silent, and so on. Everyone understood that the sacrament itself *owned* all of the power; priest and people were coming *to* that power and trying to become a part of it. The "churchy" music created the impression of power being scattered and diffused. (It still does, but only if would-be celebrities are kept in check.)

Glory and Praise and the whole reformed-folk repertory have been responsible for a radical redistribution of power. What power the liturgical event once contained is now handed over to individuals, who take turns showing off their newly acquired strength:

Priest. The reformed-folk repertory creates a casual ambiance which permits the priest to spend every moment of a liturgy trying to manipulate a congregation with the power of his charm.

Congregation. That "now" repertory in *Glory and Praise* and similar books — virtually untouched by any indebtedness to the past — reassures the congregation that the Catholicism of history, church authority, experts, and authorities of all kinds have no power over them.

Musicians. Folk musicians are big winners in this redistribution of power. The music itself allows them to pull a large portion of the liturgical "time" to them. If all the music in *Glory and Praise* and derivative publications could be stretched out and measured by the inch, you would find that several hundred feet are for the congregation but miles and miles belong to the special performers, the local stars who must always be placed where everyone can admire the way they feel the meaning of words. The congregation, awestruck, merely assists.

The technical difficulty of most reformed-folk music allows musicians to maintain their portion of the new liturgical power. By any measure, by any standard of congregational music, most of the music found in *Glory and Praise* must be classified as "difficult for the congregation." The composers of this music did not really intend to write "assembly music" or "congregation music." What they skillfully composed was "group music" or "soloist music" — very subtle, very quirky music for the special performers in the front of the church; the congregation tags along.

Sing to the Mountains by Bob Dufford, S.J. — with its frantic leaping and jumping in all directions — is perhaps the most notorious specimen of this congregational music which no congregation could ever sing, but a much more famous example is *Be Not Afraid* by the same composer. At the beginning of this song, the congregation must wait in silence for precisely three full measures of music and one partial measure before coming in on the weakest possible pulse; in other words, while the group or soloist plays an introduction, the congregation must think "1+2+3+4+/1+2+3+4+/1+2+3+4+/1+2+3+4 You shall." At the words "with youuuuuu . . . through it" the congregation must again get out calculators and hold "you" for the exact number of micropulses before quickly snapping in with the rapid pitches on "through it." And those sustained notes! One of the main characteristics of the style, they test human endurance to the utmost. Congregations cannot hold a pitch for that long without fainting.

The whole style of *Be Not Afraid* could be described as "studied whimsy." The group or the soloist up front whimsically feels the meaning of the words; when one "feels," one lingers, one moves unexpectedly. That dreaming and drifting from note to note, all carefully specified in the notation on the page, does not make life easy for the poor congregation. Musical whimsy of this sort is quite difficult for an assembly of people to reproduce.

Hail Mary: Gentle Woman by Carey Landry requires special attention here because it provides a superior example not only of musical whimsy, but of whimsy gone berserk. The congregation never really knows when to come in, because the musical rests, the entrances, and the sustained notes are somewhat unpredictable. Indeed, the unpredictability of the music is almost malicious.

I once heard *Hail Mary: Gentle Woman* sung by a soloist at a concert — very effectively, very beautifully. The composer had quite nicely spaced the sung portions and the instrumental portions in a manner that suggested an improvised scene. ("Oh, I shall feel the meaning of the words here. Now I will pause a moment during an interlude, in order to think about the text and then, when I am ready, I shall feel some more of the words in my song . . . ") It was wonderful theater, a dreamy little tableau, but it was not assembly music.

Assembly music is big and broad and plain and klutzy and even crude at times, in order to accommodate the big crowd that has to sing it. The sounds, the notes, present themselves one after another. The rhythms are often "square." Most of all, the music has a secure predictability, which gives everyone the confidence to stay together.

Be Not Afraid and *Hail Mary: Gentle Woman* must be rehearsed by a group or by Mr. Caruso; these performers must carefully study the "blocking" (pause here, linger there, dream at this point, regain consciousness at that point, watch this sixteenth-note, observe those rests, etc.). These special musicians, as close to the microphone as possible, sing this music. They master the rhythmic intricacies and flicks. The congregation, which cannot keep up with the nimble sophistication of the soloists' music, is really left out of the picture.

The theologian, the liturgical expert, or the member of the parish liturgy committee will move his or her index finger up and down the words of a song like *One Bread, One Body*, count up the appropriate doctrinal references, and then declare the composition to be an imperishable masterpiece. But nobody, certainly no mere musician, is allowed to evaluate the work as assembly music. Look at the melody: "One bread" (pause, gasp) — "one body" (pause, gasp) — "one Lord of all" (pause, gasp), and so on. It seems to be suffering from a debilitating case of emphysema. The bewildered congregation can never quite figure out how long those pauses last because each musical gasp has an ever-so-slightly different length. ("Is the pause over yet? When do we resume singing?") This "irrationality" of the pauses is no accident and is just one part of a calculated effort to make the melody sound impulsive and casual — as if the singer is a little tipsy and is flitting carelessly from one sound to the next. The words of *One Bread, One Body* may be great post-adoration eucharistic theology but very few congregations can follow the steps of this delirious melody. Check what is happening in any church or chapel that uses *One Bread, One Body* or anything like it and you will find that a song of this type is usually performed as a pleasant, beautiful aria for soloists — who want the attention of the assembly rather than its voice.

Designer Music

"You simply do not understand. Go to St. Wilbur's and you will discover just how wrong you are. At St. Wil's you will find a loving, caring parish. People from all over come for the liturgy. They bring their children. You will not hear any of that 'churchy' music amid medieval gloom at the liturgies there. Everything is so loving and caring and full of zest. The music from *Glory and Praise*, of course, makes this all possible."

Chastised, I decided to go to St. Wilbur's, one of those parishes described as "thoroughly postconciliar" or "contemporary." The first thing I noticed was the size of the choir/folk group; it was substantial. The second thing I noticed was that this musical ensemble up front did nearly all of the singing. The rest of the congregation, for the most part, just watched in silence. (This is usually the case with "contemporary" music.)

I could not force myself to sing *I Have Loved You with an Everlasting Love* by Michael Joncas, but I marveled at the total unashamed narcissism of it all. The tempo marking for Tom Kendzia's *I, the Lord* instructed me to sing the Voice of God "Passionately, with conviction," but I had neither the passion nor the conviction to pretend that I was God. These two songs, like most of the other music at this Mass, had nothing to do with the liturgy of the day or even the liturgical action.

At St. Wilbur's, Father Hank presides — and the word "presides," with its connotation of passivity and neutrality, is the perfect verb. Except for the token "Through Him and with Him . . . " he sings no dialog with the congregation. He is merely the invited guest who interrupts all the singing with his talking. By now, Father Hank must surely realize that the musicians are trying to neutralize him. Perhaps this is why he takes every opportunity to give some indication that he really does belong there. He constantly calls attention to himself by adding personal touches to the ritual (especially effective is the hands above the head posture, like Superman about to take off). In private he explains that his personal liturgical "style" is his joy in the Resurrection coming out; but even his best friends discovered long ago that what is really coming out is his joy in being Father Hank. The man is certainly trying hard to be liked and I am trying to adjust my ego to his — and the egos of the featured musicians. It is not easy.

Like the "typical" parishes before Vatican II, St. Wilbur's prides itself on the narrowness of its music for congregation, its sweet songs. The congregation at St. Wil's, most of the time, is only permitted to hear or sing famous contemporary music by famous composers and famous groups. Touching that fame makes everyone part of something big and bold, something that gives them an exhilarated sense of being alive and independent of the past. (What is famous at St. Wilbur's may, of course, be completely unknown at the Protestant church across the street.) But even though this repertory may be limited in style and the lack of truly "functional" liturgical music may be hard to rationalize, St. Wilbur's still boasts. By limiting themselves mostly to famous music by famous composers and famous groups, the congregation at St. Wilbur's becomes a part of that fame, if only on weekends. They would consider it an insult to sing anything, no matter how useful, composed by a mere "anonymous."

St. Wilbur Catholics have been trained to live lives of obedient, unquestioning consumers. Society teaches them that the latest contemporary product will give them powers and freedoms that their parents never knew. The media guarantees, absolutely, that, if you buy the latest designer jeans, modeled by beautiful and skinny youths, you too will become beautiful and skinny. If you sing the latest designer songs, you too will attain the same level of piety attained by the designer composers. St. Wilbur's is indeed a "contemporary" church, almost to the point where they need the cultural equivalent of the ticker tape to keep up with the endless fluctuations in fashion. Today's designer song can quickly become yesterday's passing fad.

Orthodox Christians, Anglicans, and indeed the majority of Christians go to their churches and know what to expect there. The service will unfold. It will have its own life and logic, its own dynamic power. The worshiper and the clergy and the musicians will, in a "horizontal" relationship, work to move that religious event forward. The music, majestic or mediocre, will help that forward movement. St. Wilbur Catholics go to church and know that, in many cases, the experience will resemble a talent show or amateur hour. Here the "unfolding" consists of individual performers doing individual, sometimes unrelated things which seem to require audience participation. The whole situation is "vertical," with canonized celebrities on top and the congregation down below. Those on top dominate and control; those on the bottom sense that their presence in church, their participation, and their singing serve only one purpose: to reinforce someone else's ego. This is what Ego Renewal is all about.

6

The People

They're Hopeless

The Methodist minister steps into his pulpit, takes a deep breath, and then delivers an eloquent sermon especially crafted for "the members" of his church. The Baptist minister, before giving his sermon, pauses for a moment as he looks at "his congregation." He knows almost everyone by name; after all, they hired him. The Roman Catholic pastor, standing in his pulpit and ready to preach his sermon, looks at a completely different landscape; out there in front of him, he sees a vast herd of humanity which he calls "the people." Of course, Catholic pastors and parishioners do use words such as "the assembly" and "the congregation," but in unguarded moments the expression, the very revealing expression, that slips out is "the people" — the mob lined up in row after row of pews.

In one sense, "the people" implies something quite honorable. "Catholic" means universal. The doors of the Catholic parish, the "universal" parish, are open to everyone: rich, poor, young, old, and every ethnic group (in theory, at least). "The people" is everybody, and not a social caste at prayer. But then in another sense, this honorable term, "the people," has also come to mean something problematic and unflattering: the gaping flock, cattle, the crowd of sullen and uncooperative strangers slouching in the pews, the mixed bag of those who take the faith seriously and those who do not. "The people" — just the sight of so much human diversity — would discourage anybody who had to deal with them, especially the pastor who leads them spiritually and the musician who places musical pearls before them every week. Discouragement can easily slip into a form of unconscious contempt for the mob in the pews — who ignore the church's authority when it suits them, who continue to sin with undiminished vigor, and who flaunt their independence by not singing in church.

During those early days of liturgical change, the pastor in some parishes would march up and down the aisles of the church, while a colleague was saying Mass, and sing the hymns at the top of his voice; now and again he would stick his head into a pew filled with silent parishioners (as if to say, "Get with it, you slackers! *Sing!*"). But nothing happened. "The people" did not sing. He preached sermons on the virtues of participation. He bought missalettes and guitars. Somebody told him that flutes provided the best support for congregational singing; he bought flutes. But still, most of "the people" would not sing. As singers, the Catholic laity was judged to be hopeless, and their silence would have to be covered over with the sound of a folk group or Mr. Caruso.

The priests, music directors, and liturgists who have reached the "hopeless" verdict about "the people" (but will never admit this in public) need to be reminded of certain inescapable realities, which are contained in the following story, the parable of the bus:

A chartered bus is going down a highway late at night. Everyone on the bus is a stamp collector or the spouse of a stamp collector and they are all going back to their homes after an exciting weekend at a stamp collector's convention. Someone in the front of the bus begins to sing some old, familiar songs. Soon, almost everyone is singing. Long afterwards, they remember the ride home as one of the most enjoyable features of the trip.

Another vehicle, a public bus, slowly makes its way through the streets of New York City during rush hour. It is packed with strangers, united only by their need for transportation. Someone in the front of the bus begins to sing some old, familiar songs. A few passengers smile at the singer; most ignore him. After a few minutes of this solo singing, the bus driver waves to a police car; the singer is then arrested for disturbing the peace.

Mass in a Catholic parish is usually the liturgical equivalent of that bus route through the streets of New York. The bus accepts anyone with the fare. The other bus, the one filled with stamp collectors, is an enclosed private club. People who are not stamp collectors or their spouses might feel somewhat uncomfortable about riding in it. A "universal" church cannot always have it both ways; it cannot keep its doors open to "the people" and, at the same time, expect the kind of robust congregational singing associated with "private," homogeneous congregations or "clubs." Perhaps everything comes down to a simple set of facts which go something like this: A multiethnic, universal church might get all of "the people" to sing some of the time; it will certainly succeed in getting some of "the people" to sing all of the time; but nothing will ever persuade all of "the people" to sing all of the time. The problem of diversity is absolutely overwhelming — and yet a compromise is possible.

In the past, Catholics in Eastern Europe and what is sometimes called Central Europe had worked out a compromise that reconciled the liturgical needs of a universal church and the "private" needs of a particular ethnic group. At some Masses the congregation vigorously sang religious songs in the vernacular (German, Polish, Czech, Slovak), while the priest took care of the required texts in Latin. People who did not wish to sing could attend other Masses that proceeded with hushed reverence and without any music. And then there was the option of the supremely "universal" High Mass in Latin, often a splendid spectacle. This arrangement (i.e., different methods of liturgical expression) made it possible for the church to keep its doors open to everyone and for "the people" to sort themselves out according to preferences and even mood.

The Orthodox churches and the Eastern Rites have compromised on this issue by not compromising. "The people" simply go to "the liturgy." These ceremonies are a continuous fabric of singing. At certain points, the congregation weaves its own sound into the musical texture. (To be more precise, those who wish to sing will sing; many will not make a sound.) It does not matter if a few worshipers contribute to the music or if everyone in the church sings. The liturgy is the liturgy.

Roman Catholicism used to know all about the idea of letting liturgy be liturgy. (Like the Orthodox, it knew how to make "the people" feel that they were actors on a cosmic theater set.) But the church is rapidly moving away from this way of doing things to a system which tries to appease each constituency and subconstituency within "the people." In other words, it is moving away from a ritual which simply *takes place* (the historic method) to something that is *presented to* a constituency. The theologians may say otherwise, but many members of the laity have the impression that, in the "new" Mass, the priest, musicians, and assistants seem to be presenting a show *at* the congregation. Let me give the reader two "pictures" which clarify this important distinction between the event which "takes place" and the one which is "presented to" a congregation.

In the 1950s I attended the somber Tenebrae service during Holy Week in Philadelphia's Catholic cathedral. A choir of seminarians, seated in the front of the church, elegantly chanted one Latin psalm after another, without accompaniment. Now and then, a priest would appear, beautifully chant one of the readings (again, in Latin), and then disappear into the sacristy. Aside from seminarians, there was a total of about six members of the laity in the congregation. The time of day was inconvenient for most people; the cathedral had made almost no effort to publicize Tenebrae or explain it. But nobody worried about the small "turnout." Nobody was embarrassed. Liturgy of all sorts just "was," whether two people were there or two hundred.

My second picture takes us to a large urban university. I was strolling past the university's large chapel and heard some impressive music coming from it. I decided to follow the sounds to their origin. There, inside the chapel, I beheld a robed and paid choir of about twenty, under the direction of the finest organist within a radius of a hundred miles. As I stood there at the entrance of the edifice, I froze in a mild form of terror, because the five or so clergymen who were conducting this interdenominational service were all intensely staring at me with a mixture of rage and hope. I was now the third member of a congregation of three and my toes were curling.

Tenebrae "took place." The interdenominational service was "presented to" a congregation. In the first event, everybody, including the six laypeople in the cavernous church, was part of an action which moved forward, in one direction. In the second event, the service moved toward the congregation, which was not there.

Roman Catholicism is in no position to restore Latin Tenebrae in every parish, but it should try to restore an "essence" that all six of us laypeople instinctively understood as we attended that ceremony in the 1950s: the sense of being part of something that was taking place. Today, the church has heavily invested its energies in a policy of reaching constituencies by presenting them with something they are supposed to like. The liturgy does not seem to proceed with its own inexorable logic; instead, the sacramental Mass recedes into the background while, in the foreground, little musical "happenings" are aggressively presented for participation. What is hopeless is this policy, not "the people."

Notre Dame Study

Today, the "liturgical system" in a large number of Roman Catholic parishes and chapels does not work properly, at least not with the same confidence and assurance found in the majority of Orthodox and Protestant churches. "The people" sense this; that is, their instincts tell them that something has gone wrong. Maybe some Catholics express their anxiety about this by not singing.

The above statement sounds impressionistic and a bit like the grumblings of a chronic complainer. But the impressions and the grumblings have reached the status of scientific "fact" in a project entitled the *Notre Dame Study of Catholic Parish Life*, a "comprehensive survey of Roman

Catholic parishes in the United States . . . conducted by the Institute for Pastoral and Social Ministry and the Center for the Study of Contemporary Society of the University of Notre Dame" (1984–89). Over a thousand parishes cooperated by filling out questionnaires for the project. Teams of observers, specially prepared by the directors of this project, visited thirty-six parishes. Then, the researchers, analyzing the surveys and other data, discovered what the laity has known for years: Catholic liturgy in the United States often does not turn out the way it is supposed to, especially the music. When the observers "inspected" the liturgies at various churches (chosen as a representative sampling), they found abundant evidence that "important elements of the Mass structure are sometimes omitted or distorted by misunderstanding. Often the freedom given to the local community to plan and adapt the liturgy results in poor or altogether inappropriate selections of prayers, readings, and especially music" (Report No. 5, p. 4).

Collectively, "the people" are quite shrewd. They may not know much about theology or the subtleties of liturgical symbolism but they can instinctively detect "poor or altogether inappropriate selections of prayers, readings, *and especially music,*" which they might protest by not singing. The researchers who put together the *Notre Dame Study* found that an overwhelming majority of the congregation sang at only about 12 percent of the Masses they visited; at another 18 percent of the Masses about two-thirds of the congregation joined in the singing (Report No. 5, p. 7). In a survey conducted for this same *Study*, 37 percent of those who responded expressed dissatisfaction with the music in their parishes; 40 percent were dissatisfied with the singing (Report No. 6, p. 2). These percentages, it is important to remember, are averages. In some parishes, the "dissatisfaction rate" is higher than in others. Also, the survey collected opinions from loyal Catholics who go to church regularly, the sort of people not given much to complaining about their church; "fallen-away" Catholics or those who have just taken a spiritual leave of absence were not polled.

Writing in the journal *Worship*, Mark Searle, one of the authors of the *Notre Dame Study*, reports that the observers sometimes found a "lack of conviction about the role and purpose of liturgical music."[1] They did come across some "remarkable exceptions" but the "overall impression" was one of "mechanical and listless performance [of liturgical music]." And then, Professor Searle casually drops a one-sentence description of what the observers discovered when they attended the "new" Mass in different parts of the country. (Please read this slowly.)

Rarely was there an atmosphere of deeply prayerful involvement.

The "deeply prayerful involvement" of the laity during Mass used to be something that persuaded many people to convert to Catholicism. Apparently, that "atmosphere" is hard to find these days, but, as Professor Searle correctly adds, "the people" are nevertheless content. The great majority of them say, in surveys, that they like their parish liturgies (the prayers, the readings, and the singing), even without the "prayerful involvement," yet in some cases the evidence suggests "a serious problem in liturgical music, although the precise nature of the problem is not altogether clear."

The *Notre Dame Study* is a fine piece of scholarship, but in the future sociologists will use the section on liturgy as an example of research skewed by sincerity. The researchers, working from the highest motives, intended to find truth but they ended up adjusting what they found, in order to conform to principles established at Notre Dame University, specifically its departments of liturgy and theology. To see this bias coming to the surface, we must look at a later section of the *Study* which deals with a "No-conflict Traditional Parish" (Report No. 9, p. 9). The authors describe what they probably consider to be a backward ethnic parish "in an economically stagnant mill town." According to the *Study*, the pastor at this parish, a church that is perhaps a synthesis of several examples, "admits to being conservative and tradition bound. He aims the Mass at people over 50 with an eighth-grade education. Liturgists describe it as a privativistic Mass, one that does not celebrate the community."

Those last five words — "does not celebrate the community" — say more about the slant of the *Notre Dame Study* and the "nature of the problem" of liturgical music than a hundred books. The academic liturgical specialists and the more impatient members of the clergy do not want priest and people in a church worshiping together, offering thankful praise together. They want a community which celebrates *itself* — a gathering of people who come together to show what they can do as a group and who somehow perform in a unique and special way (as befits unique and special people).

As everyone in education knows, college and university departments tend to develop certain unquestioned ways of thinking, certain orthodoxies which no one may contradict. (An English literature department at an Ivy League university is much more thorough about punishing its dissenting professors and students than is a Vatican-sponsored department of theology.) Notre Dame is no exception. The observers sent by that university to study the liturgy in the parishes were somehow trained to detect boredom levels, congregational attentiveness, and rapport with the priest, but they were also trained to block out reality and only see the orthodoxies acceptable at Notre Dame. The observers were supposed to look for "fellowship" and a "gathered community" as signs of the liturgy envisioned by the Second Vatican Council, but all too often they only found "the people" — everybody and anybody, the crowd, the "mixed bag," the backward mob. The orthodoxies so thoroughly expounded at the university were usually not there in the parishes, in the real world. "The people" were preventing the formation of the aware "gathered community." And so, we can detect a slight tone of exasperation running through some reports in the *Notre Dame Study*, and it sounds something like this: Why do "the people" resist "fellowship" and identification as a gathered community? Why can't "the people" sing? Why can't they behave just like the Notre Dame University community in the chapel, at Sunday Mass?

Despite all of its flaws, the *Notre Dame Study* provides a useful portrait of the "new" Mass for exactly what it is: a success with failures — or a failure with successes. It shows all the warts. But, unfortunately, the original *Study* may be "lost" because a condensed book version of the separate reports — *The Emerging Parish: The Notre Dame Study of Catholic Life since Vatican II* (1988) by Joseph Gremillion and Jim Castelli — may receive a wider circulation. In this bound edition, some of the warts are edited out; the book gives the impression that "the people," excessively happy with the way they worship, will be even happier when the priest establishes more rapport with them and when everyone drinks coffee after solemnities. The negative results of the *Study*, if they have to be mentioned, receive a brief sentence and the assurance that all problems go away with planning.

When analyzing the *Notre Dame Study*, it is important to put three texts side-by-side: Mark Searle's article in *Worship* on the *Study* (which he helped to write), the original *Study*, and the book version. Editing gives three very different shadings to the data. The first bluntly acknowledges the existence of troubling developments, human failure, and the imperfect world; the second seems to go back and forth between positive and negative data; the third, in its relentlessly cheerful outlook, paints a picture which is not suggested by the original research.

What Do They Want?

Freud once complained that he had analyzed women for forty years and he still did not know what they wanted. The researchers for the *Notre Dame Study* could go on analyzing the Catholic population for the next forty years (without Freud's male chauvinism, of course) and still never find out what "the people" want or how to solve that "serious problem" called liturgical music. You can't want what you don't know. The average

Catholic congregation in the United States is somewhat hesitant on the subject of liturgical music because it has really not experienced enough options to formulate what its wants.

The energetic promoters of "contemporary" music have no hesitations on this matter. "The people" want *Glory and Praise*, maybe blended with a few standard hymns or maybe unadulterated. It is as simple as that. But the *Notre Dame Study* does not support that contention at all. The teams of observers sent by Notre Dame to look at the parishes noticed that what is loosely classified as folk music "emerges with mixed results. Often it is associated with very enthusiastic participation, but the participation is by a limited part of the congregation; equally often, the congregation appears quite unresponsive" (Report No. 5, p. 7). "Contemporary" religious music produces impressive results when used by a homogeneous group, a parish within a parish, but it is quite useless for "the people." Also, we should remember that the six or sixty individuals in a parish who fervently proselytize this music often turn out to be the same featured singers who stand up in front of the unresponsive congregation and perform.

"What do 'the people' want?" is a question that leads past the crisp and neat tables of sociological data, past the theological propositions, and directly into the swamp of intuition and hunches. After years of observation, reading, and study, my own intuitions are still lost in the darkest part of the swamp, but I can see in the distance two pieces of dry land. Let me describe them:

The most successful example of vernacular music for congregation introduced after Vatican II is the Our Father which is based on Gregorian chant. When performed without accompaniment, it is usually the strongest, most powerful moment of congregational singing.

I once visited a thriving suburban church and I was not at all surprised to come across, once again, that struggling-invalid singing so common in Catholic parishes. But at one brief point, the Responsorial Psalm, the whole church seemed to light up with singing; the booming sound of the congregation was astonishing. Afterwards, I asked the organist to reveal the secret of her success. She told me that she took a simple melodic formula that she thought was Anglican plainsong and, for most of the year, used it as the congregation's refrain at the Responsorial. The words changed from week to week but the congregation heard the same melodic idea. After a while, this melody became like a comfortable old shoe. Some in

the congregation were under the false impression that they were
singing an ancient chant of the church.

The common ingredients in these two "success stories" are subtle:
This music — special, distinctive — evoked a sense of *pride in ownership*.
The singing had an *effortless quality*; without displaying any hint of being
self-conscious, the music flowed easily into and out of the ceremony. The
music seemed to be *part of the ritual* and not something irrelevant added
just to keep everyone busy. There was *no coercion* ("Now we are all going
to sing this hymn and you better participate"). The melodies *sounded
important*, as if they had existed forever. They were *familiar* tunes which
had been *memorized*. Perhaps the inner secret of this "success" was that
the music just seemed to *take place*; it did not sound like something
presented to the congregation.

Pride in musical ownership is an exceedingly rare concept in the
Catholic parish, except among the folk musicians. Most of the time, "the
people" are simply told to sing this and sing that. But "this" and "that"
are just something printed in a missalette which is thrown out at the
end of a season. Trash music belongs to nobody. Pride in ownership
could be slowly developed over the years if the church started with the
youngsters, but this is not the case. I have seldom heard of a Catholic
school which puts a good hymnal into the hands of its students and
tries to develop a love for the church's best music. In the whole United
States there are probably no more than three dioceses which could pull
together a festival of their youth choirs, because parishes seldom bother
with such things.

Another complication is that, since the late 1960s, Catholics have
regularly heard preaching with mocking or humorous asides about the
old Requiem Mass, Latin, the way children used to be prepared for
First Communion, and so many other things they had once proudly
cherished. "The people" have been led to believe that they had mis-
takenly invested their spiritual energies in a fraud. Their missals, their
rosaries, and their fond memories of chant are like worthless stock
in a company that went bankrupt. The modern, postconciliar Catholic is supposed to be a cultural refugee who owns nothing musical.
I know of parishes where the music director is under strict orders to
avoid any and all music which might awaken a sense of continuity
with the discredited Catholic past. From the tower of the Unitarian
church not far from where I live, I can hear the bells play *Adoro Te
Devote*, an old neo-Gregorian tune; but at a certain Catholic parish I
know, the music director may not ask the congregation to sing this same
beautiful melody, even if the English translation never goes near the

unfashionable idea of adoration, because the music sounds "too Catholic."

The researchers who gathered the information for the *Notre Dame Study* must have been startled when they found Gregorian chant surviving in a few parishes; they had to concede (perhaps reluctantly) that "there is no reason for thinking that chant will inhibit full congregational participation" (Report No. 5, p. 7). This is a backhanded way of saying that congregations sing chant, Latin and English, very impressively. Any parish or cathedral would find it immensely useful to exploit this love, this pride in ownership, by introducing a small repertory of "effortless" chant — Latin or English, authentic or newly composed, perhaps unaccompanied, and definitely without amplification. (The music is available in the better hymnals.) It would be even more profitable if congregations could again sing the church's most ancient form of folk music: the chanted dialog between priest and people or between cantor and people (maybe a simple Amen or Kyrie). This is where congregational singing should begin. Once that core chant repertory is established, all kinds of other music can be successfully added, including music I dislike.

The principle at work with this "successful" chant is not nostalgia or antiquarianism. Rather, chantlike music is the original people-music of Catholicism. It appears to be a natural and organic part of the ritual. But, alas, the sort of individuals who decide how Catholics will worship have been trained to think of chantlike music as something which will "inhibit full congregational participation." The current fashionable theory is that "the people" want self-celebration and musical excitement; they want to be hammered into "a people," an aware "gathered community" — and chantlike music is not an effective tool for hammering.

Before anyone can answer "What do they want?" in music, another question must be asked first: "Who are they?" Who are "the people"? The answer goes back to the fourth century, A.D. In the year 300, a bishop had to conduct worship in a secret place or behind bolted doors; he was an officer of a small, persecuted sect. When he looked around at his small flock, he probably recognized each face. In 313 the emperor Constantine issued an edict tolerating Christianity and this began the process which led to the establishment of Christianity as the Roman Empire's official religion — the state church, the public utility for everybody. By the fifth century, a bishop was presiding in front of the local population, including the pickpockets, the hastily converted, fanatics, and those who were neither hot nor cold: in short, "the people."

During the Middle Ages, the nave of a church sometimes was treated as an extension of the town square outside. While the liturgy was going on, "the people" indulged in superstitious practices and talked; they wandered around the church because there were few places for them to sit down. (Pews, a relatively late addition to Roman Catholic churches, would have divided the congregation into classes and that would have started feuds.) In 1562 the Fathers of the Council of Trent, fed up with this type of behavior, asked bishops to put an end to "unnecessary and profane talking, strolling about, loud noises, and shouting" by the congregation during Mass.[2]

Centuries ago, the clergy in the East and the West were probably shaking their heads and calling "the people" hopeless; to protect themselves from the rowdy congregation, the clergy had to put up some kind of wall across the entrance of the sanctuary. This "hopelessness" of the mob-congregation helps to explain more than a millennium of Christian art. The magnificent Romanesque and Gothic cathedrals, the overpowering grandeur of the Baroque basilicas, chant, Renaissance polyphony, the Masses of Haydn and Mozart (with orchestra), and all the rest were part of a desperate campaign to get "the people" to shut up, to treat the church building as a sacred space. The campaign produced results, eventually. Roman Catholic congregations, in general, are much better behaved than they were in past centuries, although they now chat in church after Mass — something considered absolutely sacrilegious just a few years ago.

"The people" go far back in history. They are everybody and anybody, the kind of rabble that used to follow and pester Jesus of Nazareth. They are what makes Roman Catholicism "catholic." But they have enemies: a new class of Catholics who are determined to reshape the rabble into disciplined and attentive communities which sing disciplined and attentive music. I refer to those supreme masters of sadism, the *liturgical experts*. Roman Catholicism, which survived the Dark Ages and the bubonic plague, may not be so lucky with this menace.

The Experts Will Transform the Mob

An anonymous wag once defined the modern liturgical expert as "an affliction sent by God, so that those Catholics who have not had the opportunity to suffer for their faith might not be deprived of the opportunity to do so." Years ago, it used to be that liturgical experts were scholars who could effortlessly translate Greek, Latin, and Old High Slavonic, but today everybody can be an expert, everybody can be an affliction. There are, of course, honest liturgical experts — fine individuals who might work for a church or teach; unfortunately, their voice is often drowned out by the amateurs and noisy theorists who seem to come up with one unworkable scheme after another.

The way to tell the difference between the "good" experts and the "bad" ones is simple. The "good" liturgists take a humanist approach; they start with the reality that the church deals with an assortment of imperfect human beings called "the people." The "affliction" experts, however, know about every possible aspect of liturgical science except human nature. Despite their public displays of prodigious theological learning, they are really social architects; they start with the conviction that they can remake society and human nature through the *architecture* of liturgy. This is, I admit, a somewhat bewildering statement, but it will make sense upon reading the following digression on the cultural origins of the modern liturgical expert.

"It was a fake and a failure. It has not stood the test of time."

From the indignant tone of voice, you would have thought that the professor of art history had just made a pronouncement on municipal corruption or the Nazis. The man was so angry I thought he would spit.

For perhaps a minute the professor silently scowled at the image projected on the screen in the darkened lecture hall, as if he wanted his students to join him in contemplating the total awfulness of the picture in front of them. He then decided to move on. A series of images flashed across the screen. Finally, after about the tenth slide, the professor issued another pronouncement.

"I think you can see from these examples how completely hideous all of this was. Yes, it certainly has not passed the test of time."

In the dim light, about a hundred students clicked their ballpoint pens and scribbled a brief reminder into their notebooks: "The stuff stinks. Has not passed test of time."

The date of the lecture was somewhere about the year 1970. I, a visitor at this big university in the Northeast, had quietly slipped into the darkened lecture hall to hear a few minutes of the class. And what monstrosities had aroused such indignation in this professor? Architecture from the late nineteenth century and early twentieth century — government buildings, homes, and (most of all) the paintings and sculpture that embellished them. The students were taught that the architectural extravagances shown on the screen were filled with artistic lies: Greek columns, Roman arches, Gothic decoration, and other historical allusions; true architecture expressed its own time and did not raid other styles for ideas. Besides, this eclectic decorative nonsense had no function. The only practical thing to do with such architectural confusion was to tear it down and put up something functional.

The professor who was passing on these cultural doctrines to his class was an ardent disciple of the International Style — the new, purified religion of architecture which gave the world the glass box skyscraper and the housing project; most of this cult's major prophets came from Europe. Walter Gropius, one of the founders of the Bauhaus in Germany, stressed the importance of applying the ideals of this nondecorative, stripped-down architecture to the design of furniture, dishes, and all the things that people use in their daily lives. "Start from scratch," he advised his students; the past has nothing to offer. Ludwig Mies van der Rohe perfected the coldly severe glass-box building and taught his disciples the beatitude, "Less is more." Le Corbusier promoted the idea of "the slab in the park," the skyscraper-apartment building standing alone and detached from its neighbors; his writings gave the International Style much of its theoretical and philosophical justification.

When the International Style reigned unchallenged, some of the finest examples of architecture in the United States crumbled under the wrecker's ball, in order to make way for glass-box office buildings and housing projects. Magazine advertisements showed how new plastic and aluminum panels could hide old architectural gingerbread and other "eyesores." "Victorian" was an especially dirty word and demolishing anything Victorian became a matter of civic pride or even public hygiene. All of this destruction went forward in the name of progress but also in the name of society's moral improvement. There was, after all, something inherently evil about an architecture which did not try to be "of its time" and which contradicted the values of engineering logic. Such architecture, and the urban fabric based on it, had to go. Le Corbusier, after all, had shown the way for this sort of progress. His so-called Voisin Plan of 1925 called for the demolition of a large portion of Paris. The crooked old streets, the cafes, and the Beaux Arts structures would all be pulverized and replaced with straight highways and massive architectural slabs, the skyscraper apartments of the future.

Perhaps the strongest moral justification for the International Style was its socialist commitment to buildings that would serve *people* and improve society. The ultimate mission of the architect was to design humane housing for workers and apartments for the poor. The world would be a better place, once it was redesigned along the principles of the International Style — and as soon as the old order was bulldozed.

During the 1960s, the International Style enjoyed immense prestige; it became not only "the architecture of our time" and "the architecture of the future" but also a form of scientific truth, embodied in building materials. Between the years 1962 and 1965 the Second Vatican Council met. A certain amount of cultural seepage, from architecture to liturgy, was inevitable. Let us just say that those who had the job of implementing the council's decrees — the liturgical experts — quite often promoted an agenda which originated not in the Basilica of St. Peter but in the Bauhaus. Page through books, articles, and especially the texts of speeches written by the new liturgical experts after 1962 and, when you come to the word "liturgy," substitute "architecture." In a large number of cases what you are reading sounds as if it could be a treatise by Le Corbusier or a manifesto from the Bauhaus. Maybe it was unavoidable that the principles of Liturgical Renewal would begin to sound like the ambitions of Urban Renewal.

One word which shows this link between the International Style architects and their imitators in the field of liturgy is *clutter*. For both the architect and the liturgical expert, clutter represents loss of control, pollution of the clean environment, independent and unauthorized expressions of ideas. The liturgical experts fret about whether the singing of *Glory to God in the Highest* will "clutter up the Entrance Rite." Singing anything in Latin during a vernacular liturgy, they declare, is "macaronic," and there is nothing more confused, more cluttered than macaroni. In the sterilized postconciliar liturgy, clutter is not only a dangerous bacteria, it is repugnant.

What makes the utterances of the new experts so impressive is the tone of righteous anger that runs through every sentence — pure, fist-clenching anger. Anger dazzles; it gives a moral dimension to what might really belong in the category of personal taste; it allows the International Style liturgical experts to inflict shame upon the cowering Catholic audience (1) for having once submitted to the pleasures of liturgical clutter, (2) for not producing the liturgical New Jerusalem immediately, and (3) especially for belonging to a church which had once tolerated those interior decorators of worship, those public enemies of true liturgy, *musicians*. The International Style liturgical expert, to put it diplomatically, detests the musical expert — the trained, historically aware, skilled musician who produces the aural equivalent of the gingerbread "eyesore" and clutter.

We can see faint traces of this hostility in the pages of Joseph Jungmann's masterful work, *The Mass of the Roman Rite: Its Origins and Development* (English translation, 1951, 1955). Pius XII supposedly kept this book on his desk. It was probably consulted by many bishops who attended Vatican II; Jungmann himself was one of the advisers at the council.

Beneath the book's scholarly detachment, the reader can detect that Jungmann, an Austrian Jesuit, is frustrated by the Roman Rite, as it was in 1949 when he first published his book. In his opinion, Catholic congregations, mere spectators and listeners, are alienated from the sacred rites. The Baroque-style liturgy, whose influence was still powerful in 1949, annoys him. Originally, this type of Baroque grandeur provided the faithful with a spiritual splendor, "but it is a splendor whose greatness is self-contained and whose arrangement is as immutable as it is puzzling; and in the midst shines the Blessed Sacrament, a precious jewel for which this traditional setting appeared just, right, and necessary."

Jungmann very subtly organizes the "conclusions" of the *Mass of the Roman Rite* around the central theme of corruption. As the author sees it, far back in history liturgical form followed liturgical function and "the people" had an essential role to play. Gradually, however, musicians pushed the laity aside and singing became "the art-function of a small group." The ideal and simple rituals which had once existed soon disappeared under embellishments and useless clutter, most of which was music.

Sometimes Jungmann sounds as if he wants to get rid of "the people" and return Catholic liturgy to the catacombs and assemblies of the chosen few. He reminds his readers that the policy of opening the doors of a church to everyone results in "a situation where at our divine services every sharp boundary between church and world is broken down, so that Jew and heathen can press right up to the steps of the altar and can stand in the very midst of the faithful at the most sacred moment." Early Christians, Jungmann points out, would have found this "incomprehensible." The church can get away with the mob-scene congregation, "so long as the faithful are only onlookers and listeners at a sacred drama." The mixed bag congregation of "the people" encourages passivity, and this "will be substantially and actually overcome whenever and insofar as they [the ones who really belong in the congregation] take up a more active role." What he implies is that the supposed passivity here can only be "overcome" by the exclusion of the outsiders: the indifferent, the sinners, the tourists, the "Jew and heathen" who clutter up the assembly with their presence and prevent the faithful from participating.

Jungmann's corruption theory of liturgical history — the era of ritual purity and participation followed by the era of Baroque embellishment and alienation — is widely accepted today as fact. The decrees of the Second Vatican Council are seen as a vindication of his point of view; they supposedly put an end to the corruption which Jungmann had, in restrained terms, deplored. Now, we have to remind ourselves that the council's documents nowhere encourage this interpretation of history; if anything, they leave the impression that business will continue as usual, but with some wonderful improvements. Yet the International Style liturgical experts, lacking Jungmann's broad scholarly vision and flexibility, insist that the *Constitution on the Sacred Liturgy* identifies embellishments and art music as the source of all liturgical ills; they want the church to return to the type of liturgy that existed before the musicians corrupted it (actually the type of worship before the church admitted "the people" into its ranks).

This corruption theory received something close to official approval in a German edition (1967) of the Second Vatican Council's documents. Karl Rahner and Herbert Vorgrimler, in their editorial commentary on the *Constitution on the Sacred Liturgy*, state that genuine art, as found in traditional church music, is "of its very nature — which is esoteric in the best sense — hardly to be reconciled with the nature of the liturgy and the basic principle of liturgical reform." The sort of music identified with Christian worship for centuries, especially compositions by the great masters, is alien to true liturgy. The council may have insisted that "the treasure of sacred music is to be preserved and fostered with great care," but, according to Rahner and Vorgrimler, this does not mean that the preservation is to be done "within the framework of the liturgy." (In other words, preserve and cultivate this "treasure of sacred music" in the museums, not in the churches.) The council fathers recommended that choirs should be encouraged, "especially in cathedral churches." Rahner and Vorgrimler interpret this to mean that fine choirs should exist *only* in cathedrals and even then their principal job would be to support congregational singing.

Rahner and Vorgrimler stress that the "new" Mass would have little room for what they call "actual church music," the kind of music which the musicians had composed in the past. That sort of thing would have to go now. Henceforth, the liturgy could only provide a place for what these editors describe as "so-called utility music," which does not really exist yet and will have to be invented; the church will have to begin all over again.[3] (The appropriate scriptural quotation here would come from the gospel according to Gropius: "Start from scratch." The past has nothing to offer.)

This is all very puzzling. The documents of the Second Vatican Council praise the beauties of the pipe organ; they indicate that Gregorian chant should receive an honored place in worship; the council fathers recommend that "higher institutes of sacred music" be established where musicians would study the esoteric art of "actual church music." Yet Rahner and Vorgrimler confidently describe a liturgical future which will really have no need for inspirational organ music or chant or musicians trained at higher institutes of music. Perhaps these two theologians can be excused for missing all the nuances in the *Constitution on the Sacred Liturgy*, because they were completely enthralled by the idea of the

International Style governing all aspects of life. Rahner and Vorgrimler were acting like idealistic architects of the 1930s dreaming about the coming of that clean, purified world of tomorrow, in which architecture, cities, furniture, appliances, silverware, dishes, and liturgies would all be products of honest Bauhaus simplicity. They saw the *Constitution on the Sacred Liturgy* not as the working of the Holy Spirit but as another example of the International Style Zeitgeist.

The Rahner-Vorgrimler vision of liturgy in the future is, in a way, quite beautiful and appealing. They have in mind the liturgical equivalent of workers' housing designed by Mies or Le Corbusier — plain dwellings (all in the shape of cubes), smiling laborers in spotless overalls, straight paths leading to the factory, everything germ-free and clean, everything at right angles to everything else (including the inhabitants), and not a single superfluous decoration in sight, not so much as a geranium in a pot. Rahner and Vorgrimler will allow music into this functional environment, only if it helps the workers to respond, in unison, at functionally correct places in the functionally correct workers' liturgy; any other type of *artistic* music is unthinkable, since it introduces an element of the mysterious or, even worse, the decorative. Le Corbusier described a building as a "machine for living." In the Rahner-Vorgrimler vision, liturgy is an efficient machine for worship. One does not decorate a machine or help it to move by playing esoteric music over it.

Rahner and Vorgrimler remain quite calm as they describe what amounts to an angry act of violence (i.e., cutting off this gangrenous limb called "actual church music"). In contrast, *Père* Joseph Gelineau lets some of his French anger show. A liturgist, a composer of psalms for the congregation, a persuasive speaker, and (like Jungmann, Rahner, and Vorgrimler) a Jesuit, Gelineau demands liturgical utopia now. He can be somewhat recondite in his books and speeches, but his message is really quite simple and could be phrased thus: "For centuries the Catholic church knew nothing about worship. Nothing. It completely ruined the idea of liturgy. Composers added to this ruination by composing masterpieces and other decorations which have no place in authentic liturgy. For about one thousand and six hundred years the history of liturgy has been a saga of nonsense, misunderstanding, perversion, and decadence. Nobody did anything right, until the arrival of...Joseph Gelineau."

When the Second Vatican Council was putting together the *Constitution on the Sacred Liturgy*, there was a mad scramble to find this perfect participation music, and the *Psalms* of Father Gelineau looked like an act of providence, a gift of manna for the starving multitude. This would be the liturgical music of the future, if not for all time. These *Psalms* are certainly well constructed compositions which try to convey the spirit of the Hebrew originals. Some of the melodies are charming and the English adaptation is very good; the *Psalms* would be useful in any parish. But there is a troubling question about a conflict of interest that needs to be asked. Is a composer who dismisses about a millennium and a half of church music someone who cannot stand competition? Does he sense that any comparison between the older church music and the products of his own modest talents might prove distressing? These issues need to be raised, but nobody dares to question a liturgical expert, especially an angry one.

In the United States, every International Style liturgical expert, at one time or another, pays homage to an article entitled "Music as Art in Liturgy" by Rembert Weakland, archbishop of Milwaukee.[4] The author, a Benedictine archabbot when he published the article in *Worship* in 1967, is an accomplished musician (a graduate of Juilliard) and a first-rate scholar (he helped to prepare the text for the New York Pro Musica's production of *The Play of Daniel*, a medieval drama). The International Style experts frequently invoke his name as the expert above all experts and try to include him in their ranks by quoting from "Music as Art in Liturgy," but the archbishop's modesty and tolerance really disqualify him for membership among the "affliction" experts.

In the article, Archbishop Weakland informs his readers that "there is no music of a golden age to which we can turn, because the treasures we have are the product of ages that do not represent an ideal of theological thinking in relationship to liturgy." Gregorian chant, the product of an era which had misunderstood the theology of worship, can offer nothing to the modern church. Looking back to the past for musical solutions to today's liturgical needs "ends in a *cul de sac*, even if we try fruitlessly to abstract from the bad theological opinions on liturgy that gave birth to the music."

This is Gropius all over again: "Start from scratch," because the past has nothing to offer. Archbishop Weakland states this in absolute terms and without qualification. There is *nothing* useful in the past. Zero. We must presume that even the do-re-mi scale is suspect. Corrupt theology produced corrupt liturgy which produced corrupt music. All of this must go.

Like Rahner and Vorgrimler, Archbishop Weakland seems to demand a lobectomy. The liturgical and musical past was simply wrong and must be cut out, in order to save "the people" from the infection of artistic decoration and mystification. In the past, the church justified artistic music "by describing it as a gift to glorify God — the sublimist creative act of man being given back to God. It [church music from the past] is like a package wrapped in a golden cloth with a golden ribbon. Whether the people understood the contents of the gift is secondary."

"Package," "golden cloth," "golden ribbon" — this is undiluted Bauhaus contempt for decoration. One must strip away unnecessary wrappings and ribbons. Get down to the functional essence of things, the bare bones. Of course, the unstated and thoroughly embarrassing fact here is that "the people" *love* packages and ribbons and gold and things they do not completely understand. But, according to Bauhaus dogma, this kind of bourgeois delight in frivolity must be rooted out, for the good of humanity.

In 1967, when Archbishop Weakland's article appeared, there was a nasty fistfight between the Ancients, church musicians who looked to chant and Renaissance music for guidance, and the Moderns, who believed that music from the remote past had absolutely nothing to offer the church after the Second Vatican Council. The fistfight became very nasty indeed at the Fifth International Church Music Congress, which was held in Chicago and Milwaukee in the summer of 1966. At this convention, the first such gathering of musicians after the close of the Second Vatican Council, the Ancients and the Moderns caricatured one another's positions. Audiences were rude. Tempers flared. As the Ancients tell it, the Moderns refused to listen to the wisdom of history and experience; they only wanted to twang guitars and sing peace songs. (The Vietnam War was raging; confrontation was everywhere.) The Moderns remember a different story. They say they were just defending themselves against arrogant Europeans and elitists. The Moderns' crusade for musical freedom, they claim, seemed hopeless and it looked as if they would be silenced by powerful forces of reaction within the Vatican, but then Rembert Weakland, a Benedictine archabbot at the time, stood up and defended them; thereupon, the Ancients, hissing and licking their wounds, retreated back to their European basilicas. American Catholicism's way of life was saved. (The truth is, both sides acted abominably. But perhaps the crisis of the Vietnam War made everyone irritable back then.)

In his article, Archbishop Weakland continued the fight that broke out at the convention. (It must be mentioned here that some of the Ancients had become insufferably smug and needed to have a brick thrown at them.) He attacked the position of the Ancients by reminding them that the past does not provide some kind of magic-wand music which automatically solves all musical problems for all time. The church needed to change its musical priorities.

Up to this point, all of the archbishop's observations are on target, but the article takes a turn for the worse:

If, on the other hand, the liturgical experience is to be primarily the communal sensitivity that I am one with my brother next to me and that our song is our common twentieth-century response to God's word here and now and coming to us in our twentieth-century situation, it [music] will be something quite different. We will not expect to find the holy in music by archaism, but in our own twentieth-century idiom.

At the rhetorical climax of the article we do not find words like "Christ" or "worship" or "sacrifice" or "thanksgiving for redemption." Instead, the highpoint is the expression "communal sensitivity." The liturgy becomes the community sensing itself. Because the editor or the author left out some important qualifications here, the article leaves the impression that, during Mass, God merely looks on while the congregation senses itself, partly with the help of music.

Some readers may have come to a screeching halt at the archbishop's use of the words "our own twentieth-century idiom" of music. Exactly what does this mean? Rock? Jazz? Stravinsky? Lawrence Welk? Messiaen? Country and Western? Rap? The author does not say. He gives no examples.

In a sense, Archbishop Weakland is correct. Liturgical music cannot be chosen just for its historical significance or for its long-ago-and-faraway sound. It must be "contemporary," and this word has a broad interpretation. Today, "here and now," it so happens that a thoroughly "contemporary" musical composition which speaks eloquently to a contemporary congregation might be something written yesterday or a motet from the sixteenth century or Gregorian chant or a nineteenth-century hymn. Modern people can "understand" a wide variety of musical idioms.

Archbishop Weakland's theses about "our own" liturgical music, despite its overheated rhetoric, does leave room for accommodation. Perhaps because of this slight amount of flexibility here, the true believers in International Style liturgy have quietly rejected his insistence on the music of "here and now." Instead, the experts continue the quest for the *real* golden age of liturgical music. They exhaust themselves searching for this ideal music which must have existed somewhere and which the musician cannot possibly create. One expert tells us that, in order to find this golden age, we must go back, beyond Pius X, beyond Gregory and Augustine, beyond the corruptions, back "to the dawn of our Christian beginnings, to the first halting syllables of that new song that burst forth from the first assemblies, because I believe that the Apostolic church has much, oh so much, yet to teach us about the meaning of our song, and that we won't understand our singing until we go back to our biblical roots."[5] At this point, one is tempted to ask the expert, "Would you please hum a few bars of this perfect Apostolic music?" But such a practical request would spoil the abstract beauty of the rhetoric here. Also, we should be on the alert about the expression "our biblical roots" in reference to church music. Often these are code words for music in the reformed-folk style which, so the experts tell us, begins the long road back to the ideals of biblical music, after centuries of useless decorating by musicians.

Another expert also goes back to the dawn of Christianity for the golden age of liturgical music. This music, he tells us, must have been so simple, so prayerful, so uniformly correct, but it all came to an end quickly because of the cantor, the original corruptor of church music. In the very beginnings of Christianity, according to this expert, the cantor received a beautiful tradition of sung prayer from Judaism but he "betrayed the role of prayer leader for that of musician.... It is such a betrayal, clearly in contradiction of our Judeo-Christian heritage, that we must now seek to reverse."[6] The church must go back in time, back before the betrayal, before the serpent-musician slithered into the Garden of Eden. And where might we find this pre-betrayal music today? What does it sound like? The expert is silent on this point and with good reason. As soon as liturgical music has a *sound*, it comes from musicians, who are the everlasting betrayers.

The historical evidence does not support this slander about the wicked musician who single-handedly twists sung prayer into mere art. The fact is that throughout the centuries church musicians did what they were told to do. If the pastor or the king wanted violins for the liturgy, the musician wrote music for violins. If those in charge wanted embellishments and clutter, the musician embellished and cluttered. The musician always had to follow the orders of the authorities (ecclesiastical or civil) who, for their part, wanted liturgical music that would communicate a message to "the people." The "betrayer" of the musical golden age, if we want to think of it that way, has always been the person who gives the orders and issues the paychecks.

The skilled, historically aware, musician — that favorite bogeyman of the liturgical expert, that "betrayer" of sung prayer — is the sort of person who knows the precise techniques and principles which would make congregational singing much more vigorous, but he or she does not always feel welcome in the Catholic church. Musicians who take their profession seriously will hear some Catholics use the word "professional" as a term of contempt in reference to music ("The choir sounded too professional"). Organists who spend hours trying to polish their performance of a prelude and fugue by Bach must listen to condemnations of "musical performances" during a liturgy.

Many of the church's dedicated musicians seek refuge and sympathetic fellowship in the American Guild of Organists (AGO), a stately, nondenominational association which represents thousands of organists who think of themselves as dedicated professionals. But, as far as many liturgical experts are concerned, membership in the AGO is the badge of betrayal, a sure sign that the musician only wants to turn the church into a concert hall by bringing back preconciliar music. In 1987, the director of the Office of Worship for a Roman Catholic diocese wrote to the AGO's journal and announced that this association of musicians could not possibly understand what was happening to Roman Catholic music today, "as long as it identifies with those who would have us turn back a clock that in fact turned upside down the worship life of more churches than the Roman Catholic one!" It is useless, the director goes on, to "long for those Egypt flesh-pot days" when church music was supposedly so beautiful but was in fact so thoroughly wrong.[7]

Here, at this point, the reader must step back, as it were, and take a good look at what the liturgical authorities are really saying. From Jungmann to the above-mentioned director of the Office of Worship, they constantly repeat the same message and it could be phrased as follows: "St. Ignatius Loyola, St. Benedict, St. Francis of Assisi, St. Clare, and all the rest — the dummies! Why could they not plainly see that the musicians had turned the worship life of the church upside down? What was the matter with them? Why could they not see through the fraud of their flesh-pot church music? What was the matter with those fools? Why didn't anyone have the sense to hire a director of the Office of Worship who would set them straight?"

Of all the doctrines of the Catholic church, one of the hardest to take is the new dogma of the liturgical and musical parenthesis: the golden age of liturgy and music in the very earliest days of Christianity, followed by the age of the parenthesis, when congregations were alternately beguiled by flesh-pot music or snubbed by musicians, followed by the dawning golden age of participatory perfection. It is so hard to believe that this clock of history wipes out all memory and makes everything obsolete every time its second-hand moves forward.

The Glass Box Cracked

It now gives me great pleasure, *delicious* pleasure, to report that in the space of a few years the whole International Style has, in a manner of speaking, collapsed into a pile of rubble. The coldly severe geometric form, in glass or raw concrete, is no longer the one and only acceptable "look" for contemporary architecture and definitely not the sacred symbol of progress that it once was. In fact, the International Style is now openly ridiculed, even hated. "Less is more" certainly has its virtues but, as the architect Robert Venturi put it, "Less is a bore." One glass box is intriguing. A whole downtown of glass boxes is boring.

The recent issues of *Architectural Record*, a professional journal for architects, provide ample proof that, today, "our own" contemporary idiom of architecture now includes new skyscrapers with pointed or flamboyant tops, towers with clocks, housing that tries to "recall" old styles, a shopping center with the ambiance of an old Italian town, Greek columns, Roman arches, mansard roofs, New York apartment houses that try to look like something built in the 1920s, old railroad stations beautifully restored for new uses, and, of course, the modern style in all its brash assertiveness. This return to older styles in architecture (and also in music and painting) goes by the name of Postmodernism; back in the 1960s this synthesis of the old and the new would have been considered absolutely impossible, culturally *illegal*, a lie.

Roman Catholicism caught the International Style fever about thirty years after most architects came down with it, and an ecclesiastical postmodern reaction was inevitable. Some of the most doctrinaire liturgical experts have even become a little less tense about the church's cultural past. At the local cathedral, one might hear "actual church music" — Gregorian chant, Renaissance motets — and lightning has not struck the building. A university chapel might use selections from a Renaissance Mass one Sunday and reformed-folk music the next. Some hymn books and missalettes will place a chant Kyrie just a few pages away from the kitsch "Voice of God" song. I remember when *any* use of "old" music, *any* "going back" was shrilly denounced as treason, but it does indeed look as if Roman Catholicism has not surrendered to a total International Style purity.

Yet, at the same time, this cultural "adjustment" appears to be stuck in its preliminary stages; breaking away will be very difficult. Roman Catholicism has always had to communicate through the signs and symbols of culture, and the Second Vatican Council communicated many of its liturgical ideals in language that suggests International Style severity. The world can go through all kinds of modernist phases and postmodern reactions but perhaps for many years to come the spirit of the "new" Mass will be confused with the cultural outlook that produced the glass box, the "slab in the park," and brutalism in concrete. History does indeed linger.

One essential characteristic of the International Style which will linger — something built right into the style — is its "unpopularity" or, to look at it another way, its limited ability to "appeal," to enchant ordinary people. A prominent example of this is Brasília, the capital of Brazil; this city was started from scratch in the 1950s and designed along the strictest principles of the International Style. With its bleak vistas that look like something in a surreal nightmare and its geometrically precise buildings that seem to obliterate all signs of human life, Brasília is perhaps the most functional city in the world but also the most hated; diplomats fly into it, take care of business, and then fly back to the clutter of Rio de Janeiro as soon as possible; the bureaucrats who have to live in Brasília consider it a graveyard. Another example of the International Style's failure to "appeal" is the apartments that Le Corbusier designed for Marseilles; the residents, not at all grateful for the uncluttered spaces he gave them, lost no time in filling up their apartments with room dividers, moldings, fake fireplaces, and (the ultimate desecration) wallpaper.

Back in the 1960s, those early efforts to unclutter the Mass, although quietly tolerated, were definitely not "popular." Attending them was like stepping into a meat freezer — or a lobby by Mies van der Rohe. In spite of the singing and the on-cue spirituality/participation, there was something cold about the whole experience. All of the incessant talking at the congregation and the singing, shaped by the ideals of functional simplicity, only seemed to create vast stretches of emptiness. What had once appeared to be unfathomable and untouchable now simply looked bare. (Especially bare was the efficient robot-talk of the English translations.) "The people," trapped in the eerie landscape of a liturgical Brasília, lost no time in filling the blank spaces. The folk phenomenon, the charismatic movement, "contemporary" religious music, liturgical dance, and those ad libs by the priest are popular efforts to put back some clutter and charm into the liturgical emptiness.

To be sure, this "redecoration" process, some of it theologically garbled, gives the experts apoplexy, but there is little they can do. The International Style mandarins of liturgy must suffer an ingeniously cruel form of punishment: They got what they wanted in the way of changes; audiences at conferences cheer their pronouncements as articles of faith; but, at the same time, nobody pays much attention to them. "The people" and the local clergy, dashing off into all directions and experimenting with liturgical Postmodernism, "do their own thing," no matter how appalling, while the experts lament.

"In our church, somebody tapes real flowers on the cross during the Good Friday ceremony, to remind everyone of the Resurrection." (True story.)

"In our church, the priest once processed to the altar while pushing a wheelbarrow filled with donated food for the poor." (True story.)

For many amateurs in the parishes and chapels, this is what Liturgical Renewal is all about: inventing gimmicks which, although theologically confused and sometimes downright appalling, are always cute. The amateurs can proceed with unshakable confidence in their gimmick inventing because, as they claim, the books, articles, and speeches by the great liturgical experts gave them permission to "do their own thing."

The amateurs are, of course, mistaken — and yet not very far from the truth. If you look at so many of the commentaries on liturgy and religious music from the last twenty years, the implied message is that the restraining traditions of the past are bunk, all parameters are gone, local initiative ("your own thing") is what matters most. The unintended message is "invent cute stunts."

Some members of the "liturgical establishment" are becoming quite angry because everybody seems to misunderstand their idealistic, bookish vision of a liturgical utopia. They can walk into almost any parish and notice immediately that the congregation does not behave like the "aware, gathered community" described in the academic literature. They certainly must notice that only a fraction of the congregation does any singing. This may explain why, in many recent commentaries on liturgy, you can see, just below the surface, rage and frustration. "The people" refuse to follow their script. The clergy is uncooperative. Musicians are betrayers. Nothing is working according to plan. Liturgical Renewal must begin all over again.

In Christianity's early days as a state religion, the hierarchy must have realized that small, self-selected groups could be trained to perform certain liturgical tasks properly, but "the people," jealous of their independence, could not be tamed. They were the human race in all its complexity; they could not be treated like soldiers on parade. In the oldest rituals of the church (the kinds of liturgies that still survive in the East) congregational singing was designed to be somewhat open-ended, so that members of the congregation could drift in and drift out of the singing, whenever they felt like it.

Church musicians discovered long ago that you do not tangle with "the people" and they have scars to prove it. When Palestrina and Mozart conducted their lovingly crafted liturgical compositions, they must have looked out of the corner of one eye at the congregation: at the restless youngsters, the men leaving early, the bored, the pious ones who were paying more attention to their private devotions than to the ceremony. One cathedral organist told me that he will hear members of the congregation defiantly slamming their hymn books shut at the final note of a hymn, every time the singing goes on for more than two stanzas. Anyone who has worked as a musician for the Catholic church will develop calluses, in order to survive. Abuse and failure come with the job.

The modern liturgical experts, unfortunately for them, are innocents who naively believe that they can succeed where Catholicism failed for the better part of two thousand years. It is all so simple, they declare. If the introductory rites are designed cleverly, the heterogeneous crowd will automatically be galvanized into a prayerful and attentive community. With careful planning there will be a clear purpose to the rites and not a meaningless succession of one thing after another. If every last word of every last reading and prayer is linked, like electric circuits, to every last song, the congregation will tingle with awareness of the brilliant game of associations. (It will be like the bead-game in *Magister Ludi* by Hermann Hesse.) Refreshed by this invigorating workout with word-idea connections, the aware, attentive, and gathered community will then go out into the world and work for peace and justice. . . . It's magnificent, all of it, but it's not catholic. In the real world, the universal church, which is by definition a human zoo, will always be a much more frustrating and sloppy enterprise.

When reading the books of the International Style liturgists or when listening to one of their speeches, Catholics should be on the alert for telltale signs of pathology: the unusual preoccupation with words like "clean" and "clear," the dictatorial tendencies, the obsession with an almost military form of functionalism, the total inability to deal with lack of cooperation from "the people," and — here is where music comes in — the distrust of the poetic and the beautiful.

The Layer Cake

Four thousand people who call themselves Protestant and live in the same area will take themselves to a variety of places on Sunday morning: the fundamentalist Baptist church, the Quaker meeting house, the High Church Episcopalian establishment, the Salvation Army, and so on. Four thousand people who call themselves Roman Catholic and live in the same neighborhood will find themselves in the same parish. Seated in the same pew will be the union leader, the union-busting employer, the nun with a degree in theology, and the saintly man who puts a dollar bill under the statue of the Infant of Prague for good luck. (I remember when it used to be a dime.) They are "the people." What kind of music should the church offer them?

In Edwin O'Connor's novel *The Edge of Sadness* (1961), the priest who narrates the story is thinking about the sermon he will give. He remembers the old pastor, a monsignor who, years before, delivered sermons to a "solid, homogeneous band... whose wants and needs were fairly uniform and simple." But all that had changed, because the laity had changed. The modern sermon, "in order to be effective, must be comprehensible to a congregation composed of lawyers, stevedores, educators, doctors, scrubwomen, politicians, bankers and baby-sitters — in short, to an incredible layer cake of intellect and imagination. And when you talk about what matters most — that is, when you talk about Almighty God — how do you talk to a layer cake?"[8]

What kind of music is the most appropriate for a layer cake?

The wise Catholicism of history (East and West) decided that the most appropriate music was something that seemed to come from a source outside the layer cake — music which gave the impression of being universal and beyond the narrow tastes of one constituency. This was the theory behind Gregorian chant (which supposedly could be at home anywhere in the world), but in practice the church did allow room for music that sounded "local."

The church's newest policy, in many cases, is to pretend that the "layer cake" does not exist, or perhaps *should* not exist. Sometimes there is a strong tendency to homogenize the faithful by musical force: that is, to make all individuals express their beliefs only in "contemporary" music or to make everyone a "blended" Catholic who has to identify with little bits and pieces of music borrowed from all over the cultural map. Sometimes there is another strong tendency to separate the layers: to give the African-Americans, the Latinos, the suburbanites, and so forth segregated forms of spiritual expression in music. But perhaps the most common practice is to go to somebody's idea of the lowest level of the "layer cake" and find the appropriate music there.

Catholics in my part of the United States are using a version of the Lamb of God that is possibly the most imbecilic succession of musical tones ever assembled — and also very tricky to sing. (I still have not been able to discover who wrote this merry-go-round ditty. Bozo the Clown?) Whenever I ask why this musical joke is being foisted upon the human race, I get the same cynical answer: "Well, they like that kind of thing. And besides, you have to remember where 'the people' are at"; that is, at the cave-dweller stage of development. The faithful are starving for spiritual nourishment symbolized in music. What happens? Somebody says, Let them eat dog biscuits.

The standard hymnals and even the missalettes contain examples of music that sounds important and would certainly remind the congregation that they are part of something important, but that repertory is frequently off-limits, because it would *offend* the congregation. Today, according to a popular slogan, "The Mass is the people" (which is a little like saying, "Baptism is the baby"). Therefore, church music is the people. Therefore, any music which seems to come from *outside* the people or *above* their "lowest common denominator" will hurt the feelings of the congregation, the cave-dwellers.

Sometime in the 1960s I was practicing the organ while the sexton, a Cuban refugee, was mopping the floor of the church. After a few minutes of practicing, I began to play a composition which featured the melody of the Gregorian hymn *Veni Creator Spiritus*. Suddenly, the Cuban man dropped his mop and came dashing up the stairs of the organ loft. When he got to the organ (a little out of breath), he started singing the grand old hymn, which he had learned as a youngster. For a few brief minutes we were united by a Latin hymn dealing with theological complications we could barely follow. What united us was the sound of something uncommonly beautiful, something which did not come from Cuba or the United States but from the "highest common denominator," something not part of the layer cake.

Will a scene like that ever be repeated again, at least in the United States? Nowadays, most American Catholic youngsters are carefully protected from any music that even sounds like *Veni Creator Spiritus* (in Latin or English), because such music would offend them. The Cuban sexton and I felt honored to be part of this important-sounding music when we learned it in our youth. The current thinking, however, is that Catholics only want to see their own particular cultural "layer" represented at a liturgy; they are hurt and alienated by something which does not come from them. The youth "layer" is folk music of the kind found in *Glory and Praise* — nothing else; the egghead-snob "layer" is music like *Veni Creator Spiritus*, even in the vernacular.

What the Second Vatican Council called the "treasure of sacred music" (chant, the glorious choral works, organ music, etc.) was, in many ways, part of a complex program to deal with an extremely complex situation: the heterogeneous congregation of "the people," who come to the church in different social "layers" and who refuse to be homogenized. This "highest common denominator" music was the church's very imperfect way of coming to terms with the stubborn independence and, indeed, the anarchy of "the people." At the same time, this music reminds the congregation that their spiritual values originate in a source that is higher and more important than their particular tribal "layer" in the world.

I saw "the people," in spite of all the pressure on them to conform, still surviving in one of those downtown churches in a shopping district. Worshipers came and went; some directed their attention to the statues and the candles rather than the Mass; doors banged. The priest asked us to sing a couple verses of a hymn, without any accompaniment. The sound of the singing was rather ragged, but in its own way as beautiful as a choir of angels.

I saw "the people" in a big cathedral, one of those "beached whales" isolated in a corner of a downtown area; there was not much of a parish left. The man in the pew in front of me was drunk. Not far from him were a few bums from skid row, which was nearby; out of respect, they were not drunk yet. Around the edges of the great basilica one could see a bag lady here and there with all of her earthly possessions next to her in the pew. The Puerto Ricans occupied territory to my left. Asians sat behind me. The beautiful people who lived in nearby luxury apartments took up their positions away from dangerous-looking characters. Tourists, eccentric artists, disenchanted intellectuals, laborers, all manner of forlorn characters, two Protestant friends of mine, my wife, mother-in-law, children, and I — we all gathered as the assembly on a hot Sunday morning in June. Everything was done tastefully; the music was very good. The hymns, however, were not exceptionally robust, since many in the congregation could not read English or did not feel inclined to pick up the music book. Then the cantor — a real cantor, not one of those leaders of song — began to chant the Alleluia, a sensuous Gregorian melody and one of the longest in the book. For a moment I was stunned. What was going on here? Didn't he know that "the people" are babies and should be given babies' music to sing? The cantor finished and then, miraculously, the bums, the drunks, the bag ladies, the beautiful people, and all the rest of us were somehow carried along by the choir as we sang this grand Gregorian melody in all its insane, irrational complexity. The floor shook.

Roman Catholicism is in the process of dividing its forms of worship into smaller liturgical boutiques, each of which caters to a select clientele. There is really no other choice today. But the church, if it continues to show the kind of shrewdness it had in the past, will resist the temptation to fragment itself totally and will hold on to some forms of worship for "the people," at least in a few places. And what will be the artistic criteria for this kind of non-boutique liturgy? What will be the sure sign that the structure of the liturgy is for "the people" and not a "layer"? The bums — the skid-row alcoholics, the homeless, the down-and-out. Follow the bums on Sunday morning and see where they go to church. They will feel unwelcome at the trendy parish where Father Chuck gathers the faithful around his commanding personality; they will walk past the university chapel where white suburbanites celebrate themselves. But they will enter the church or cathedral with the good choral music and the ceremonies which just "take place," without the over-eager-puppy-dog hospitality. The bums know that this type of liturgical ambiance is for "the people," especially the independent, those who do not want to be boiled in the melting-pot; they know that a Renaissance motet or a chant Kyrie is appropriate for the rich and the wretched of the earth, for the wise and the foolish, but maybe not for those who see the church as the elect organized into small cells.

There is much to be learned from the bums.

7

The Stick and the Carrot

Challenge and Response

An acquaintance of mine told me an intriguing story about his student days in a Benedictine preparatory school back in the 1950s. The monks, anxious to get this thing called Liturgical Renewal off the ground, regularly assembled all the boys in the school for High Mass in Latin and had them sing various parts (Kyrie, Gloria, etc.) — a practice that was considered quite "far-out" at the time. While the boys were singing, a rather grumpy monk, with a long stick in his hand, would patrol up and down the aisles of the chapel. When he came across some recalcitrant lad who was not singing, the monk would give him a good poke with the stick. Thus encouraged, the boy would join in the chant at that point ("... *et ascendit in coelum* ...") but, as soon as the monk was out of sight, the youth would again defiantly shut his mouth.

The historian Arnold J. Toynbee might have interpreted this scene in the Benedictine chapel as yet another example of "challenge and response," that eternal principle of history, that begetter or destroyer of civilizations. From the challenge (the environment, the need for water, the threat of invasion, etc.) comes the response (the civilization). In that Benedictine chapel and on the low level of the atomic particle, we find a hint of this same endless struggle. *Challenge*: the renewal of the faithful, the necessity of expressing and reaffirming belief, the turmoil of youth. *Response*: a stick.

There has never been a time in history when Roman Catholicism was not being challenged, from within, by the threat of sagging faith. Even in apostolic days (and the New Testament makes this clear), it looked as if the zeal in certain Christian communities was going flat. Over the years,

108

the church used to respond to these internal threats to the faith perhaps by starting new religious orders or even by invigorating the faithful with impressive art and music. The Fathers of the Second Vatican Council were not really doing anything unprecedented when they once again responded to the challenge of complacency. Stressing continuity and tradition along with change and renewal, they confidently predicted a great awakening of the faithful through liturgical participation, especially singing. The church merely had to present the congregation with clarified and simplified rites, which matched the cultural values of the local population, and this awakening would automatically begin. Religious singing by the congregation, the *Constitution on the Sacred Liturgy* states, would have to be "skillfully fostered" so that the "voices of the faithful may ring out" during worship (Article 118) — and that ringing out would symbolize the vitality of the heretofore drowsy congregation. It was all a simple matter.

The bishops, priests, and liturgical experts who had the job of implementing this ambitious agenda of Vatican II approached the task from two directions. Sometimes they took the council's yearning ideals and fashioned them into very long, very heavy "sticks" which prod the congregation to pay attention. But sometimes these same implementers have put a "carrot" on the end of the "stick," in order to lead the congregation onwards, and this "carrot" is usually the cultural bias of a particular group.

Clarity

While I waited for Mass to begin in a particularly grand church I was visiting, I admired the stained-glass windows and the way the sunlight poured a soft glow on the decorations in the sanctuary. Natural light, I meditated, gives the worshiper the sense of being in something organic and alive; sunlight "plays" with architecture by revealing a feature of a building one moment and obscuring it the next, by giving the impression that walls and columns can be lifted up and moved when the light moves. Suddenly my thoughts were interrupted. Somebody pulled a switch and the entire interior of the church, from the tip of the ceiling to the floor, was transformed into blazing sunshine. Harsh, unyielding lights — the kind of lighting one might expect in a baseball stadium for a night game — erased every shadow and bleached out every stained-glass window. This interior space, which was supposed to be a place of prayer, now looked more like an operating room ready for bypass surgery. I was so unsettled by the searchlight illumination that I wanted to escape as soon as possible but, at the same time, I was not surprised.

The latest trend in Catholic churches is to illuminate them during a service to the point of painfulness. This building just happened to be an especially violent example of Catholicism's new obsession with clarity.

The late William M. C. Lam, a respected designer of interior lighting, was one of the first to realize that this kind of unrelenting artificial sunshine will just overload the viewer's brain with more "information" than it can possibly absorb.[1] Unyielding brightness in all directions, oddly enough, only leads to a confusion of "messages" and a lack of clarity. Lam's most famous lighting project, the Washington, D.C. subway system, deliberately allows for shadows; it withholds "information." His masterful arrangement of the lights makes a distinction between a restful background and the more important "information" which needs to be seen clearly. The subway lighting gives this potentially hostile space a warm, inviting quality with a mellowness that puts the public at ease.

All of this talk about light and its effect on us — what could be classified as the "psychology of environment" — means nothing to the "contemporary" Catholic, because shadows and nuances in lighting suggest old-style Catholicism, which tried to obscure the importance of the congregation. New-style Catholicism requires an intense, total brightness in illumination and, indeed, a corresponding brightness in words, ideas, ceremonies, music, and all things which are part of worship. Justification for a blinding brightness in everything, it could be argued, was even demanded by Vatican II in the *Constitution on the Sacred Liturgy*, specifically Article 34:

The rites should be distinguished by a noble simplicity; they should be short, clear, and unencumbered by useless repetitions; they should be within the people's powers of comprehension, and normally should not require much explanation.

Those are shining ideals, but it may take centuries to fix the wreckage caused by those few innocent words. In the real world, things are not necessarily appealing just because they are clear. "Useless repetitions" certainly made the old Latin rites dauntingly complex but "repetitions" can also be a delight; in fact, verbal repetitions in a text (e.g., *mea culpa, mea culpa, mea maxima culpa*) can provide just the right flourish which transforms routine words into something resonant and memorable. (Consult the speeches of Winston Churchill.) Rituals watered down so that they seem to be within everyone's "powers of comprehension" cease to be rituals and become sessions for dispensing information, which everyone is required to comprehend. Somewhere in the process of making religious rites so elementary that they need no explanation, "clarity" and "simplicity" have been transformed into sticks which force a distracted congregation to pay attention.

The first indication that this quest for clarity could lead to disaster came when the English-speaking bishops of the world set up the International Committee on English in the Liturgy (ICEL) and gave it the task of translating the official Latin of the Mass into "clear" English "within the people's powers of comprehension." A few perceptive individuals realized from the start that, let us say, the opening prayer of the Mass (the Collect) for Trinity Sunday could never compress its theology into a "clear" statement which everyone will understand. Furthermore, deceptively simple words of the Mass like "Lamb of God" and "kingdom" are highly complex concepts which 99 percent of the faithful really do not follow. (Academic specialists who apply the literary principles of deconstruction or semiotics would have also warned about the futility of searching for a "clear" language which produces a single meaning understood by everyone.) But the ICEL ignored all such hesitations about complexities that really cannot be made "clear," ignored all suggestions about keeping a form of English which suggested the presence of an Almighty God, and proceeded to shape the English text of the Mass along the principles of the purest International Style and Bauhaus simplicity. "Through my fault, through my fault, through my most grievous fault" of the Confiteor was simplified to one "through my fault." The Presidential Prayers of the Mass (such as the Collect), intricate and deferential supplications to the Almighty, were translated so that they would sound like a "Dear Sir" letter from one businessman to another. All the ambiguous "poetry" of the Latin Mass (with its infinite number of "meanings" for every individual) was compressed into small cubes of English prose, "within the people's powers of comprehension."[2]

Many of those public housing projects erected in the 1950s and 1960s, in order to give people clean dwellings (designed according to the most rigorous ideals of International Style simplicity), have turned out to be massive blunders. Some of the worst examples of these apartment buildings in places like St. Louis, Newark, and Boston have had to be dynamited, literally. Those ICEL translations of liturgical texts — with their bleached-white clarity and their stingy verbal minimalism — are also in the process of being officially dynamited (or at least the prayers spoken by the priest are going to be changed). They are so beyond rehabilitation they have to be demolished.

Unfortunately, all the dynamite in the world will not be able to dislodge Roman Catholicism's new preoccupation with "clarity" anytime soon. Intense, total brightness — which allows the worshiper to be bombarded with "information" — has become an accepted part of Catholic culture and a potent antiseptic which will supposedly kill the germs of "private devotions" and "folk Catholicism" (e.g., old ladies praying privately during Mass). What might be called "historic Catholic devotion," the kind of piety which so impressed a Protestant Thomas Merton when he visited Corpus Christi Church in Manhattan, is a form of charismatic energy, without stress; it flourished in the gloom of a Gothic cathedral, it flourished in the sunny Rococo churches of Bavaria, but it will wilt under the glare of "clarity" and intense artificial lighting.

This emphasis on a static and unyielding visual brightness has a parallel in the contemporary insistence on an aural brightness as well. In most churches, the worshipers are never any more than a few feet away from a loudspeaker which incessantly pounds clear "information" into them. I once attended a liturgy in a famous church and found myself almost in pain from the sound of bright, clear, intense amplification. The celebrant's voice — a bishop — was the biggest thing in the building. It was everywhere. There was no escape. Loudspeakers all around the nave enabled the Gigantic Voice to occupy every pew, every corner, every square inch of space. Talk, talk, talk everywhere, and at a volume that musicians would call *fortissimo*.

Now and then in this liturgy, the bishop stopped talking and at that point the songleader, quickly jumping in with a few seconds of music, would become the Gigantic Voice, the invisible monster hovering over the congregation. The songleader's repertory consisted mostly of short, peppy musical intrusions. The incessant talking at the congregation, the snappy singing at the congregation — all of it was "information" and all of it was blasted through microphones. I longed for those few rare moments when a "natural sound" — the unamplified organ or the choir — floated through the great building. I yearned for shadows, for release from the steady hammering of talk, talk, talk. But there was no escape. "Clarity" in worship is interpreted to mean constant "loud volume," so loud that everything is garbled. After a while, garbled loudness sounds like shouting and nobody pays attention to it.

Roman Catholic liturgy in the United States has become a heavily processed affair. Very little is left in what could be called a "natural state," because every spoken word and every note of music are converted into artillery fire shot through amplifiers. The whole liturgical environment, from the lighting to the music, crackles with technological static. The excessive amplification and speakers set up all around the building completely destroy the sense of "here" and "there." The liturgical space disappears; the disoriented Catholic in the pews has the feeling that he or she is inside an enormous radio.

Liturgical music used to be part of the fabric of Catholic ritual; today, it is used most often as a stick which maintains the illusion of an excited congregation paying attention to "clarity." The typical liturgical pattern is: talk, talk, talk — quick, thrash the congregation with a peppy Alleluia, which lasts fifteen seconds; talk, talk, talk — quick, thrash the congregation with an Amen; talk, talk, talk, etc. Crashing into the talking with so much volume and with so little music is unnatural and without any historical precedent, but it does give the impression of alertness.

A few years ago I was visiting a parish church and all of a sudden, right in the middle of the liturgy, there was a power failure. The lights, the microphones, and the organ all went dead. Fortunately, it was during the daylight hours and because of the light from the windows the ceremony could continue. At the very moment the electric lights went out, I think my blood pressure and my pulse rate lowered; muscles in the back of my neck relaxed. The congregation, suddenly aware of what it sounded like, sang beautifully. You could almost sense the stress and the tension draining out of the liturgical environment — until the priest, in a state of panic without his technological crutches, began to shout every last word assigned to him. Talk, talk, talk became shout, shout, shout. Tension returned.

Perhaps this is the place to disseminate a few heresies:

The Catholic congregation does not need to hear every single word of a ritual with vibrant immediacy (especially words that come back week after week). A Catholic who tries to listen attentively to every syllable of the Mass — this is what some experts demand — will be driven insane from the cascade of "information" and have to be taken out of the church in a straitjacket. The priest who, *without amplification,* chants the Eucharistic Prayer of the Mass from the main altar of a cathedral may not be very audible in every pew, but this prayer and this message will come across to everyone with resplendent clarity.

One theologian, Father Kevin W. Irwin, beautifully summed up the matter this way: "The issue in liturgy is less verbal understanding and mental comprehension by the mind and more a shaping of attitudes and allowing one's imagination to be engaged in symbolic acts, which by their nature are not oriented to comprehension alone."[3] This insight was the taken-for-granted wisdom back in the days of the Latin Mass. Whether the wisdom will spread very far is another matter. All of those priests and songleaders standing behind a microphone will not easily give up the power that comes from dispensing their version of "clear" information.

The Requirement

Go to any shopping mall. Everywhere you look, in every direction: convenience! A McDonald's next to a supermarket with instant foods in every aisle next to the highway with cars that take drivers anywhere, anytime. A nation of convenience! Convenience everywhere. Convenience for the sake of convenience. Convenience, so that we may be allowed time for more convenience. Blessed convenience, how I love thee!

Right along the street, not far from the automatic bank teller and the automatic car wash, we find the Roman Catholic parish, and long before the first McDonald's hamburger was fried, the church, supremely conscious of the attention span of the faithful and their busy schedules, had developed its own ingenious convenience culture. The liturgy that droned on for hours in the Orthodox churches and the Eastern rites was condensed in the West to more manageable proportions. Aristocrats were allowed to choose their chaplains on the basis of how fast the priest could say Mass. Some readers may remember the days when parishes offered seven relatively short Masses just on Sunday morning. They may also remember the relaxation of fasting rules for receiving communion, the greater use of the Vigil Mass ("the Sunday Mass transferred to Saturday evening"), and permission to celebrate the liturgy in the afternoon and evening — all modern changes which have helped to make the times of worship convenient for just about any schedule.

The dark side of the church's convenience culture is a little-mentioned fact of life which does not fit very well into the idealistic designs of Liturgical Renewal: the requirement. The old canon law required Roman Catholics, under pain of sin, to *attend* Mass on Sundays and Holy Days of Obligation. The newer version of canon law (1983) insists that the faithful are bound by obligation to *participate* at Mass on Sundays and Holy Days. This law receives a somewhat elastic interpretation today but at one time the "Sunday obligation" was treated as a very stern stick indeed. Catholics who missed Mass, because of carelessness, were not in the state of grace. If you were not in the state of grace and died, you went to hell. That was that.

I can remember the early Sunday Mass at a Catholic college for men back in the 1960s; one would find half-inebriated lads, hanging over the pews and ready to pass out, after a night of general debauchery. They may have broken all ten commandments a few hours earlier, but there they were, fulfilling their obligation. I can remember the strange sight of St. John's church in downtown Philadelphia, one of a couple of places in the archdiocese permitted to have a late afternoon Mass on Sunday.

The building would be packed with those who had missed the last Mass in their parishes. Sometimes a crowd would be standing on the steps leading to the front door because they could not fit inside. From time to time a new worshiper would arrive and ask people on the steps, "Where is the priest now?" "He's not at the Gospel yet," someone would answer. (Translation: "Stand on the steps with us. You can still fulfill your Sunday obligation. If you had shown up after the Gospel, it would have been too late; you would have missed Mass.")

My favorite Sunday obligation story was told to me by a retired F.B.I. agent about the interrogation of Joseph Valachi, a vicious Mafia criminal and, in the 1960s, a government informant. During one interrogation, Valachi went on at great length about a particular Mafia chieftain (in the United States) who was old, gentlemanly, self-educated, and, according to one rumor, an ex-seminarian. One day, this don gave Valachi and a partner a contract to rub out an annoying competitor, whom we shall call Bugs Rafferty. Valachi and his associate went about their task with professional thoroughness but they failed. Every time they got near Bugs, the police were too close or there were too many innocent bystanders. Discouraged, they returned to the Mafia boss's house that night, in order to ask for an extension. They met the don in his study, a room lined with books. (At this point in his story, according to my F.B.I. friend, Valachi became excited and exclaimed, "There were books on the shelves about *Julius Caesar*!") The old don was understanding when he heard their story. They could try again next week, he said. "By the way," he added, just as Valachi and his accomplice were about to leave, "Did you boys go to Mass today?" (It was Sunday.) Why, no, said Valachi. They had been too busy trying to assassinate Bugs Rafferty (and, besides, Valachi had no use for religion). The old man shook his head. "Rubbing out Bugs is important for business," he said, "but going to Mass on Sunday is important for your soul."

The liturgical experts turn crimson with rage whenever they have to discuss this routinized, perfunctory "showing up" at Mass. They demand that the faithful come to church willingly and celebrate joyously. They are furious with the sort of Catholics who just sullenly present themselves for roll call and give every indication that they want to break ranks as soon as possible. "The people," for their part, want salvation but they also want to get home and put the roast in the oven. Resounding participation does not come easily to a laity who, for centuries, have often thought of their presence at Sunday Mass as another installment of their religious taxes.

The result of all of this maneuvering around obligation and convenience is the McDonaldized liturgette, in which everything is squeezed down to the smallest possible proportions and served up in the shortest possible time, with a smile. There is, of course, something to be said for the quick and the concise. McDonald's restaurants thrive because they serve reasonably pleasant food in less time than it takes to read the menu. But the McDonaldized liturgette thrives because it quickly dishes out something unpleasant: *requirements*, especially musical ones. The required opening hymn sets up the required "Good morning" and monolog from the celebrant, which, after a clumsy transition, shifts to the required Penitential Rite and so on. The liturgette may proceed with an honest sense of religious purpose, but a stronger sense of obligation and chore sometimes permeates every moment and turns every note of music into a painful requirement.

Brevity can be beautiful. Routine can be virtuous. The idea of a Sunday obligation, intelligently interpreted, can provide a sign of continuing commitment. In the past, Roman Catholics could deal with the pressures of obligation and routine because the church provided them with gradations of liturgical "impact" — from the quietly reassuring Low Mass to the bigger High Mass for important occasions. The contemporary church, especially where the liturgical experts are in control, mistakes quiet routine for indifference; it demands that noise and energy should somehow continually shake up the calm that comes with a settled routine; it pushes the whole liturgical experience to a higher level of "attentiveness," week after week. The result is burn-out.

I can remember attending, in my younger years, the Latin Mass and listening to the parish choir — five or six tone-deaf sadists — scream bloody murder from one end of the service to the other. (In those days, it was not at all unusual for a parish of five thousand souls to have a choir which consisted of five people.) "Wasn't that singing awful," I would say to my family as we walked home, and everybody would respond, perplexed, "What singing? Was there singing?" They never heard a thing. To be honest, sometimes I never heard a thing either. Like my family, I was trained to see liturgy as a "process." We, the faithful, were accustomed to filtering out unpleasant noises in the "process." The church understood this and used to leave ample opportunity for the faithful to "tune out" an annoyance and indulge in their private meditations. "Tuning in" and "tuning out" were not only acceptable, they were necessary for the self-protection of the captive audience fulfilling an obligation. In France, the Netherlands, and Central Europe the church sometimes promoted all kinds of music (congregational, choral, and instrumental) which encouraged "the people" to abandon their private thoughts and pay attention. In Ireland, the United States, and, to a great extent, Italy — countries with a history of unremarkable church music — "the people" protected themselves by descending deeper and deeper into private prayer during Mass — so deep, in fact, that even the experience of good liturgical music began to be seen as an intrusion, a *distraction*. ("Distracting music" meant anything you might find yourself listening to with some pleasure.) I can still remember the Catholics who, before the late 1960s, used to become indignant at the very thought of musical *distractions* in church.

Younger readers cannot imagine how shocked some American Catholics were when the church asked them to snap out of their liturgical trances and sing *loud music* during Mass. I happened to be sitting next to a very fine organist as he tried to get a Catholic congregation through *Praise to the Lord* during one of those early versions of the "new" Mass. Right in the middle of this hymn, an intense young man came storming up to the organ and shouted, "Stop that noise! It's so loud, I can't *think*."

When you attend a Roman Catholic service today, you can be sure that there will be no distractions whatsoever. You will not be permitted to escape unpleasantness or incompetence by retreating to your private thoughts. Nothing will distract you from watching and listening to the special individuals up front who know more about God than you do. If perchance your mind wanders into thoughts of eternity, awe, or holiness (or lunch), Big Brother or Big Musician behind a microphone will interrupt and insist that you pay attention.

The deal used to be this: the church would use the stick of Sunday obligation but would leave "the people" alone during Mass. It was a fair trade, but the church has now changed the rules of the game. The new requirement is both obligation and excited involvement, the stick *and* the stick.

The parishioner enduring yet another repetition of *Praise to the Lord* may not be aware of much excitement, but the typical Sunday liturgy is an extremely ambitious undertaking calculated to create the impression of something thrilling. The lighting, the rousing music, and the volume of the amplification are all part of a plan to keep the congregation constantly uplifted. But *excitement* and *required routine* do not quite click together; it is also very hard to produce an exciting required routine at perhaps four to seven parish Masses every weekend.

Obligation, routine, and convenience, by themselves, cause troublesome distortions in Catholic liturgy and then matters are made worse by the church's historic commitment to *excellence*. Roman Catholicism, at least in its theoretical ideals, is the church of excellence surpassing excellence and spiritual attainment beyond the commonplace. In the West, the church insists that its clergy have to be the best — which is interpreted to mean celibate males. The church names its buildings after saints whose heroic lives are held up as models of spiritual excellence for all to imitate. The church used to commission the greatest architects, painters, sculptors, and composers and tell them to provide beauty which would astound the faithful; the best church with the best faith required the best art.

The sung Latin Mass used to be one of the church's most striking symbols of heroic greatness. Catholics my age or older can usually remember some High Masses that were times of consolation and healing, but also reminders of spiritual greatness to strive for and mountains to climb. (What triggers the memory is that distinctive mixed smell of incense, burning beeswax candles, flowers, and furniture polish on the pews.) At the same time, we Catholic veterans of the Latin era also retain the memory of the weekly parish High Mass with the bargain-basement imitation of musical greatness; the results were ghastly.

Even with the High Mass virtually gone, the church's liturgical "greatness syndrome" persists to this day, but the obsession has changed from a longing for an aesthetic excellence to a longing for the congregation which performs excellently. "The people," acting together like a disciplined chorus line, will now provide the greatness. They will sing hundreds of responses, just like the Byzantines and the Orthodox; they will sing hymns, just like the Protestants. "The people" shall be driven, like cattle, to participatory greatness, every Sunday and every Holy Day of Obligation.

Somehow, for the sake of their own sanity, Catholic clergy and congregations need to be reintroduced to the lost virtues of mediocrity. The word is, I will admit, loaded with bad associations, but in healthy, honest mediocrity there is strength, even excellence. At this point, I must ask the reader's patience as we probe, in the following paragraphs, this idea of a virtuous mediocrity, without ever defining it adequately.

Roman Catholics who attend a memorial service in a mainstream Protestant church will, afterwards, sometimes grumble about the inordinate *length* of the ceremony (one hour!) but, when it comes to the music, they respect what they hear. "Now, why can't we Catholics have music like that?" is the common response, "It was excellent." A musical technician like myself knows perfectly well that this "excellent" music is often quite mediocre — honest and plain stuff, but nothing to write home about. For approximately five hundred years this mediocrity has been the secret of success for the music in most Protestant churches. A few good hymns and a few simple responses, backed up by a choir and accompanied by an organist who keeps everything at a reasonable speed, will always make an excellent musical impression.

It would be so refreshing if a prophet could arise in every Catholic diocese and proceed to do the following: (1) smash the idols of excellence, including most of the microphones and (2) lead repentant sinners back to the forgotten virtues of mediocrity. The musical prophet's plan of action would be summed up in an expression used by Father Robert Hovda, a commentator on liturgical matters: *homely music*. Cathedrals and the many churches with good resources have an obligation to take the one musical talent and multiply it fivefold, but the "typical" parishes should get out of the business of trying to sound excellent all the time; instead, they should concentrate their musical efforts on good, wholesome, plain, homely music, in particular, music sung from memory. This homely material, ironically, can be found in the topnotch Catholic hymnals, such as *Worship III* and *Hymns, Psalms, and Spiritual Canticles*. A simple Kyrie, a litany, many of the older Protestant hymns, songs from Taizé — you cannot get more homely than that; and yet, behind the "mediocrity" in this music there is a reverberating profundity, especially when the music is sung unaccompanied or with a minimum of instrumental support.

The leadership at most Catholic parishes and chapels disdains the very notion that they should humble themselves by using homely music. They want congregational excellence and they want it every week. For example, a parish committee on liturgy, after rejecting a dozen examples of homely music for the congregation, will choose a song like *Gather Us In* by Marty Haugen — a respectable composition. The decision to incorporate this song into the parish repertory seems to be based on solid grounds. After all, the resident liturgical expert has checked all the biblical references in the text; the local music director has pronounced the melody pleasant. But nobody calculates the titanic *ambitions* of this song. The words of *Gather Us In* run across the page like the text of a Gilbert and Sullivan patter-song. Images and whole concepts seem to shift in every phrase. The singer's left brain has to process the ideas that go racing by in the words; the right brain tries to dance along with the frolicking melody. *Gather Us In* would make a useful anthem for choir or a hymn for a small congregation straining for spiritual excellence but, like so many of the "modern songs for the modern church," it is a mouthful.

The Roman Catholic church, back in the 1960s, tried to launch the musical equivalent of the Great Leap Forward. One week there was silence at Mass; the next week the congregation was supposed to sing four hymns which took Protestants four centuries to develop. Congregations in the United States, with rare exceptions, never struggled through a stage of musical apprenticeship or even infancy. With very little preparation, they went immediately into the "advanced class."

Most parishes should go back, as it were, return to the primitive state they never really knew, and try to go through a stage of development that they missed. They need to lower their expectations. This could begin with two important steps: reducing the artificial lighting and reducing the amplification. With lighting and amplification lowered, a greater use of unaccompanied, chantlike singing would make sense. The most homely church music ever written, the most folklike of all music for congregation is any kind of chanted dialog (preferably unaccompanied) involving priest, cantor, and people.

Complexity is easy; simplicity is hard. Parishes, alas, will find it much easier to go on scheduling a complex assortment of read-left-to-right hymns, which few people sing, and nursery school tunes, which nobody likes, since this will give the impression of great accomplishments and, at the same time, hide failure. It would be very frightening for most churches to go back to a "natural state," if only temporarily. Simplicity, especially without the hype of amplification, is scary — and besides, Catholics have a habit of equating simplicity with indifference or lack of resolve.

An example of "scary simplicity" is the Penitential Rite chanted from beginning to end, without amplification and without loud accompaniment. Some kind of simplified Gregorian formula would sound *stupendous* — but also raucous, primitive, mediocre, and homely. Homely music does not sound excellent, and for this reason those who make liturgical decisions reject it.

In the earlier part of the twentieth century, when parishes reached for excellence, they said they wanted a Renaissance Mass by Palestrina and the Gregorian Propers at the High Mass. Often they fell flat on their faces trying to approximate that level of excellence. Today, the excellence to which so many parishes aspire is that rich, creamy sound of "contemporary" church music. "*I Have Loved You* by Michael Joncas — that is it!" some Catholics say, "That is the kind of music we must have today." They swoon over the melody and the way the notes, gently and gracefully, float downward, like feathers in the still air. But if you ask them to sing back to you those same floating musical feathers (especially at "ev-er-last-ing love"), they fall flat on their faces. The music is too pretentious, too demanding. They cannot remember how it goes, even after several minutes of coaching. The Te Deum in Latin is easier to learn than *I Have Loved You* and half the songs in the reformed-folk repertory.

In the parishes, the pastor and the planners look at two piles of music. The first contains primitive music: the classic hymns, chant, the service music in the better hymnals. But it all looks so "mediocre," so "dead." The second pile is the reformed-folk repertory; there are enough scriptural allusions on each page to make a biblical scholar dizzy and the choreographic gestures in each musical phrase are extravagantly exquisite. This folk repertory may be difficult for "the people" to sing but it gives the impression of striving for an excellence of some sort (in this case, a perfect imperturbability, Grade-A cream). Just on the basis of the immense ambitions in this music, the reformed-folk repertory will frequently be given preference; it will elbow-out the "mediocre" competition, music written with "the people" in mind.

Nicely "mediocre" music (homely and yet classy) ... music that easily insinuates itself into the liturgy ... even some kinds of "boring" chant which nevertheless has an eternal and hypnotic sound ... quiet serenity ... silence, no music — all of this will seem natural in an environment pinched by obligation and convenience. Tumultuous musical excitement or the feverish emotionalism of reformed-folk music makes sense as an occasional option, here and there, now and then, but on a regular basis (at every Mass on every Sunday and Holy Day of Obligation) this kind of enforced excitement will most assuredly encourage a large number of Catholics to hate any form of liturgical music.

A Cultural Carrot

In the late 1960s, everyone thought it was going to be so simple. The church would stop trying to impose a European, Roman form of worship on the whole world and, instead, would let liturgical practices evolve from indigenous cultures. Like a carrot on the end of a stick, regional cultural values attached to the Mass (especially the music) would lead the faithful to a higher understanding of the sacred rites. In Africa, drums and dances would become a normal part of the Mass. In Asia, gongs would look perfectly normal. And in the United States...

"Indigenous American Culture" — what is that? Years ago, the cultural values of the American rich and the well-born used to trickle down to the multitude below, but not many people today check to see what the Vanderbilts are doing before they pick out a wardrobe or design a house — or a church. In our time, a common perception is that nobody has a monopoly on the one and only high culture. Everything, we are told, is relative; one person's idea of a "cultural value" is as good as another person's. As a result of this relativism, culture has exploded into thousands of competing cultures. Anybody who wants to learn what each mini-culture considers to be important will have to go to the one place in our civilization where all the values come together and fight it out: the magazine rack, especially the bigger ones. The "American Way of Life" or the "Culture of the United States" reveals itself in the magazine rack, that riotous parade of publications devoted to competing notions about fashion, cooking, obscenity, obesity, profundity, frivolity, news, movie stars, and so forth, *ad infinitum.*

One Protestant church might gather together its entire congregation from the sort of people who subscribe to *House Beautiful* and who keep back issues of *Fortune* and *Forbes.* Another might confine itself to the cultural level found in *Popular Mechanics.* The Roman Catholic church has the unenviable job of trying to deal with the whole magazine rack, the whole store. Some of "the people" subscribe to *Better Homes and Gardens;* some are avid readers of *Guns and Ammo.* Before the Second Vatican Council, the church gave the impression that its liturgical life rose above the petty fashions of popular culture but today it gets right into the thick of things. To use a somewhat confused image: the church is constantly plugging into the energies found in different areas of magazines on the rack, constantly shifting from one category to another, from top to bottom, from this side to that, constantly searching for what "turns people on."

If the official liturgical books published by Rome were sold on magazine racks, they would be found right there in the small "good taste" section. The Vatican's Latin edition of the "new" Mass, the *Missale Romanum,* should go next to classy publications like *Traditional Home, Colonial Homes,* and *House Beautiful.*

Another section of the magazine rack is devoted to what could be called ripened sexuality. For men there are the magazines clustered around *M: The Civilized Man, GQ: Gentlemen's Quarterly,* and *Playboy.* For women there are *Vogue, Cosmopolitan, Playgirl,* and so on. Protestant denominations regularly plug into this section of the magazine rack. *A Mighty Fortress Is Our God* sung in a Protestant service sounds bold, confident, mature — and assertively male or female. All the glands have developed and are secreting hormones.

A good many Catholic parishes and chapels stay clear of the energies in the ripe-sexuality magazines. Instead, they find it much more comfortable (and less threatening) to plug into the many, many publications dedicated to a ripening sexuality: *Tiger Beat, Teen Beat, Teen Machine, Teen Idols, Super Teen, Wow,* and all the rest. Here in this part of the magazine rack we find page after page of soft boys who have just shaved for the second time. Sexual danger lurks in every photographed smile, yet the whole effect does not seem terribly threatening.

The last teen heartthrob magazine on the rack touches the edge of the soap territory: *Soap's Sexy Stars, Soap Set, Soap Opera People, Soap's Loving Couples.* The ripening process is a little more advanced here, but not complete. All the intricacies of the sexual couplings in these television dramas would seem to indicate an advanced state of reproductive maturity, and yet most of the characters still act like babies, spoiled rotten.

If the music of the famous Catholic folk "groups" and the reformed-folk composers were sold in stores, it would go on the magazine rack, right there between *Tiger Beat* and *Soap Opera People*, or perhaps next to the paperback romance novels (the ones about Tammy and Teddy and their first high school crush, not the more aggressive "bodice-rippers"). This is the one and only territory in modern culture where that dreamy, heart-squeezing sentimentality belongs. This is the cultural soil from which grew *Be Not Afraid* and *Yahweh, I Know You Are Near*.

At a certain age, a little immaturity combined with a lot of innocence looks cute. At a later age, however, the same immaturity looks sickening. It is truly sickening to see men and women in some churches desperately clutching their copies of the latest "contemporary" songs because, they insist, there is nothing else in the universe. It is stomach-turning to see adults trying to sustain their pubescent innocence well into their ripened years, by means of reformed-folk music. They are so pathetically afraid of maturity. Yes, it is true that Christians must become as little children, but must they also, in order to be saved, maintain a state of perpetual adolescence?

Usually, in a section of a store that is away from the clamor of all the competing magazines but closest to the cash register — a privileged spot — we find the scandal sheets, the tabloids: *Globe, National Enquirer, The National Examiner, Sun, Weekly World News*, and so on. The headlines scream loudly about the latest man-bites-dog story but most of the sensational news seems to be about a few predictable topics: the British royal family, unusual pregnancies ("Baby Born With Bullet in Chest"), invaders from outer space ("Family Held Captive by Space Aliens"), crash diets, psychics who predict the future, and the cavortings of movie stars and other celebrities.

Over the centuries, Roman Catholicism has played the role of the tabloid church. It really has had little choice in the matter. A substantial number of "the people" want signs and wonders; they want sensational headlines about the saints and Mary. These tabloid believers make pilgrimages to Fatima and Medjugorje, but Jerusalem is far down on their list of places to visit. If we can judge from the catalogs of organizations and publishers which cater to tabloid Catholicism, they have little interest in love-thy-neighbor brotherhood or in alleviating the social miseries of our time.

The history of Roman Catholic liturgy and church architecture, until recently, could be described in part as a constant fight between the church, which has a specific spiritual duty to perform, and the millions of tabloid believers who have their own agenda. In the past, the church managed to keep the tabloid believers under control by stunning them with liturgical beauty. Lately, the church has tried to neutralize them by turning them into an "aware gathered community." They are not impressed.

Tabloid Catholics are the kind of people who, if they owned the White House, would put vinyl siding on the exterior and that plastic, fake-wood paneling on every interior wall. They have a ravenous appetite for religious music of the most personal, egotistic sort — soggy songs which embarrass even the practitioners of the *reformed*-folk style. At the same time — and I do not understand this contradiction — they also have an extremely sensitive appreciation of beauty; they are the ones who will support any effort to bring great liturgical art and music into the church. Maybe they instinctively understand realities which have eluded the wise music professor and the liturgical expert who is weighted down with academic degrees. Maybe the tabloid believers are the only ones who realize that a single pilgrimage to Lourdes is a lot more powerful than a thousand attentive repetitions of *Now Thank We All Our God*.

Good taste, teen romances, and the tabloids take up a large proportion of the space on the magazine rack, but all of this is small potatoes. For the real clout in contemporary culture we have to look at one particularly disturbing assortment of magazines in an area of the rack which seems to be devoted to photographs of tantrums in a madhouse: *Rock Pix*, *Rock Scene*, *Guitar World*, *Hit Parader*, *Metal Madness*, *MM: Metal Music*, *Power Metal* (which calls itself "The nastiest magazine on earth"), and all the rest. We are now in rock territory, and for proper perspective here, we should recall that all of these lurid and — yes, indeed — *nasty* magazines represent just a few souvenirs in printed form, a small extension of the mountain of material in the local record store and the radio station.

Rock is it. Rock and its derivatives dominate contemporary culture. Rock is more than just music; it is a way of life, a philosophy, a system of social and artistic values; it sums up an era. This is the age of rock.[4]

Rock's domination of daily life became painfully apparent to me recently when I had to spend a day doing various chores. At the garage, while I waited for my car to be fixed, I had to listen to rock music of the most violent kind and at an earsplitting volume. ("Does that radio stay on all day?" I asked the mechanic. "Yeah," was the answer. "It keeps me goin'.") My next stop was a toy store. There it was again: rock at full volume, and behind the cash registers the monosyllabic youths with that hostile, beat-up look on their faces. At the drug store I tried to pick out a sympathy card while a rock chanteuse, blasting at me from speakers in the ceiling, wailed inconsolably, "I wanna feel your body." Rock pursued me to the delicatessen, the gift shop, the post office, the hardware store, and the shopping mall. I could not escape it. No matter where I went, I was socked in the face by rock noise.

Quite a few people born after about 1960 now refer to rock as "regular music." (The young devotee who has acquired a taste for 1950s rock tells us, "I'm really into classic rock from the fifties but, sure, I still like regular music.") Every other type of music — Bach, Beethoven, jazz, folk — is not regular music from the regular culture and is, therefore, peripheral. We now find that at some wedding receptions a rock group presides and detonates one musical explosion after another. If you ask these musicians to play the *Anniversary Waltz* or *Here Comes the Bride*, you get a sneer and mumbled reply which refers to the stupidity of your request. They only play "regular music."

Rock is almost exclusively singer-music. At the center of the stage and in front of screaming fans, the singer writhes in a manner which suggests the agony of an artistic form of childbirth and, at the same time, the ecstasy of an unshared eroticism; he squeezes, he twists every fiber of his being; he sweats. As he sings, his lower jaw is thrust forward in a most unnatural manner, as if to show intense suffering, the personal pain necessary to feel the meaning of the words. (I refer to the rock singer as "he" because macho, male singers dominate rock.) The appeal of his performance partially depends on the glitter of the mise en scene and on the mystique that comes from his unrestrained lifestyle, but the big criterion of excellence is how he *feels* the words that he sings.

Rock and its derivatives are today's "regular music," which consists of an interaction between the suffering, feeling singer, under a spotlight, and the audience, which watches. The music itself and the words that it carries sometimes disappear into the background; the main event is the *watching* of the dramatic tableau performed by the great ego (who holds the mystic scepter of media power, the portable microphone). The public buys recordings of this "regular music" and passively listens to it but cannot really sing it around the piano in the parlor or while they are working. This music is much too spastic for the amateur public to sing.

Sometimes it looks as if Roman Catholicism has already adjusted to this cultural phenomenon of the passive audience which derives its pleasure not from singing but from watching rock performers. For example, the music of the reformed-folk variety may not have the relentless, driving one-TWO-one-TWO rhythm of rock but it has a lot of other things in common with it: the narcissism, the soloists who have to be watched as they feel the meaning of words, and the consistent, studied indifference to formality. Mod Masses sponsored by the most thoroughly mod Catholic organizations sometimes look like mini rock concerts.

Strangely enough, rock has even insinuated itself into churches that keep their musical repertory fairly conservative and traditional. The booming amplification and the constant succession of "stimulating" songs are somebody's idea of how to make boring liturgy as exciting and as relevant as a rock concert. The pope himself is now treated as if he were a rock star and media celebrity. The papal Mass of the pope on tour sometimes looks like Catholicism's answer to the rock concert competition. One must always admire the way the papacy, throughout the centuries, has managed to beat the contemporary culture at its own game. Yet, sensitivity requires that one must wince at the possibility of divine services being turned into something that Broadway producers call a "star vehicle."

Future generations will, we are assured, laugh at the current brands of rock, heavy metal, and rap and find it all charmingly old-fashioned. Or will they? Will the values of rock become so "regular" and so omnipresent that society will see anything "non-rock" as irrelevant or a threat to the established order?

"You can't use classical music or chant when there are lots of kids in the congregation. They just go blank. They've been raised on rock." In the past twenty years, words like that have probably been said more times than the Hail Mary. The pseudorock of "contemporary" church music is now thought to be a very big orange carrot which will entice the young to church. From nursery school through college, most Catholic "kids" are trained to think of reformed-folk music as *theirs*: the church's answer to rock and the *only* genuine, sincere music of Catholicism. The problem is, they are also being trained to curl their upper lips at any "style" of liturgy which does not appear to be under their control.

The Old Carrot

One day, when I am flipping through a library's card catalog, I shall not be startled if I come across a new subject entry for a genre of creativity: "Catholic Church, cranky memories of." For a while there, one could not visit a bookstore or read a magazine or check the theater listings without running into yet another autobiographical recollection of the Catholic church as a Chamber of Horrors, wherein one finds (or at least used to find) concentration camp schools, blazing-bonfire sermons on hell and/or masturbation, psychotic nuns, and other gruesome specimens. Memoirs of this sort (really love-hate tributes to a spiritual parent) go back to Joyce's *Portrait of the Artist as a Young Man* and beyond; starting in the 1960s this phenomenon looked as if it would grow into a service industry. These public confessions about the ordeal of Catholicism or how it loused up your libido were once all the rage, but that seems to have peaked. Today, it is sufficient to display a bumper sticker which proclaims, "I survived Catholic schools."

An integral part of this self-examination art form for Catholics is the book or drama which evokes memories of that densely textured Catholic culture which existed before the Second Vatican Council. Sometimes the remembrance of things past is lighthearted and funny (e.g., the St. Fidgeta lampoon by John Bellairs[5] and the musical *Nunsense*). Sometimes acid eats through every syllable (e.g., Christopher Durang's play *Sister Mary Ignatius Explains It All for You*). But, whatever the case, it would appear that the Catholic population, obsessed by its culture and what that culture does to people, has an abundance of reasons for laughing at itself. Maybe this has been going on since the days of Chaucer's *Canterbury Tales*.

Yes, Catholics do the darndest things, especially if their memory goes back to the days before the Second Vatican Council, and then they want to ponder these religious doings in a highly morose form of brooding disguised as comedy. But an interesting thing: the laughter stops at the Mass. Anyone who examines this creative output devoted to the Catholic laity's "cultural memories" will have a very hard time finding (1) unpleasant remarks about the Latin Mass of the past or (2) pleasant remarks about the "Good morning" English Mass of the present. The literati, the intelligentsia, "creative types," and the sort of laity who make their living by thinking in public generally do not conceal their disappointment with the talky "new" Mass in English, compared to the "old" Mass in Latin. Examples of this disappointment turn up in Peter Occhiogrosso's highly informative anthology, *Once a Catholic* (1987). Twenty-five practicing or nonpracticing or former Catholics — a very broad range of personalities — tell about their religious odyssey in this collection of autobiographies. The church's "new" liturgy, which was supposed to recharge the world with spiritual energies, produces no excitement, no sense of renewal; the "new" Mass is hardly mentioned and, when it is, gets very bad reviews. (Conservative commentator Michael Novak: "It feels more like a meeting of the Lions Club. The liturgy has been made over into a celebration of our being together — how lucky we are to be together with one another! It's awful.") Some of the prominent individuals quoted in Occhiogrosso's anthology kick the Catholic church up and down the stairs for its past sins and offenses, for its cruel insensitivities, for its innumerable failings, but criticism of the old Latin rituals is conspicuously absent.

For centuries, the church had used liturgical rites which seemed to belong to a culture above regional culture; these ceremonies, in spite of their imperfections, were like a luscious carrot dangled in front of "the people." The intellectual and the anti-intellectual could be drawn into the rich fantasy world that these Latin rituals encouraged. Then, suddenly, the carrot was gone. The "creative" and "thinking" laity had to make the adjustment from austere solemnities in Latin (which commanded their respect) to interminable talking in the vernacular (which sounded patronizing). These disappointed individuals are not reactionaries who want to restore the old Latin regime completely, and public hangings as well. They do not want to "go back" to a style of worship that badly needed revision but they show traces of bitterness at the way the church has abruptly changed a serious act of worship into a low-grade variety show.

Sir Alec Guinness, the famous British actor, converted to Catholicism in 1956. In his autobiography, *Blessings in Disguise* (1985), Guinness sums up the attitude of many "creative" Catholics who have had the chance to compare the church's old carrot with the new rites which emerged after the Second Vatican Council.

...I find the post-Conciliar Mass simpler and generally better than the Tridentine; but the banality and vulgarity of the translations which have ousted sonorous Latin and little Greek are of supermarket quality which is quite unacceptable. Hand-shaking and embarrassed smiles or smirks have replaced the older courtesies; kneeling is out, queueing is in, and the general tone is rather like a BBC radio broadcast for tiny tots (so however will they learn to put away childish things?). . . . The Church has proved she is not moribund. "All shall be well," I feel, "and all manner of things shall be well," so long as the God who is worshipped is the God of all ages, past and to come, and not the idol of Modernity, so venerated by some of our bishops, priests and mini-skirted nuns.[6]

In an essay "Confessions of an Ex-Catholic," the writer Pat Conroy offers a different perspective: the nostalgic memories of the "creative type" (or the intellectual) who never quite got over the sheer power of the church's old carrot, the liturgical culture above the local culture:

I left the church but she has not left me.
This seems to be the Universal condition of ex-Catholics. We said our goodbyes but did not totally escape. . . . I loved the poetry of the church prayers. . . . I loved Gregorian chants, the sight of nuns at prayer on Good Friday, the sanctus bells, the covered forms [i.e., statues] of saints during Lent, the drum roll of the confiteor with all the sadness and elegance of a dead language filling a church and entering my bloodstream at the ear, and the sunburst of gold when the priest raised the monstrous chalice at the Consecration. I loved the ceremony,

the adherence to tradition, and the astonishing continuity of it all. The Church equipped me with a limitless arsenal of metaphor. I have never recovered from the vividness of its imagery, from the daze of its language. But I have never had a single day when I wished to be a Catholic again.[7]

Show the above quotation to the International Style liturgical expert or the red-hot worshipers of the idol of Modernity and you will receive one of two reactions. The first is the polite smile concealing disgust: "Well, those people were just cultural Catholics. They fell in love with the cultural baggage — the Latin, incense, chant, and all that. They never understood the religion underneath the cultural decorations." The second reaction is spoken through very tense lips: "You can't please everybody. And besides, those people really left the church for reasons below the belt."

The trap here is ingeniously constructed. The believer who expresses the slightest sympathy for the church's liturgical past is a *cultural* Catholic who has been dazzled more by the antiques than by the faith itself. Catholics who walked away from the church because they could not stand being treated like tiny tots at Mass really left because of the pelvic issues. The prevailing message is that the Catholic culture of old, with its emphasis on solemnity and awe (fear), was wrong from the start and has finally been repudiated. The new modes of worship, especially "contemporary" folk music, have absolutely no cultural values which get in the way of the true faith.

In 1987, the editors of *U.S. Catholic* conducted a somewhat unscientific survey of its readers and one of the statements presented was the following: "The Mass means more to me today in the 1980s than it did in the early 1960s." Sixty-four percent of those polled agreed with the statement; 29 percent disagreed; 7 percent had other answers.[8] That settles that. Majority rule wins, and the majority is happy.

But look again at the statistics. The fallen-away and other "disappeared" Catholics were not asked for their opinions. Also keep in mind that many Catholics who go to church regularly are quite cautious about giving scandal; the parish liturgy may make them feel miserable but they will behave like good soldiers and tell any nosy pollster that everything is fine. No matter how one looks at these percentages from *U.S. Catholic* — as accurate or as suspect — it is still amazing that 29 percent of those who responded admitted that the Mass of the 1980s was a disappointment compared to the Mass of the early 1960s.

A large portion of the Catholic population of the United States is "disappointed" with the way they are forced to worship and perhaps these people have learned to express their dissatisfaction by a time-honored method: withholding donations. In 1987 Father Andrew M. Greeley, the famous sociologist and author, and Bishop William McManus released an extensive report which reveals that Roman Catholics in this country are contributing half as much of their income to the church as they did twenty-five years ago, while Protestant contributions to their churches have remained at about the same percentage. According to this report, *Catholic Contributions: Sociology and Policy,* in the early 1960s Roman Catholics gave a little more than 2 percent of their income to the church; Protestants gave about the same percentage. By 1984 Catholics were giving only 1.1 percent of their income to their parishes; the percentage of Protestant donations remained the same.

Catholic Contributions does not contain any statistics or "hard data" which could explain this dramatic drop in contributions. Penny-pinching Catholics were not asked why they were giving less. Father Greeley suggests that the laity may be using the reduced donations to protest the supposed incompetence of bishops, the closing of so many Catholic schools, and especially the church's official position on birth control.[9] But could this "lay anger" and "partial alienation" (Father Greeley's terms) also be attributed to annoyance with the demystified, "Good morning," tiny-tot Mass? The report briefly entertains the possibility of unhappiness with the "new" Mass and quickly dismisses it because all the statistics show that a large majority of the Catholic population heartily "approves" of the English Mass and other changes. And yet, approval of "the changes" is one thing; approval of the way they are implemented is something altogether different. It is entirely possible that a significant number of Catholic laypeople are dropping pennies into the collection basket, instead of dollars, and holding back on their singing because they resent being treated like tiny tots when they attend Mass. (My own hunch is that Catholics slice off a third of their donation whenever the priest begins Mass with "Good morning," two-thirds if he begins with jokes and remarks about the weather.)

An acquaintance of mine reports that a newly installed bishop, during an address to priests in his diocese, made a very revealing observation. In a few decades, said the ultraconservative bishop with a smile, all the Catholics who can remember the better moments of the "old" Latin liturgies will be dead or senile. Once those people are gone, dissatisfaction with the liturgy will disappear. Nobody will be around to compare "old" and "new." His Excellency could have added that younger generations, which have only known the tiny-tot banalities, will never be burdened with the curse of cultural Catholicism. In other words, they will never think back, after they have left the church, and remember wistfully: "Ah, how we used to love to hear Father Chuck say, 'Good morning'! Didn't

you just break out in goosebumps when Mr. Caruso used to sing so powerfully into the microphone that he drowned out the entire congregation!
Oh, how I miss those unmemorable songs we refused to sing!"

Most of the impressive "old culture" that ex-Catholics remember
selectively has been erased or banished to the distant edges. The im-
penetrably austere ceremonies, the covered statues during Lent, nuns in
picturesque habits, exotic chanting, and most of the other cultural manifestations which seemed to flaunt a defiantly confident faith are nearly
gone. There will be very little "cultural Catholicism." At the same time,
of course, there will also be a lot less in the way of obsessively precise
liturgical requirements, outmoded practices, cumbersome costumes for
nuns, and unhealthy attitudes disguised as the faith eternal.

Sister Mary Dynamite, one of those nuns who could brilliantly run
the Pentagon and IBM at the same time, found a way to put some extra
energy into the liturgical singing of the middle-class area where she lives.
Once a year she would bring together four parish choirs plus the choir
of the church where she was music director and have them sing some
challenging music at a Solemn Mass: maybe portions of a Mozart Mass
with orchestra, maybe Gregorian chant. All the ideals of the "new" Mass
were faithfully observed and the congregation had plenty of music to
sing.

By any measurement, this once-a-year fling was a huge success.
Parishioners were generously supportive; in fact, the church could barely
hold the crowd. Choir members were refreshed by the musical challenge.
Everybody was moved by music which gave a deeper meaning to words
that were recited every week. Sister Mary Dynamite proved once again
that the better music of "cultural Catholicism" — in all its seductive
beauty — is as potent as ever, provided you have the resources to do it
properly. The "old carrot" still works.

Unfortunately, I have to report that the good sister was harassed out
of her job. (One diocesan official, an enraged layman, complained in
public about this dangerous cultural witchcraft being practiced upon an
unsuspecting congregation.) To the great disappointment of the parishioners, the nun had to take her talents elsewhere. She had failed to realize
that this type of music may be immensely popular with the laity (for
certain occasions and certain places) but it also does something rather
unpleasant to Father Chuck, Mr. Caruso, and the liturgical expert: it rips
the stuffing out of them; it knocks them down to the level of the congregation — but I am getting ahead of myself. This is discussed in the
next chapter.

8

Mr. Nice Guy

The New Triumphalism

Historians will someday conclude that the decision to "turn the altar around," so that the priest would face the congregation during Mass, did more to unglue Roman Catholicism than the Protestant Reformation. This changing of the furnishings in the 1960s has accidentally revealed to all the world a dark secret which the church had managed to conceal for centuries: *The male priest, in most cases a bachelor, is just another flawed human being.*

The liturgical experts work themselves into a state of fury when they remind everyone that, in the old days, the priest used to say Mass "with his back to the congregation." But that is a modern interpretation. For centuries priest and people, offering the Mass together, thought they were facing the same direction; symbolically, they were pointing themselves and their prayers toward the unseen God.

The liturgical experts work themselves into an even greater state of indignation when they refer to the altars which used to look like a shelf stuck near the back wall of the sanctuary, away from the congregation. In ancient times, the experts remind us, the altar was free-standing and the Eastern churches have always kept it this way; priests in these churches have always faced the congregation. Before the Second Vatican Council, even the pope continued the custom of celebrating Mass *versus populum* (facing the people) at the high altar of St. Peter's in Rome.

But, here again, the experts got it wrong. The Eastern churches, worried about all the attention that would be given to the man standing behind the altar, usually "hide" the sanctuary. Priest and people are deliberately kept apart by a wall, the iconostasis, so they cannot get to know one another. The exposed, free-standing altar in St. Peter's and other Roman basilicas was probably the model followed when Catholic churches and chapels, starting in the 1960s, began to rearrange their sanctuaries, but back then nobody seemed to notice that these altars in the Eternal City are under a baldacchino and in a space that is separated from the congregation. Also, nobody wanted to hear that the custom of priest and congregation facing a "shelf" altar may go back to the days when Mass was said in the catacombs on the tombs of the martyrs.

Long ago, Catholicism, East and West, understood that the structure of the church building had to be set up in a way which emphasized the entire assembly's prayer to the God who was unseen yet present. Priest (on one side of a screen) facing people (on the other side) — that solution has worked well in the East. Priest and people facing the same direction — that arrangement can be very effective, especially in a small space. Priest and people, eyeball to eyeball for the entire duration of the ceremony — that is asking for trouble; it sets up a kind of magnetic field, an "I-you" tension, instead of the liturgical "us." What has happened now, with the turned-around altar and the priest constantly dead-center, is that "the people" seem to pray *at* him, not *with* him. His own loudly amplified prayer seems to be addressed not to the unseen God but back to the congregation.

At the thoroughly modernized Mass in the modernized church, "the people" try to pray, but their first order of business is always an evaluation of the man standing behind the altar and looking at them; it is very difficult to escape his dominating presence. The sanctuary has been designed so that his personality — all of his inadequacies, his failings, his quirks, and his good points — will be exposed to a sustained public scrutiny. ("My, he's getting so ... plump ... thin ... old ... bald. He's certainly a ... charmer ... politician ... mama's boy ... jerk.") This process of evaluation can go on for the entire duration of the liturgy, because everything seems to be aimed, like beams of light, to the priest's face. Even the music often gives the impression of being something which is bounced off his presence.

In the old days, "the priest" approached the altar with much bowing, breast-beating, and protestations of unworthiness; he left his personality back in the sacristy. "The people" assembled behind him. Together they offered "the Mass." Today, "the priest" is almost gone. He has been replaced by Mr. Nice Guy, who strides into the sanctuary as the triumphant President of the Assembly. He stands and sits at the architectural climax of the entire building. Everyone's eyes are on him. His face is the center of attention. The celebrant becomes a celebrity. "The priest" develops a stage character. A star is born.

Any television producer knows that one of the least appealing and most boring things that can appear on the screen is the talking head, the lone man or woman who is saying something to the audience and is televised from the neck up. The longer the same talking head remains on the screen, the more boring it becomes.

The central reality of Roman Catholic worship since the 1960s is the talking head. Catholic journals and books can go on for page after page with disquisitions upon the meaning and message of the new, revitalized forms of worship, but all of the idealist theorizing does not match what a congregation actually experiences, what really happens, and that is the priest standing behind an altar: the talking head. Sometimes the talking head yields the center of the screen to another talking head, such as a reader; sometimes the singing head, the massively overamplified leader of song, occupies the center of the screen. But these are only cameo appearances. Lighting, amplification, and the layout of the sanctuary will always force the worshiper's attention back to the main head that talks, the priest. The talking head does not preside over a collective, communal form of prayer; it intercepts prayer. The congregation senses that it is offering a collective prayer only when the talking or singing head moves away from the microphone and the center of the screen.

Roman Catholicism, the Eastern churches, Anglicans, Lutherans, and other Christians have a history of making sure that one head would not draw all of the attention during a service. So many of their liturgical and musical traditions deliberately "confuse" the worshiper and "scatter" his or her attention so that the face of the presiding clergyman would get lost in all the activity. They tried "every trick in the book" to make sure that the liturgy would not be an almost constant, frontal presentation of heads. In the older Catholic rites, for example, the priest chanted some prayers from the side of the sanctuary; deacons also occasionally stood sideways when they chanted. When an Anglican priest delivered prayers from a side kneeler, the congregation could only see part of his face; sometimes, when he aimed his prayers toward the back of the sanctuary, the congregation just saw the back of his head. The Baptist minister seemed to be looking at the floor as he addressed the Almighty; the congregation only saw the top of his head. The idea behind some of these strange movements was to give the impression of directing prayer to that unseen God, who was the *real* "presider," but in many cases the clergy just instinctively sensed that they had to break up the deadening monotony of one head facing a parallel group of heads.

Some Protestant denominations, it is true, invite the worshiper to pay close attention to the minister who preaches dramatically for an hour or more, but that is the *persuasive* head, which tries to make a point. The talking head — which appears to be reading to the congregation and the congregation appears to be praying to it — is a new development in Christianity.

Of course, nobody ever said that being a star, a talking head, would be easy. Out there, in the great beyond called the congregation, are eyes, hundreds of them; they are all fixed upon the priest. The eyes follow his every move; often they find him wanting. Some priests who have left the active ministry probably could not stand having their faces watched by so many eyes. Some have managed to endure the eyes, in spite of an aching shyness; they make sure that the liturgy moves along with finger-snapping efficiency, so they can get away from the eyes as fast as possible. The rest of the clergy seem to be thrilled by all the eyes looking at them. They love it. To descend into a vulgar expression, they lap up the attention like you wouldn't believe. Somebody once said that "ambition is the ecclesiastical lust," the celibate clergy's substitute for sex. According to this theory, priests lust after promotion to pastor; pastors lust after promotion to bishop, and so on. But ambition, this old-fashioned sex substitute, is awfully tame stuff compared to the new salivating for liturgical attention.

A recent unexamined cliché goes something like this: "Years ago, *the Mass was the priest*. He monopolized everything. All that has changed. Today, *the Mass is the people*." This kind of talk is so dishonest. A tour of the churches in any diocese will show that, in most cases, *the Mass is still the priest*, and with a vengeance. He now enjoys more visibility, more celebrity status, more control than at any other time in history. Nearly everywhere, the priest is the triumphant monarch. The entire service pivots on him — not his role but his personality. His face may be the only decoration allowed in the stripped-down sanctuary, or else all of the decorations lead your eyes to his face. His voice, which has been magnified to superhuman proportions, is louder than the choir, organ, and singing congregation combined. In some cases, churches and cathedrals have been designed so that they will look like a throne room for an emperor. All of this is supposed to be "presiding" but it is really the new Triumphalism. The old Triumphalism — the ecclesiastical arrogance and haughtiness, the plumes and the splendor — assured a frightened faithful that, despite innumerable threats from the modern world, the church was in glorious shape, thank you. The new Triumphalism takes that glory away from the institutional church and bestows it upon Bishop Mack, Father Chuck, and their lay associates — whose personalities are supposed to be much more stunning than the old "cultural Catholicism."

The first moment of Triumphalism, the first grabbing of attention, comes with the "Good morning" (i.e., "Welcome to my presentation") and the little rapport speech at the beginning of the liturgy. The liturgical experts claim that these warm-up remarks *build community*; "good liturgy" will not take place unless the priest builds the community with his welcoming words. The *Notre Dame Study of Catholic Parish Life*, especially the book version, is adamant on this point. Even though the researchers who put together this project never brought up the matter in surveys ("Do you like standing there while the celebrant softens you up with introductory pleasantries?"), the *Notre Dame Study* insists that the warm-up speech is absolutely essential to *establish rapport*. But is "I-you" rapport compatible with the "us" spirit of liturgy? The *American Heritage Dictionary* defines "rapport" as "relationship; especially one of mutual trust or emotional affinity." There is no reason — theological, historical, or practical — to believe that the Eucharist is a rapport session, during which priest and congregation generate electrical currents of mutual emotional affinity, back and forth. There is, however, every reason to believe that liturgical rapport, especially right at the beginning of Mass, turns worship into an ecclesiastical version of *Hello, Dolly*.

Rapport means power: a presiding "I" who controls the assembled "you" through displays of rehearsed rapport. In the continual rapport process between the presider and the presided-over, awareness of the unseen God can get lost. Music too can get misplaced; instead of doing its job in the ceremony, it becomes a symbol of happy rapport and everyone's triumph.

The rapport Mass is no aberration among the lower clergy. It starts at the top. Let us go to a famous cathedral and watch the way one particular prelate shows the priests of his diocese how rapport will allow them to "steal the show."

At Midnight Mass the prelate charges into the great church; he shakes hands on his way up the aisle. The chorus, organ, timpani, and congregation are supposed to be jubilantly gathering the faithful in song or announcing the theme of the Mass, but a stronger impression is that they are proclaiming the arrival of the star performer, the prelate. The man reaches the sanctuary and the music stops. He begins his rapport monolog, which I paraphrase: "Thanks, Bob [a word of thanks to the music director]. Wasn't that music great! Well, I see the mayor is here, so that means we can begin, officially. [The audience giggles.] I also see lots of people standing in the aisles because there are not enough seats. Sorry about that, folks."

This opening chitchat is supposed to make everyone feel at home, gather the community, and automatically produce postconciliar liturgy.

But maybe the prelate's little warm- up speech comes across with a completely different message: "This is *my* show, everybody, and *I* own the
building."

The thoroughly traditional, old-fashioned way of getting this prelate
or any priest into a church for Mass — the Entrance Rite — is a mar-
velous study in ways to upstage the clergy. Just to make sure that the
approaching celebrant does not turn this moment of entry into his own
personal triumph, the traditional ceremonies require him to take care
of the incense job first and to wait until all the preliminary music is
finished. In the old days, he had to do this "entrance waiting" (maybe
twenty minutes) in a chair that was somewhat hidden on the side of the
sanctuary. By "cluttering up" the entrance of the priest or prelate with
"one thing after another," these traditional opening ceremonies deliberately make him look rather small by comparison and, to use another
metaphor, they also kick him in the teeth.

The liturgical experts ceaselessly moan about this wretched *clutter* of
the traditional Entrance Rite but even they sense the need for "belittling"
the presider. Some of them wisely suggest that the celebrant should
enter with discreet instrumental music; then, after his warm-up remarks,
everyone should sing the more jubilant "hymn of gathering." But the
larger the ego, the less the priest or prelate wants to hear about littleness
or discretion. A liturgy in the new Triumphalism style must always begin
with the immediate assertion of power: (1) *triumphant entrance hymn*,
(2) *opening warm-up remarks*. With this arrangement of "events" the first
song becomes a kind of coronation music for the entering presider and
a grand introduction to his opening remarks, but it does not begin the
liturgy.

Back to Midnight Mass: The prelate's introductory chat has knocked
the liturgy right off its tracks. Somehow, he manages to get back to
the Penitential Rite, in this case the Asperges or sprinkling with water.
Down the main aisle the prelate races, as if he were putting out a fire.
The choir, in a concession to tradition, sings the Gregorian chant for the
Asperges, but not in the other-worldly, mystical chant style. No indeed!
Remember, triumphant Mr. Nice Guy presides here; chant is for wimps.
The Asperges chant is changed so that it will sound like a college football
fight-song. After all, the clergy and laity have gathered in the cathedral
to be uplifted and electrified by triumphant Mr. Nice Guy *and by the
music, which is an extension of his triumphant personality*. There is no
room for any music which suggests human submission to something
greater than the star prelate.

In the new Triumphalism, *the Mass is the individual*, and even the
music for it must be conveyed to the congregation by triumphant in-

dividuals. This is why, just a few paces away from the prelate, we see Mr. Caruso triumphantly substituting for the congregation. Whether the assembly is singing *Silent Night* or a response, the loudest sound comes from Mr. Caruso's amplified voice "on top." Congregation, choir, instruments, and even the prelate accompany him. (In this style of worship, triumphant individuals take turns performing in front of the audience.)

At this Midnight Mass there are enough musicians to put on a production of *Aida*, but this is not a sung Mass. Except for one brief moment, the prelate sings none of the liturgical texts assigned to him. There is no sung dialog with the congregation, and for good reasons. With the real sung Mass, the priest cannot act like Mr. Nice Guy. He cannot toss in a few cute remarks at the beginning and at the end. Also, if he chanted the Collect or the Preface ("Lift up your hearts," etc.), a few thousand eyeballs in the cathedral would focus intensely on his Adam's apple. Imperfections in his singing technique would be mellowed and modified if they were allowed to echo naturally (i.e., without amplification) through the stone arches of the building. (A high ceiling covereth a multitude of musical sins.) But today, in the name of clarity, every single syllable of the liturgy must be bloated through amplification. If the prelate were to sing into a microphone, the slightest imperfection in his voice would be enlarged a thousand times in size to the point where it would sound hideous. He wisely decides not to sing his section of the Midnight Mass. Most of the congregation, following his example, also does not sing.

There are no villains at this Midnight Mass. The prelate means well. The musicians get an A rating. Everyone is working hard to do what "the people" (it is presumed) really want, and that is to be uplifted by larger-than-life heroes in the sanctuary. The further presumption is that modern Catholics want to be treated like children in the presence of a liturgical Santa Claus/priest who reassures them with rapport and then says, "Welcome to my magic toyland, let me personally guide you through its wonders, let me thrill you with *explanations*."

Since the 1960s, Roman Catholics have witnessed the evolution of the Solemn High Explanation Mass. In this type of liturgy, almost the entire service appears to be one continuous band of explanations spoken into a microphone. In the more elaborate examples, someone comes out before the liturgy begins and explains what is about to happen. Then the priest enters and in his opening chatter explains what is about to happen. The recited Penitential Rite should be an admission of human sinfulness but it too sounds like a list of explanations of what God does. Each scriptural reading which follows will begin with a short explanation of what it means. The homily explains the explanations. Everything continues in the same explaining manner until the Communion Reflection, which recapitulates the meaning of it all. Explanations are useful but the motivating idea behind the overkill in the Explanation Mass is *the triumph of the explainers* who have been endowed with the spiritual gift of clarity; their job is to rescue the congregation from the dangers of nebulous poetic perceptions.

Music — esoteric, irrational, poetic — has a very limited place in the Explanation Mass. Music greets the priest, the Master Explainer, with a rousing welcome at the beginning and bids adieu to him at the end. It is allowed between the explanations, but it must have a "clear" sound (as if it were explaining something). Other-worldly, chantlike music is frowned upon, because it suggests that religion cannot be completely explained by the victorious explainers. When music does make an appearance at the Explanation Mass, it usually has to take care of its business quickly and escape before it is mowed down by the next explanation. This is why congregational singing at a Catholic liturgy often sounds like an interruption, a sudden crisis which has tumbled into the talking-explaining.

Some Catholic organization should establish a "Sidewalk of Triumph" outside of its headquarters. Every so often, a bishop or priest who has done the most to advance the cause of the new Triumphalism should be invited to have his handprints immortalized in this Sidewalk of the Stars. The first person to be so honored would be a certain monsignor who plunges into the congregation at the Sign of Peace in the Mass. Up and down every aisle he goes. Grinning and with his robes flowing in the turbulence he creates, the monsignor attacks every pew, shakes every hand he can reach, kisses every baby. The man looks as if he is running for president. This crowning moment of rapport can take longer than the distribution of communion. Monsignor is an extreme case, but there are also less obvious ways to cause the same damage, to turn public worship into a solo recital. For example, some no-foolishness conservative priests favor the trick of continuous amplification; every time the assembly tries to say a prayer or recite the Creed or even sing a hymn, the priest's brutally amplified voice dominates "on top." Forty-five minutes of this never lets anyone forget who is in charge.

More liberal priests (ones who constantly emphasize that the Mass is essentially a ceremony for sharing bread) like to grab everyone's attention with their personal reshaping of the familiar liturgical texts — so uniquely reshaped that the congregation never knows what to expect next. (My favorite: "And may He, the Lord, who is with us all be with you." Uh, what was that again?) A university chaplain I knew had the

simplest trick of all for making sure that everyone remembered he had
top billing; he would begin Mass just with one little word: "Hi!" (Now
how does a congregation proceed to the confession of its sins after an
opening line like that?)

A Protestant bishop, after the morning service, goes home for lunch.
His wife says to him at table, while they are eating cantaloupe, "By the
way, dear, during your sermon today you made a perfect ass of yourself."
The Protestant minister, at a meeting with the church's board of trustees,
is told that people cannot stand his style of preaching; he has got to go.
These methods of "natural correction" do not exist in the Roman Catholic
clergy, at the top or at the bottom. From the day he is consecrated, a
Catholic bishop (as the joke goes) never gets a bad meal and never hears
the whole truth, especially about himself. The pastor and the priest, after
the morning liturgies, go home to adoring housekeepers. Moreover, the
bishop and his priests are protected by what I call the Headwaiter Effect,
a phenomenon based on an episode in the British television series *Fawlty
Towers*. I explain in the following paragraph.

Two women, of a certain age, are eating lunch in the dining room
of Fawlty Towers, a hotel run by a comically inept staff. The women
complain about the meal. The service is wretched. The meat is leather
and of questionable origin. Right in the middle of their complaining, the
headwaiter appears at their table. He is tall, imposing; "authority" seems
to be written all over him. "Is everything all right?" he asks mechanically.
"Why, yes," the ladies respond. The headwaiter moves on to the next
table with the same question. The women meekly resume their meal
in silence.

Nobody complains to the headwaiter, especially if the man radiates
the mystique of office. Nobody complains about the new Triumphalism; maybe everyone assumes that this is what modern liturgy is about:
victorious explainers allowing an audience to share in the joys of clarity.

The Brakes

How should the presider preside? Does he begin with "Good morning"
or "May the Lord be with you"? Probably before the last apostle died,
the church discovered that there are two basic solutions to this presiding
perplexity:

1. *The Protestant Option*. Let a community choose its own liturgical
"style" and have a say in picking its own presiding minister from a large
assortment of candidates (married and unmarried men and women).

Indirectly and certainly not overtly, the community will also be selecting the kind of members it wants.

2. *The Roman Method.* The bishop picks the priest who will minister unto "the people," and they accept this arrangement as long as the ritual does not somehow depend on liking the appointee. The presider agrees to become a "nobody" during worship, so that he may serve "everybody." To make sure that he keeps his end of the bargain and stays a "nobody," the church puts liturgical brakes on the priest — such as vestments and a prescribed liturgical text.

Part of the history of the Western and Eastern Catholic liturgies is the history of brakes on the individuals who have some kind of role in public worship (priest, singers, assistants, and even the more "remote" contributors, such as composers and artists). The "old" Mass in Latin contained maddeningly precise instructions about the priest's bowing and other gestures. Moreover, he was required to recite every word of the prescribed texts, even words that the choir sang. At one point in this so-called Tridentine Mass he referred to himself as an "unworthy servant" of the Lord. He described himself and the entire assembly as the Lord's "sinful servants" who were ever conscious of their iniquities. Either in the actual text of the Mass or in the prescribed gestures, the old missal constantly clobbered the priest with messages about humility, constantly slammed on the brakes so that he would remain the "nobody" who served "everybody."

Even the old-fashioned architecture of Catholic churches, while certainly not felicitous in every case, ingeniously increased the priest's humility by making him difficult to find in all the artistic camouflage. The liturgical art of the past deliberately distracted the worshiper's attention away from priest, away from his personality. Every statue and every mosaic subtracted a little from his presence.

Maybe the most effective emergency brake on the priest used to be, of all things, music. The following anecdote illustrates what I mean.

A religious community I know has to depend on visiting priests to say Mass for it. Mild-mannered Father X is the usual chaplain and favorite, but when he is away the community must endure the antics of Father Kev: world-class egotist, domineering presider, and triumphant Mr. Nice Guy. Naturally, he *always* begins Mass with "Good morning" and pleasantries which have been more carefully rehearsed than his homily.

One day, the community gathered together to commemorate a distinguished friend who had died recently. They also braced themselves for pain; everybody knew that this Mass, as celebrated by Father Kev, would provide the kind of suffering that the whole congregation could offer up for the repose of the departed soul. But a strange thing happened. Instead of beginning the liturgy with some routine hymn, the whole community sang *Requiem aeternam*, the poignant Gregorian Introit for the "old" funeral Mass (and a chant that is still in the church's official books). Father Kev, who had received no advance warning about this, processed into the sanctuary; when the chant stopped he was visibly confounded and perhaps a little shaken. And then the miracle happened. He did not begin with "Good morning" and the rapport speech! He started right away with "In the name of the Father..." Gregorian chant came back at the Sanctus and at the Communio; again, it left him so "speechless" and humbled that he did not personalize the liturgy with his own darling rephrasings of the Mass text.

Every item in Roman Catholicism's immense "treasure of sacred music" (the Second Vatican Council's term) was deliberately designed to *humble* the priest, as well as the congregation. The illustrious prelate and the simple parish priest had to sit and wait patiently on the side of the sanctuary, while the choir worked its way through the Kyrie or the Credo. The priest had to stand in front of everyone and embarrass himself, for the sake of the faith, by an act of stupefying and insane majesty: chanting the Epistle, Gospel and so on in Latin. Even the composers of this "treasure" music were humbled; they had to restrain their wild flights of imagination and humbly work within the confines of difficult traditions.

By the 1930s, perhaps even earlier, there was a campaign to release some of the artistic brakes. What rankled many priests was the power of "cultural Catholicism" to lure the worshiper's attention away from the celebrant (and his weaknesses). In 1950, when I made my First Communion, I received a small prayerbook intended "for a very young child." It contained a list of instructions on proper church etiquette. ("Kneel up straight... Do not shuffle your feet.") The author of the prayerbook strictly admonishes children: "Do not look back, up at the choir, up at the ceiling.... Keep your eyes on the altar; watch the priest."[1] The intentions here were honest but they were contradictory. Many Catholics of my generation had to reconcile a schizophrenic message that went something like this: "Church music must be beautiful but at the same time it is dangerous, distracting stuff; pay no attention to it. Yes, the ceiling is richly decorated, but resist the temptation to take pleasure in it or any of the beautiful things in the church. Keep your eyes on the priest at all times, preferably without blinking (even though the church has dropped a ton of traditions on the liturgy to make sure you cannot clearly 'see' the priest)."

Any suggestion that the liturgical brakes should be loosened up used to be interpreted to mean a loosening up of faith and morals. The brakes were the faith. Then, in the years before Vatican II liturgical scholars, very discreetly, offered a way out; their historical studies seemed to prove that the restraints on the priest really did not belong in the Mass after all. The courtly formalities, the rigidities, Latin, and, most of all, the heritage of artistic music were just so much ivy which had attached itself to the surface of the Mass. This overgrown vegetation had no function. Pull the weeds off, and you would find, underneath, the pure Bauhaus structure of the Mass.

After Vatican II, the superfluous layers of vestments and ornamentation were discarded, but in the process of simplifying the Mass the brakes were released. As a result, there is really nothing left to restrain the priest's whimsy, except perhaps the bishop (who is preoccupied with other matters) and residual inhibitions about taste. More important, there is nothing left to *hide* the priest. The man behind the altar might as well be naked.

The "naked" priest will remain a distinctive feature of Roman Catholic worship for some time to come, because most of the clergy are determined to keep it that way. Anyone who sifts through the articles in the journals on liturgy and liturgical music or who listens to the lectures at various Catholic conferences might be blinded temporarily by the luminous ideals about participation and by the Greek and Hebrew words, but behind the rhetoric there is an unmistakable hidden agenda: the continued triumph of the priest and a few of his chosen lay associates, especially musicians. Every decision about liturgy — from the music to the lightbulbs — will have to pass a crucial test: if it enhances the presence of the triumphant ones, use it; if it humbles them or puts the brakes on them, scrap it.

Starting in the 1960s the Roman Catholic clergy broke a centuries-old covenant they had with "the people." Priests began to behave as if they were working under the Protestant Option; that is, they started to act as if they were elected ministers, chosen because of their ability to form rapport with a particular community. But, at the same time, they have shown little interest in parting with the job security of the Roman Method; they remain appointees. The Protestant Option, which is essentially capitalistic, depends on the invisible hand of competition to regulate supply and demand, style, and quality. The Roman Method is a more socialistic approach — benevolent and with many advantages — but it is useless without "traditions" (brakes) to regulate the product.

Today, the majority of the Roman Catholic clergy want the best of both worlds. They enjoy the "looseness" of mainstream Protestant worship; they like to think that their personal touches in a liturgy and their rapport inspire the multitude out there in the pews. At the same time, however, they abhor competition. (The bishops fear that a competing clergy might "cut prices," i.e., weaken orthodoxy to keep their clientele.) They will not let parish congregations hire priests on the basis of what rapport techniques charm and what ones repel — and, besides, the declining number of priests makes any competition unrealistic.

Mr. Not-So-Nice

"Hello, could you please help me? I'm new in town and I need a job."

The American Guild of Organists (AGO) provides a placement service in a very large American city and the volunteer who gives out the job information tells me he gets a telephone call like this a couple times a month. The caller goes on to describe his or her first-class training, letters of reference, abilities, and enthusiasms.

"I'm not really fussy about what kind of organ playing job I can get," the caller continues, "as long as it is not in a Catholic church."

The AGO volunteer explains that he is a Protestant and has worked happily at a Catholic parish for a number of years. The caller interrupts to say that a cathedral or special parish might offer an inspiring challenge, but otherwise he or she has no intention of working for the Catholic church. There are too many horror stories going around.

The word is out in the church music profession: (1) Reformed Jews are the best to work for. You learn the special skills necessary for accompanying the cantor; you show up for work, get paid well, and then you go home. It is all very straightforward and cordial. (2) Protestants can be a pain, especially if you are caught in the crossfire between the minister and the unhappy trustees. The pay is not that great either. But at least you have a clear idea of what kind of music is wanted. (3) The worst employer, generally speaking, is the Catholic parish.

The pay is all that a struggling parish can afford, and that is usually well below the poverty line.

The organist could try to hold down a second job, one that would pay the bills, but the Catholic parish might need music seven days a week for liturgies, weddings, funerals, confirmations, penitential services, and holy days.

The organist may have to provide music for anywhere from three to seven Masses every weekend; each one requires alertness and split-second timing; the repetition of the same routine every week-end has a way of draining all the energy and creativity out of any musician. After a while, you feel as if you are ironing shirts in a sweatshop.

But these discouragements are insignificant when compared to ob-stacle number one: the classic pastor. Working for the Catholic clergy must rank as one of the most puzzling challenges in human experience. The classic pastor, first of all, is a male bachelor. He may be remote or a charmer, brilliant or a dud, but he is not used to teamwork or even an employer-employee relationship. For most of his life he has only known two "slanted" modes for working with other people: subservience or dominance. (The curate is subservient; the pastor dominant. The pastor is subservient; the bishop dominant, etc.) "Horizontal" relationships, working with other professionals, making deals, give-and-take, and di-alog are sometimes difficult, foreign activities for him. (Observe the characters in fiction by J. F. Powers.) The priest who is best at dialog is usually the maverick or the saintly understanding type — the ones who are seldom trusted with pastoral power.

A few years ago, Mass was proceeding in a great church in the North-east. The pastor, enthroned behind the altar, presided as the cantor and congregation sang the psalm between the first two readings. Right in the middle of this singing, the pastor, out of the blue, shouted in a clear voice, "Oh, shut up!" Then he said something to the effect that he had had enough of this singing and it was time to move on.

For days afterwards, telephone wires in the diocese were hot from all the gossiping about the "shut up" incident. What did this *mean*? (Three different parishioners, not musicians, came to me with this story.) Ac-cording to one school of thought, the pastor had to be a boor, an art-hating Neanderthal who just could not understand musical beauty. But another group offered a much more perceptive explanation: the cantor had fallen in love with the sound of his own amplified voice. Maybe the pastor really did need to trim these musical extravagances which were getting out of hand — but apparently the priest, a highly respected man, was incapable of communicating this. The classic pastor cannot sit down with his employee and say, "Let me hear some samples of what you want to sing. Let me tell you what I want and how long I want it to last. Let's work out a compromise." He cannot enter into that kind of executive mode. Instead, all he can do is put out ambiguous signals, which the rest of the world fails to interpret, and then perhaps explode in frustration.

Find a parish where the music "works." It may be a place which encourages excellence or perhaps a healthy mediocrity prevails; whatever the case, the source of that success will not be a committee or a musician but the pastor (or perhaps his predecessor). Good liturgical music starts with the pastor or the person who acts in his place. He may be shy or a politician type, he may have a dead-fish personality or charm in abundance but the man will know how to communicate clearly and how to make deals that get the best out of his employees. He is a confident, first-rate person who is aware of the old business adage: "First-rate people hire first-rate people. Second-rate people hire third-rate people."

In the church with "successful" music (Catholic or Protestant) it is usually the case that the pastor will (1) hand the organist a list of the congregational hymns to be sung on Sunday or (2) will sit down with the organist and carefully go over the congregation's repertory, from which others will make the weekly selections. Catholic clergy and church musicians become absolutely bewildered, even appalled when I point this out ("Are you nuts? You can't expect *priests* to get involved in trivialities of this sort."), and yet the facts will not go away. Liturgical music is always superior or at least healthy when the clergy play a very constructive, cooperative role in the decision process.

If the classic pastor, as an employer, has a low reputation in the music business, a good share of the blame for this must be placed on musicians themselves. To appreciate the difficulty here, imagine this scene: On one side of a table sits the hard-nosed pastor with the stub of a cigar in his mouth. He has just received a huge utility bill. On the other side of the table sits the organist, a dreamy fellow who has just heard a recording of Beethoven's *Missa Solemnis* and is still glowing with rapture. Now try to imagine communication between these two professionals whose perceptions originate at opposite ends of the universe.

The classic musician, classically trained, comes in many varieties: maniac, prima donna, weirdo, functional atheist, human snake, scoundrel, drunk, or your basic hardworking drudge. Musicians are not the easiest people in the world to work with, perhaps because we are always bringing emotions to the surface in sounds. But why is it that a Protestant pastor will know how to get the best out of crazy musicians while the Catholic pastor will not? The root of the problem is the matter of subtraction. Classically trained church musicians practice an ancient and honorable craft of subtraction. The simplest hymn, expertly presented, takes something away from the priest, if only for a minute; indeed, the same music also has a subtle way of flattening the egos of the organist and everyone who sings it. Bach fugues and Renaissance Masses for choir are examples of subtraction at its most extreme. The best music of

Roman Catholicism, especially what Vatican II called the "treasure of sacred music," has always been a form of anticlericalism sanctioned by the church itself. No wonder most of the Catholic clergy is now so anxious to dump this musical "treasure" and to damn musicians as the "betrayers" who corrupted liturgy. The subtraction process does not win friends.

I have heard many stories about dedicated, pious Catholic church musicians who spent years developing their craft and then ended up employed by Protestant churches. I have known talented, good-natured nuns who worked as musicians for Catholic parishes and then had to quit because they found the job to be such a degrading experience. The discontent and complaints could always be traced back to subtraction. When the priest or the pastor walked into that sanctuary, he would not tolerate anything, especially music, if it subtracted one iota from his total domination of the liturgy. The songleaders, cantors, liturgical dancers, explainers, and the local composers of "contemporary" religious songs all demanded liturgical music which would add and multiply the congregation's awareness of their presence — or at least not make them look puny by comparison. Many members of the congregation also got into the addition-subtraction act by agitating for music that would make them "feel good about themselves." (An anonymous note received by an organist I know: "This parish has to get away from gloomy religious music and sing more positive folk songs, like the music they use in Florida.") A resourceful church musician could come up with a program of liturgical music which would always "sound positive" and consistently avoid subtraction, but that unrelenting emphasis on a cheery personal triumph only leads to exhaustion.

In 1987 the Reverend M. Francis Mannion, rector of the Catholic cathedral in Salt Lake City, Utah, needed a new music director for the cathedral parish. Wanting the best possible candidate, he advertised nationally. He reports:

There were 55 applicants for the position, all well trained, and some with extraordinary talent. As the selection process went forward, and I spoke with each applicant, I was led to a firm and appalling conclusion: There is a whole generation of mostly young Catholic musicians who are severely disillusioned with the state of church music in the United States and who feel thoroughly unrepresented by the nation's liturgical music establishments. Many feel that the church has sold out on them and their art. They experience incredible frustration because their training is not taken seriously. Most, as far as I can tell, are very open to the full and active participation of the people and wish to practice their art in a thoroughly ministerial and pastoral manner. They worry, with good cause, that the ministerial conception of liturgical music often involves a bias against professional excellence. They resent the fact that the term "pastoral music" is often invoked in church music circles as a subterfuge for the poor musicianship of many practicing musicians. Indeed, they observe with considerable puzzlement that many of the best known leaders, composers and recording artists in church music in the United States are more notable for their enthusiasm, charismatic personalities or marketability than for profound education, excellent musicianship or remarkable originality. These are among the reasons, in my opinion, why so many talented, highly-trained musicians are prone to investing themselves in ecclesiastical institutions with advanced music programs yet poor liturgical and pastoral wisdom. They perceive that at least in such environments the art of music is taken seriously.[2]

Father Mannion's forthright and blunt statement outlines one principal reason why Catholics can't sing: the better musicians, the ones who could provide the most valuable assistance, run away from the Catholic church as soon as they can because they are not welcome in many places. But who has pulled in the welcome mat? Father Mannion, by skillful use of the passive voice and the expression "the church," implies (correctly) that there is plenty of guilt to go around — especially upon the heads of the "pastoral musicians," those militant amateurs who are ready to make life miserable for any pastor or chaplain or trained musician they find to be insufficiently postconciliar.

The low reputation of the "pastoral musician" among the professionals has not exactly helped the efforts of the National Association of Pastoral Musicians, which really is the only functioning Catholic organization open to all church musicians in the United States (the "only game in town"). Wherever two or three refined church musicians are gathered together, the NAPM is ripped to pieces and referred to as the "pasteurized musicians" or NAPALM, the hideous defoliant used in Vietnam. But the NPM (the abbreviation it now prefers) does not quite fit the role as the monster that ruined music in the Catholic church. This conscientious organization only reflects what is "out there" in the nation and it can rightfully claim to be "middle of the road" — which is to say nothing about the condition of the road. In the books it publishes and in its journal *Pastoral Music* you will find opinions for and against everything from Gregorian chant to the guitar. This organization plainly wants all voices to be heard, and in the United States the voice of the illiterate, anti-intellectual, antitraditional "pastoral musician" happens to be the loudest.

Father Mannion is correct. The ubiquitous "pastoral musicians" (who do not necessarily belong to the NPM) mistrust musical competence; their incessant glorification of feeling over competence and trendiness over common sense pollutes the church's whole musical life. But Father Mannion does not go near one important point: most "pastoral musicians" have no power to hire and fire. If a generation of trained musicians is disillusioned, it is largely because many priests and pastors prefer to hire musicians who, for pastoral reasons, take great pride in their ignorance, their possession of pastoral awareness rather than mere technical skill. The ignorant "pastoral musicians," whatever their faults, at least have never learned to subtract.

Father Mannion's insights end with an allusion to "ecclesiastical institutions with advanced music programs yet poor liturgical and pastoral wisdom." These are code words for the higher Episcopal churches or the minuscule number of Catholic establishments where the traditions of the sung Mass still survive. In these places the art of music is indeed taken seriously but, invariably, the priest submits to "subtraction"; he allows his ego to be diminished by all the liturgical and musical traditions.

In 1982 the I. T. Verdin Company of Cincinnati announced the invention of a remarkable device which allows a parish to dispense with the services of a musician whenever it wants. For a few thousand dollars this company will install a "stereo system" that will play taped organ accompaniments of hymns over loudspeakers. The celebrant can control the hymns — turn them on or off — at the touch of a button located near the altar.

Organists in Protestant churches laughed; they thought this was a hoax. They knew from years of experience that accompanying a hymn is a live, human experience and a tape recording simply does not have the elasticity necessary to lead a congregation in song. But Catholic journals and newspapers were impressed by the Verdin contraption and welcomed the arrival of this laborsaving device. Pastors who had purchased the imitation organist even wrote testimonials praising the convenience of the Verdin invention. After all, this pushbutton appliance seemed to be the ideal "pastoral musician." It does not have to be paid, it has no ideas of its own, and it is totally under the control of the clergy. Congregational singing, of course, would not go at all well with automated musical support but nobody seemed to worry about that.

The following paragraph contains observations which have brought down howling wrath upon this author:

The pastor is in charge of the parish's liturgical music. This is part of his job. Very often, the music which the congregation hears is a reflection of the strengths and weaknesses in his personality. Musicians only carry out his instructions. Dialog and collaborative effort are, of course, essential; the shrewd pastor will make good use of consultation, consensus, and delegated authority. But, in the end, the pastor is the Chief Executive Officer who makes the final decisions. He is the captain. He steers the ship. If the ship sinks, it is his fault.

I have been royally denounced for uttering the above heresy — this paternalism, this monarchical world view. Church musicians like to think of themselves as little captains in charge of their own independent ships. But according to the principles of sound management, one person should have the ultimate responsibility of supervision, and in the Catholic parish that has to be the pastor. Unfortunately, the Catholic pastor enjoys sovereign immunity when it comes to supervising matters such as music. An executive in a business answers to a board of directors or stockholders. The Catholic pastor answers to nobody; there is no "National Catholic Hymnal" to guide him; bishops have a hands-off policy when it comes to music. As a result of all this, there are often wild, capricious shifts in a parish's music every time a new pastor takes over and exercises his unchecked authority.

I know of one place where Pastor A started a fine adult choir which supported the congregation in singing fairly standard music from a hymnal. A few years later he was succeeded by Pastor B who threw out the hymnal and concentrated on the folk repertory (which only the folk group sang). The next boss, Pastor C, was mad about Spirit-guided creativity and every week the "composer of the week" would try to teach everyone the new "song of the week." Pastor D walked in and brought back traditional music; the cycle began all over again. The congregation, a victim of one experiment after another, was like a foster child who is always shifted from one foster home to another. These good people learned to withhold their affection for any and all types of liturgical music. Why invest your emotions in something that will be taken away in a short time?

Catholic parishes would save themselves a whole list of musical troubles if they invested in one of the top Catholic hymnals, which of course contain a lot more than hymns. (I discuss them in the *Appendix* at the end of this book.) A parish with an impressive song/service book in the pews could continue to chase musical fads, but congregational singing would improve immensely if the parish always returned to its official hymnal for a core repertory.

The idea of using a song book for an enduring core repertory is the kind of practical, commonsense wisdom that Protestant churches discovered centuries ago. Even the *Notre Dame Study of Catholic Parish Life* (Report No. 5, p. 8) noted that congregational singing is always stronger in the places that use hymnals rather than missalettes. But in spite of all the advantages of a hymnal, only a tiny minority of Catholic parishes now use them. The problem with these books is that they put limits on power; they establish the fact of a collective wisdom which is larger and more enduring than the whims of one pastor or musician. The hymnal subtracts power.

There must be hundreds of Catholic pastors who would have every justification and the enthusiastic support of their flock if they murdered their parish music directors. The organist who cannot count four beats evenly, the failed conductor who is forever trying to tackle masterpieces that he cannot handle, the tyrant music director who is more brilliant at scolding than at playing music — they are often found at the church where the pastor is a living saint and hungers for the beauties of good music. This pastor has tried dialog, consensus, and all the rest, but the musical agony continues. Firing the musical perpetrator may be impractical for one reason or another.

I can offer no suggestions for these situations where the musician, who cannot be replaced easily, assumes the role of Mr. or Ms. Not-So-Nice, except perhaps this: Discover the joys of silence and unaccompanied singing.

The Bitter Half

I thought my head would split from the noise. The priest insisted on enunciating every syllable of the Mass with obsessive precision, as if he were dictating a letter to a very dim-witted secretary. The amplification of every word and every note of music was so loud and so persistent it was malicious. As I was walking out of the church after Mass, I met an acquaintance. "You look a little pale," she observed. "That liturgy," I replied, "was hard on the nerves." "So you noticed it too!" she shot back. "*Man* this, *men* that — every other word was *man* or *men*. Wasn't it disgusting! You would think that women didn't exist."

Now, how did I miss that?

In 1960, a priest had to play the role of the anonymous "nobody," so that he might conduct worship in a way that suggested "everybody." Women in the congregation could feel sorry for this poor priest who had such a difficult job to do. After the Second Vatican Council, a coup d'etat took place and the Catholic clergy, seizing control of the liturgy, gave themselves a visibility and a prominence they had never known before. Thus began the triumphant reign of Mr. Nice Guy and his parallel in music, the mighty songleader. Women in the congregation now watch a priest who (in many cases) invites all the world to love him, to adore him as a rapport object; they must contend with a new thought which goes through their heads: If being the priest at Mass is all a matter of building community by exposing your personal charms and by generating rapport, why exclude women from the priesthood? They can do that sort of thing, too.

We need perspective. We have to remind ourselves that, in past centuries, Roman Catholicism once played an important role in what could be called the "advancement" of women (relatively speaking). Women in Western civilization, thanks in part to the church, enjoyed a status that was (again, relatively speaking) quite high, when compared to the rest of the world. In the Catholic church, women were running hospitals, schools, and colleges long before the rest of society dared to give such responsibilities to the gentle sex. The church's record on women and their rights is both good and bad, but certainly no worse than the record of society as a whole. Where do matters stand now? How far have women come in the church? The answer can be found in two true stories. Both incidents took place in the late 1980s and in the same American city.

The first anecdote begins on a sad note. Father P, a missionary priest in Central America, received a telegram informing him that his aged mother had just died. Within the space of forty-eight hours he managed to return home and, accompanied by his sister who was a nun, went straight to the parish rectory to make arrangements for the funeral. Would it be possible, he asked the pastor, for him (the missionary) to celebrate the funeral Mass? Why of course, responded the pastor graciously. And would it be possible for the missionary's sister (the nun) to read the Epistle at the Mass? Absolutely not, responded the pastor. Women are forbidden in the sanctuary. That was that. Next question.

The nun who would not be allowed in the sanctuary, although aghast, just sat there and remained silent. What made her "exclusion" such a galling experience, she explained to me, was that she remembered the times, years ago, when she was magnanimously permitted to enter the sacred area every week; that is, when she and her fellow nuns got down on their hands and knees and scrubbed the marble floors in that very sanctuary. (When I asked a Russian Orthodox acquaintance of mine why women are not allowed behind the iconostasis, the old man replied without hesitation, "Because they are polluted by menses.")

The second anecdote begins with a happy occasion. A young nun who has just taken her final vows has invited her relatives and friends to celebrate the occasion at a liturgy in her family's parish church. The congregation assembles in the church but nobody can quite figure out the nature of the ceremony. The sanctuary seems to be filled with women who are reciting prayers and leading the music. The only man in the front of the church is a priest who is seated in a distant corner; he stays in his place and watches; the women ignore him. After a few minutes, the guests in the church realize that they are attending a kind of "shadow Mass," with the new nun reciting the celebrant's words from a lectern. At communion time the women take consecrated hosts from the tabernacle and distribute them; the priest also gives out communion but, when he is finished, he immediately retreats to his remote corner.

When Catholics go to church today, they sometimes get the strange impression that the religious ceremony they witness is partly a moment in their faith and partly a "statement" or set of signals about the place of women in the church. Indeed, for some Catholics the woman-message can be stronger and more memorable than all the intentions of the ceremony itself. Even when nobody is trying to make any statement of any kind, more than a few in the congregation will still pick up what they think is the implied signal about women.

If parishes want to send strong signals about the "new" importance of women, they frequently think they have to do it by avoiding music which originated in the days when the men controlled worship. The current unspoken consensus among many Catholics is that men contaminated the church's musical life for a millennium and a half; chant (Latin or English), standard hymns, and other forms of "churchy" music are all examples of "men music," which incessantly promotes, through words or style, the idea that God is masculine. Supposedly, the parish which uses this men-music is making a "statement" that women should stay in their place, the one they occupied before the Second Vatican Council. The thinking is that women will now have to bring things back into balance by promoting liturgies and liturgical music which remind everyone that God has Her feminine side too.

To restore this lost balance, to assert a "feminine presence" in rituals dominated by men, many religious orders of women have thrown their energies into church music that suggests the "feminine" — or at least does not proclaim something too "masculine." The kind of "feminine" music they seem to prefer, especially in their chapels, is a symbolic way of filling the whole sanctuary with their presence, even though they are not allowed to officiate at the altar. Nobody, to be sure, has ever come up with a scientifically convincing description of a "masculine music" and a "feminine music," but many contemporary Catholics, by tacit agreement, accept the notion of a musical "feminine presence" — which balances male domination — in the *beautiful song*, a close cousin of the sweet song. The liturgy which features gentle, loving, sweet, and beautiful "contemporary" songs effectively sends the message that women matter. (Sweet beautiful songs, unfortunately, always have a limp, wilted quality which makes them frustrating for a congregation to sing.)

In 1983, the National Council of Churches published *An Inclusive Language Lectionary: Readings for Year A*, a new translation of readings for church services.[3] The main feature of this largely Protestant effort was a scriptural text free of all male-centered language which might give the impression of excluding women. This *Lectionary*, however, "includes" women at the cost of neutering all the men in scripture. With consistent ruthlessness, the translators and editors went through the scriptural texts and cut out almost anything which suggested a male presence, while leaving the female characters largely untouched. (For example, the biblical story of the *man* born blind is changed to the *one* born blind.) The same type of mentality (or anger) which produced this *Lectionary* is also at work in the liturgical life of the Catholic church, but in this case the "male presence" which must be neutered is not a biblical character but music with a strong, assertive, imposing "churchy" character, presumed to be male.

Starting with Joseph Jungmann's *Mass of the Roman Rite* (1950), modern liturgical commentators have routinely devoted at least part of a book or a speech to an expression of their annoyance about the "old" Mass because of its aloof transcendence, its "miracle" of transubstantiation, its dramatic words of consecration, its adoration — all at the expense of the congregation, which was supposedly reduced to the status of passive witnesses. A few women in the Catholic church agree with this interpretation of history and have infused it with an especially venomous anger. Behind their denunciations of the "old" Mass is the unspoken assumption that those transcendent, "miracle" rituals constantly reinforced the unique superiority of the male sex, constantly reminded the faithful of a unique male potency to perform secret magical acts. The men needed music — unique, mystifying, transcendent — which would enhance the illusion of their unique powers, and that music would be Gregorian chant or almost anything remotely connected with the heritage of artistic church music.

The modern "inclusive liturgy," which broadcasts signals in all directions about sexual equality, is always the product of a debilitating anxiety, even hatred. For one of these events to take place, someone must first vigilantly and systematically remove all music which might possibly create the impression of a unique spiritual power given only to men. This determination to make the Mass inclusive and gender free, at any cost, may help to explain why some of the music heard in Catholic churches today sounds "neither here nor there" and pathetically uncertain about itself, as if it had been savagely neutered.

A surprising number of lay women in the Catholic church are extremely eager to ditch most of the church's musical heritage (of male music) and get on with the new music for the new church. They take second place, however, to the religious orders of women who, with some exceptions, have been the most diligent in their efforts to eradicate "churchy" music and the most suspicious of any music which gives a hint of continuity with the past. Perhaps the key word which will help us to understand what is going on here is "continuity." I instinctively use that word as if it defined something manifestly good. But Margaret R. Miles in her book *Image as Insight* (1985) alerts us to the different subtle connotations which "continuity" has for men and women:

Male physical experience, unless interrupted by serious illness or accident, features continuity, as women's physical experience does not. For women, the continuity of physical existence is secondary to the interruptions of that continuity caused by different physical conditions, which in turn carry different social identities and personal relationships. First menstruation, first sexual intercourse, childbearing, menopause — all these events are primarily irreversible alterations in a woman's body and secondarily changes in social identity. Change, the difference from one day to the next, the different body, perspective, and values of different times of life — these experiences of discontinuity, of being physically, mentally, and socially other than one was, characterize women's experience.[4]

Miles says she does not want to argue this point at length; she merely presents it as one of her many excellent insights. For our purposes here we can just ponder the reality that for men "physical continuity" is a treasured blessing. Women, however, must accept decisive biological changes and discontinuity as a part of life, in their very bodies. A Catholic man, even the most radical, might listen sympathetically when some people talk about the need for a measure of musical continuity in the church, although he may not agree. A Catholic woman — feminist or old- fashioned, radical or conservative — can sometimes be quite startling (to me) in her total contempt for church music from the old days. All that was in the past, she says; the church has "gone beyond" that and entered a new biological phase; there can be no "going back"; from a female perspective, continuity is male and any music which indicates continuity with the male-dominated church of yesteryear is possibly an insult to women.

According to Freud, a cigar can be a phallic symbol but, he reminds us, sometimes a cigar is just a cigar. Roman Catholicism's sacraments, especially the Mass, have become (at least subconsciously) a symbol of the struggle for sexual equality, for women's rights, and for the end of male privileges. In all the furor surrounding this struggle, many Catholics have forgotten that sometimes a Mass is "just" a Mass.

The furor will not go away with time nor will the angry ones be sufficiently appeased with more female readers, more female helpers in the sanctuary, and more music that "women are supposed to like," because the modernized rites of the Catholic church — or at least the way they have been presented in most places — boldly flaunt the maleness of the priest and his male privilege. The rapport banter at the beginning of Mass, the enthronement of the priest in the center of the sanctuary, the elimination of musical "distractions" (especially of the "churchy" type), and the nonstop amplification inexorably force the worshiper's attention to the priest's face and body, both of which are male. The worshiper is repeatedly directed to look at the maleness of the man who presides.

If a priest ever lost his mind and decided to begin Mass by singing a solo version of *Stouthearted Men*, a large number of women in the congregation would patiently endure the fiasco and pray for the poor man. A few other women would boil for hours about male chauvinism in the church. But perhaps three or four women in that congregation would go out of their way to tell the priest how wonderful he was, how so very clever and original was his song. They would implore him to do it again.

This is the way the system works.

Exeunt Omnes

I once met a scholar who told me about a saintly priest he knows in West Germany. This dedicated priest must tend to the spiritual needs of people in three or more rural parishes, since he is the only priest in the area. He starts his weekend schedule with a Saturday evening Mass in the parish he calls home; as soon as that is finished, he dashes off to another Saturday Mass in another village. On Sunday he finds himself saying one Mass after another. By the time he gets back to his home parish for the liturgy on Sunday evening, the man is so exhausted he can barely talk. Fortunately, his friend and neighbor, a Lutheran pastor, always helps him out by giving the sermon at this last Sunday Mass.

The person who told me about this interesting arrangement remembered the days when there was a priest in every parish in this part of Germany and a few to spare for the missions or study abroad.

A few decades from now someone might come across a copy of this book, read its more serious passages, and become exceedingly agitated. My earnest pondering could strike some future readers as monstrously irrelevant in a church weakened by a shortage of priests. ("While the Titanic was sinking, he was fretting about the decor in the lounge for first-class passengers.") Unless history takes an unexpected turn, the Roman Catholic priest of the future may become a sort of little bishop who hops from parish to parish on his way through the area.

How severe is the shortage of priests today? Almost as severe as the shortage of trained church musicians.

Nobody has the exact statistics, but anecdotal evidence and at least one preliminary study show that churches of all denominations and synagogues are having a difficult time finding someone competent to play the organ and train a choir.[5] For one thing, conservatories and music schools do not attract enough students to fill all the available jobs. (They never did.) But, more important, society as a whole does not seem to place a high value on the musical education of the young. Not long ago, in nearly every middle-class living room there was a piano; children in the family, especially the girls, were expected to endure some form of music lessons. In today's living rooms we find an elaborate stereo system, not a piano, and the children are much too busy with classes in gymnastics and so on to be bothered with piano lessons.

The Catholic church in the United States never used to worry about a shortage of musicians. It was assumed that, by divine providence, there would always be a plentiful supply of women who would be willing to play the organ for the parish. These women, motivated by dedication to the church and grateful for the opportunity to get away from their noisy families for a few hours, could be paid less than a pittance. Today, the women of the parish are trying to hold down full-time jobs which help to pay for the mortgage and the second car. On Sunday morning they want to sleep late.

Outstanding or even decently mediocre church musicians (the sort of people who can actually read and play music put in front of them) are not available in great numbers. Catholic parishes sometimes have to rely on the services of the first volunteer who walks in the door, regardless of talent. Occasionally I hear of a parish (maybe a big, healthy place) which has hired a music director who cannot read a note of music; nobody else was available, supposedly.

But the odd thing is that there are plenty of eager, highly skilled church musicians "out there." They work for businesses; they teach; they can eat three meals a day. They found out a long time ago that, if they dedicated their lives to church music (for any denomination), they would starve. The sad reality is that most churches and synagogues cannot afford to pay for the kind of music they want. To cite one prominent example, in the whole New York City area, only about thirty houses of worship (all denominations) can afford full-time music directors. The rest have to find ways to put together a full-time music program with part-time help.

Some resourceful clergymen get around the harsh economic reality that every church of every denomination faces by using a secret to their advantage: the pleasure principle. You can coax a musician to take a low-paying job if he or she can get some musical fun out of it. A Catholic cathedral or parish which advertises for a new music director will receive a stack of applications if it indicates that the job will give the employee a little money and a lot of musical pleasure. Those "lost" musicians who dropped out of the system will suddenly reappear and make all kinds of personal sacrifices, if they are allowed to play or conduct at least a tiny amount of interesting music, under favorable conditions. (More volunteer singers for the choir will also appear out of nowhere.) But when I read the job notices for music directors at Catholic parishes, so often the advertisement gives off all kinds of sour signals to the effect that pleasure will not be tolerated. The ad warns that the applicant "must be familiar with the liturgical reforms of the Second Vatican Council," and this means that the employee's only job will be to "get the congregation to sing" music of the lowest common denominator. Anyone who shows the slightest interest in musical ambitions or Catholicism's musical treasures from the past will not be hired.

An acquaintance of mine, one of those "born musicians," studied music at a university, became a crackerjack organist, and then went out into the world to earn his living in his new career: selling insurance. For at least forty or fifty hours a week he works hard in the insurance business. When he comes home, he has to take the children to the orthodontist or mow the grass or do whatever chore is lined up for him. Somehow he found the time to help his Catholic parish with music by playing the organ. The shrewd old pastor kept the services of my acquaintance by letting him and the choir director make a musical splash a few times a year: maybe some chant, maybe a choral setting of the Kyrie, maybe a big hymn which involved congregation, choir, brass, and organ. This "fun" music (mostly for choir and in small amounts) was like a yeast which improved the whole mood and self-esteem of the parish. Then, one day, after the old pastor retired, there arose a new pharaoh, a new pastor who lectured everyone on the supreme importance of the attentive congregation singing *continuously* and on the obligation of church musicians to be "flexible." (In practical terms this meant that the reformed-folk repertory, such as the songs of the St. Louis Jesuits, would provide nearly all of the parish's musical repertory.) My acquaintance promptly quit, "dropped out of the system," and devoted more time to insurance; the choir director also quit. The new pastor was puzzled when very few qualified people applied for the job of parish music director; eventually, he had to settle for someone who could barely play a keyboard.

The Catholic bishops have done their best to promote the cause of good music in the church. Many of them, for example, subsidize workshops and summer programs for musicians. They have hired some of the finest musicians in the land to take care of the music in their cathedrals. They have proved that the "official" church cares about music. But down at the level of the parishes, so often, in spite of all the effusive rhetoric, church music is treated as a chore which must be done without pleasure and definitely without any application of the intellect; when it comes to hiring music directors, many of the parish liturgists and pastors want obedient robots who will quickly get everybody through the drudgery of the required songs. There will always be a shortage of human robots.

On June 1, 1988, the Vatican issued a set of instructions entitled *Directory for Sunday Celebrations in the Absence of a Priest*. Every diocese and maybe every parish in the United States should also have on file a parallel document for music: contingency plans for liturgical music sung in the absence of a well-trained organist. There are just not enough qualified organist-music directors to go around.

Congregational singing without the support of an organ is not necessarily a "bad thing," a sign of defeat. After all, the Byzantines managed nicely without the organ, and the Orthodox churches still do. In Europe, between the Rhine river and the Russian border, unaccompanied congregational singing in Catholic churches is not unusual and it can be quite impressive. There is a certain raw power in the sound of a congregation singing without instrumental support, a certain energy from people absorbing the strength of the vibrations they are creating. The Catholic parish which has no choice and must ask the congregation to sing without accompaniment from time to time might discover that this "failure" has put new life into singing. In fact, the use of unaccompanied "barefoot music" or "peasant music" (as the exception, not the rule) could be a blessing in the disguise of artistic poverty. This type of music would definitely invigorate congregational singing in some parishes, but only when three "ingredients" are in place: (1) a music leader who has good training and a good sense of tempo, (2) a support group, such as a choir or maybe just a cadre of singing parishioners who agree to sit in one area of the pews, and (3) a repertory of plain music which does not need harmonic accompaniment. (This music is found in the best hymnals.) One "ingredient" which is not at all helpful is the guitar. Except perhaps in a small room, the guitar is demonstrably ineffective as a support for congregational singing.[6]

Alas, this type of "primitive" church music, which will be desperately needed someday, has almost no chance of developing in America. The American Catholic has come to think of congregational singing as something that absolutely must be performed by a songleader behind a microphone — someone who gets an obscene thrill from hearing his or her own amplified voice obliterating the sound of the congregation. The amplified voice of a songleader crooning into a microphone without any organ support — one of the most repulsive noises a Christian could ever encounter in church — would turn the charmingly "primitive" into the sadistically barbaric. Another problem is that the contemporary Catholic is supposed to reaffirm the principles of Vatican II by singing "contemporary" songs of the reformed-folk variety (e.g., *Be Not Afraid*) or the newer hymns with refrains (e.g., *Gifts of Finest Wheat*). In almost every case, the melodies of these songs are like drifting aromas which arise from the complex harmonic vegetation underneath; separate the melody from the harmonic background and the vocal part sounds enormously silly. Under "primitive" conditions, a congregation could sing a little chant melody or something like *Holy God, We Praise Thy Name* but that repertory of cocktail lounge "contemporary" songs needs all kinds of accompaniment props to keep it from collapsing.

Somebody could write an inspirational book about people who used to convert to Catholicism because Gregorian chant first attracted them to the church. Each chapter would have the same outline: an individual who is not Catholic happens to visit a monastery or nunnery or seminary, is flabbergasted by the chant, and within a week asks to be received into the church. (Of course, it was not the musical notes themselves that captivated these converts but the way of life which those notes symbolized.)

Somebody could write another book about individuals who lowered their estimation of Roman Catholicism because of the kind of music they heard recently in a monastery or nunnery or seminary. The atheist, for example, will look at a group of nuns floating from one "contemporary" song to another and instantly reach a verdict: "arrested adolescent development." The Protestant will observe seminarians trying to get everyone roused up with the exhilaration of the new Triumphalism and conclude: "The television evangelists can do this better." Even the devout member of the Roman Catholic laity will watch seminarians or monks or nuns wallowing in the goo of some "contemporary" song and quietly affirm: "Yes, this is where the church dumps its misfits."

"Why is the church running out of priests and nuns?" There are hundreds of reasons and a small but significant one is music. When it comes to music, all too often the seminaries, convents, and monasteries take careful aim and then deliberately shoot themselves in the foot. They deliberately promote music which has lots of sincerity but no crust, no grit, no credibility, no indication that it is wired directly to the deepest secrets of the universe. On a subconscious level, the music says that there is nothing special or distinctive or "heroic" about the religious life.

9

The End

Question: What is the condition of music in American Catholic churches today?

Answer: It has never been better and it has never been worse.

On one side of this paradox are the many cathedrals which were once immense, little-used barns but are now thriving centers of religious activity, thanks in part to the magnificent music that the bishops have encouraged. Many of the cathedrals are in a silver age of liturgical music, choral and congregational.

Silver costs money, to be sure. It takes a financial commitment to pay for music directors, organists, cantors, printed music, and all the rest. But the remarkable thing about this silver age is that volunteers help to make it possible. I have heard so many stories about the enthusiastic unpaid choirs composed of volunteers who give up an entire Sunday morning just for the opportunity to rehearse and sing good music. This enthusiasm is infectious and spreads to the congregation.

Traces of silver can also be found in the parishes, even the ordinary ones. More American Catholic congregations are singing and hearing more good music than they ever did in the past. Christian fervor, of course, is not measured by the number or the quality of musical notes, but Roman Catholics are members of the human race and their human activities are open to measurement, as well as analysis. Seen from this "human perspective," the music of American Catholicism has never been better, not because everything is perfect but because the church seems to be striving admirably to reach a musical Grand Consensus worthy of a large, diverse church which calls itself universal.

In this Grand Consensus, this harmony of diversity, one parish will

162

use the sung Latin Mass, while another will strip folk/"contemporary" music of its adolescent narcissism and develop a much healthier version of this style. Most parishes will confine themselves, more or less, to the "mediocre" music in the best hymnals and the parishes which do not always have the services of an organist will function very well with "primitive" unaccompanied music. Everyone will think it perfectly natural that one church, a place with unusual human resources, will confound the complacent and open its doors to the whole world with a brief Mozart Mass, accompanied by orchestra; a block away, music from an African-American or Latino tradition will thrive in another church. Everyone will stop trying to electrify every liturgy with loud musical excitement. Everyone will take pride in the sense of unity through diversity.

On the other side of this paradox, things have never been worse because "forces" within the church are trying to make sure that this musical Grand Consensus will die in its initial stages; they actively prevent the music of American Catholicism from going through a normal evolution.

First of all, there is the "force" of the priest — dead center behind the altar, dead center on his throne. The man is under enormous pressure. Music in the Catholic service used to rise like incense; now, with this constant centering of the priest, the music seems to be projected onto him, as if he were a movie screen. This "projecting" is always going to make him so uncomfortable that he will work vigilantly to "hold down" music and keep it from "getting out of hand." Little musical ambitions which might seem harmless in a Lutheran parish are shot on sight by many Catholic pastors because the better the music, the more pressure it puts on them.

Then there is the matter of convenience. Church music, especially congregational singing, always begins as a sensuous experience, not an intellectual one; it flourishes wherever the congregation can feel the sensuous pleasure of musical vibrations, and that takes time. The clever parish will set aside at least one liturgy where the music, expanding to "normal" proportions, can reach its full potential; another liturgy, for convenience, will proceed with no music at all. But it seems that in this the age of the transistor and electronic miniaturization parishes prefer the solution of quick "convenience music" for *every* liturgy: little doses of disagreeable musical medicine on a teaspoon. The result is a constant emphasis on hurry music which seldom gets a chance to work its way under the skin.[1]

Ah, but what guarantees absolutely that musical matters will stay at their worst is the ominous evolution of the "affliction" liturgist — from the person who helps to the officer who enforces conformity, from the expert to the *disciplinarian*. We can see the more advanced liturgical disciplinarian at work in Bernard Huijbers's *The Performing Audience: Six and a Half Essays on Music and Song in Liturgy* (1974, 1980), a book which is sometimes quoted with a reverence usually reserved for scripture.

Huijbers, a Dutch composer and ex-Jesuit, assumes the tone of voice of the prophet and begins his prophetic monolog by deploring a built-in conflict between music and liturgy. The sort of musicians hired to provide music for a church, he says, are classically trained elitists laden with too much historical consciousness; they think their job is to convert ordinary people to the love of historical, classical music for the church. But ordinary people in the pews equate classical music with "strangeness." The strange traditional music of the church alienates its "audience." Instead of trying to convert Catholics to a certain type of historical music, musicians should go to popular music and learn from its successful techniques. If pop music and folk music are properly synthesized for use in the church, the result will be an "elementary" style of music which will release the participatory energies of the common people. Naturally, all obstructions to this participation through "elementary" music must be removed. All Latin Gregorian chant will have to go. All compositions in Latin from the Middle Ages to the twentieth century must be forever forgotten.

More important than getting rid of all old music is getting rid of the God "who is sought too much beyond our world," the distant deity who is adored with fear and must be surrounded with spooky musical strangeness. "Henceforth, liturgy and church music must speak of this world, in a truly intelligible vernacular, in the music of the people," not in the music of a stern monarch-God.

Whole pages of *The Performing Audience* are so idealistically beautiful that they could be recited as a soliloquy in an acting class or even chanted solemnly. The alert reader, however, will see through the haze of utopian idealism and want to cross-examine Huijbers, to determine if he is really talking about planet earth. For example, *which* "music of the people" will lead the Catholic congregation to liturgical bliss? (This music comes in many varieties.) In recent decades, popular music has been almost exclusively soloist material for famous performers. How can this "star music" be transformed into a much easier "assembly music"? Huijbers concedes that the human race is a fabulously complex assortment of distinct individuals but then he reduces this complexity by declaring that nearly all individuals are "musical laymen" — all alike, all with the same low musical perceptions, all from the same cookie-cutter. It is difficult to take him seriously when he asserts that all of these common musical laymen will respond uniformly and positively to his idea of "elementary" music: something rhythmically snappy, precise, neat, tidy, and very Dutch.

Huijbers is correct when he says, in effect, that most people will not bother to attend a concert of sacred classical music, but he forgets that those same "ordinary" individuals will pack themselves into a Catholic church in order to hear, for example, Mozart's *Coronation Mass* sung at a liturgy. The man down the street would have to be forced, at gunpoint, to sit through a concert of Gregorian chant sung perfectly by music students at a university, but I remember the days when the farmers and the laborers — the "ordinary" people — would come from miles around to hear vespers in a Benedictine monastery. I also remember the days when a Catholic congregation listened to this "strange," historical, classical music and went home with an imperfect but important message: "We are special. We are people of destiny."

Perhaps the most disturbing aspect of *The Performing Audience* is the author's conflict of interest. Every sentence in the book subtly leads the reader to the conclusion that the climax of liturgical history is to be found in the music of Bernard Huijbers. Even the American publisher of this book is not exactly disinterested; it happens to be the world's major publisher of music in the folk/"contemporary" manner; it has a commercial interest in persuading the Catholic population to forget history and seek its musical-spiritual nourishment in "contemporary" songs. All the missalette publishers and the publishers of "contemporary" music can make substantial amounts of money when they sell music protected by a copyright which they own. They have no financial incentive for promoting traditional music in the public domain, no matter how good it is.

The musical Grand Consensus is being pulled apart by the liturgical and musical disciplinarians who are convinced that the Second Vatican Council wiped the slate clean and established a new musical orthodoxy, to which all must conform. Yes, they do acknowledge that there should be diversity, provided the resulting music sounds like the orthodox participatory music that is the direct result of the council.

But what does this orthodox music sound like? That depends on the liturgical guru-disciplinarian. Some will insist that Bernard Huijbers has all the answers. Follow his example. (His rigorously tiresome music is indeed "elementary" — some of it reminds me of doorbell chimes — but those babbling, wordy texts can only be sung by a congregation which has first prepared itself with a course in speedreading.) Other disciplinarians declare that it is not Huijbers but the famous groups who have settled the matter for all time. On and on the controversy goes.

The future belongs to the guru of the moment. There is only one point of agreement: most of the old, preconciliar music must be dropped down the memory hole. Music from the time of error must come to an end, in order to make room for the musical promised land — which happens to consist of music owned or controlled by rich publishers.

The songleader has given the order. I must sing *Here I Am, Lord*. Everyone who is a genuine, devout, actively participating Catholic knows and loves this song, I am told. You are an elitist reactionary, a mere cultural Catholic, if you dislike it. Pretty soon, all church music will sound like this. Take it or leave it.

While I am standing there having my nose rubbed into *Here I Am, Lord*, I always recall something which adds to my discomfort: one brief section of the melody reminds me of the theme song for *The Brady Bunch*, a popular television situation comedy. (The musical notes for "Is it I, Lord? I have heard you calling in the night" are, by coincidence, similar to the music for "Here's the story, of a lovely lady who was bringing up three very lovely girls.") Two thousand years of music for the Christian church, including some fine recent contributions, and all of it gets shoved aside for *The Brady Bunch*.

The disciplinarians thought they had everything figured out. Sabotage the Grand Consensus; cut down the size of that remote grandfather/king God and his "strange" music; decapitate the aristocracy of the old church music — then, miraculously, the perfect participation music would descend from the heavens. But what the disciplinarians never seem to realize is that the "ordinary" people (Huijbers's "musical laymen") are not going to wait around for somebody to announce the arrival of the musical utopia; without any points of reference to guide them, without any higher artistic ideals, many of those "ordinary" people will take matters into their own hands and pull everything down to the level of *The Brady Bunch*.

Do you have a reason to be angry at the Catholic church? Would you like an opportunity to throw a custard pie at it? Please take a ticket and wait your turn. The line is very long.

Ahead of you in line will be one very distinctive group: the liturgical and musical disciplinarians, the rapport priests, and their sympathizers. In some cases they are men and women who joined the group because they needed a career change; in other cases they are "new people" who have emerged from a midlife crisis. Whatever the reason, as part of their personal therapy, they had to kill that symbolic "parent" who had oppressed them in the first part of their lives — the church before "the changes." The hated parent's voice was music. At this point in its history, the Catholic church needs the advantages of a vigorous debate about music; it needs to retain all that is enduring and useful from its musical heritage and, at the same time, move toward the future. But rational debate is extremely difficult because so many of the church's trend-setters and official spokesmen in this area seem to be people who are fighting their own war within themselves.

In my research for this book, I went through recent Catholic journals and reviewed the speeches by assorted disciplinarians. I even recalled a homily by a member of one of the famous "groups." So many, many words. The ideals in those words were shouted loudly: *The church's worship consists of the proclamation of salvation in Jesus Christ, the community's response,* and so forth. But often those high ideals were a veneer covering a sinister agenda: the remaking of each individual Catholic into a *cultural conformist.* The "old" Catholic church respected and feared the anarchy of "the people." The "new" disciplinarians are going to shape each Catholic into someone who will approach God in the one and only *correct* way. There is, however, some disagreement about the ultimate shape of this new Catholic. Should he or she be a kitsch-person who will pray according to the cultural values of *The Brady Bunch*? Should all Catholics be trained to become attentive, thrilled members of Mr. Nice Guy's audience? Should they all be forced to become charismatics? Should they all be forced to sing?

"Liturgical Renewal," "postconciliar," and "participation," once noble ideals, are on the verge of becoming symbols of coercion. The laity, especially those who are not singing, quietly resent this.

Appendix:
Good Advice

"Anybody can complain, especially musicians and intellectuals. What do you people want anyway? Think about the future, instead of griping about the past and present. Why don't you make some positive suggestions about improving music and congregational singing?"

Whenever I am hit with this kind of challenge, I immediately go into a reflex action and start dispensing good advice. Not a word of the advice is original with me — musicians have been making these same points for years — but my suggestions are usually received as if they are a new and puzzling theory which one must approach with extreme caution. Here goes:

1. Everything begins with the pastor. His constructive involvement in planning is crucial. If the pastor or any other priest chants the liturgical dialogs with the congregation (without amplification), he gives congregational singing a significant boost. If the presider's chair is someplace other than dead center in the sanctuary, all of the liturgical music will, by some strange process, sound like an important matter.

2. Let the assembly hear its own voice, not the voice of an ego behind a microphone. Restrain the amplification. That sound of a cantor's voice sailing above the sound of the congregation and organ is perverse. It intimidates. Melt down the microphones or beat them into ploughshares.

3. Put a reasonably good musician in charge of the music. If an organist is not available, at least hire someone talented who can lead a choir. As far as possible, pay a reasonable salary. (Old saying: "You pay peanuts, you get monkeys.") Donations will increase as the music improves.

4. Occasionally, sing unaccompanied music supported only by a choir. Parishes with limited resources can produce some rugged yet impressive sounds with plain unaccompanied singing of plain music.

169

5. Maybe once a week, maybe once a month, let the music reach its full potential; let the entire assembly sense that it is doing its best to pray in song. Pull all the musical resources together and make a joyful noise in a genuine sung liturgy. But (and this is crucial) also provide another "quieter" liturgy with no music at all or less than a smattering. Giving the congregation a choice creates the impression that singing is a personal commitment and not an inescapable chore. Spreading the parish's musical resources thinly, in order to cover four to seven weekend liturgies, only creates the impression of something very cheap.

6. Hymns and songs are useful, but they can die from overuse. To keep them fresh, omit them sometimes. Catholicism's real musical destiny is in the singing of the actual texts of the liturgy, not songs which are dropped into the service. A few times a year, listening to the Gospel being chanted (without amplification) or singing the Penitential Rite can sock a congregation with an impact that is hard to forget; two perfunctory stanzas of *Praise to the Lord* lost any impact they might have had years ago.

7. Avoid "contemporary" songs that sound palpitatingly romantic (e.g., *That There May Be Bread*). Avoid the songs that go racing along at the speed of one hundred and eighty words a minute (e.g., *Gather Us In*). This type of music may be biblical or even beautiful at times but it is miserably difficult and discouraging for a congregation to sing. If these songs are requested for a wedding, funeral, or special event, by all means use them. If a sizeable number of people want this music, keep it segregated at a weekly folk Mass; do not "blend" this repertory with standard church music. The competition between an "upstairs Mass" and "downstairs Mass" will produce quality; blending produces mush.

8. Encourage music as an art. This can take many forms. Maybe have the parish choir join together with neighboring parishes for a special Advent Vespers or Mass with the combined choirs. If the parish is overflowing with talent, maybe, on a couple of occasions every year, have the choir alone sing a Kyrie or Gloria (everything within reason and within proportion, of course). The change of pace will give new meaning to the sung words; the challenge will give the choir a few necessary vitamins.

9. Good congregational singing begins with a sense of beloved familiarity and the best way to develop that familiarity is with an outstanding hymnal/service book which will stay in the pews for more than a generation (maybe next to the missalette, maybe by itself).

All the good advice comes together in the hymnal, and, at this point in history, the following four are among the best:

Worship III (G.I.A. Publications)
7404 South Mason Avenue
Chicago, Illinois 60638

The Catholic Liturgy Book (Helicon)
200 East Biddle Street
Baltimore, Maryland 21202

Hymns, Psalms, and Spiritual Canticles (BACS Publishing Co.)
P.O. Box 167
Belmont, Massachusetts 02178

The Collegeville Hymnal (The Liturgical Press)
St. John's Abbey
Collegeville, Minnesota 56321

Worship III has received high praise for being one of the most enduring and nourishing song books for an English-speaking congregation in
the United States, and with good reason; it contains some fine music.
I could guarantee in writing that a congregation would quickly fall in
love with the primitive "foundation music" in this book: for example,
the chant adaptations by Richard Proulx and Father Gerard Farrell and
the new chant of David Hurd and John Lee. (The guarantee requires a
solid choral support and the absence of someone bellowing the music
into a microphone.) This "foundation" music is not at all glamorous or
exciting but, when backed up by some sort of choir, it will sound as impressive as rolling thunder. Once that "foundation music" is in place, a
congregation will have the confidence to add on other compositions.

Hymns, Psalms, and Spiritual Canticles, edited by Theodore Marier, is
the great noble lion of the newer Catholic hymnals in the United States.
This impressive book has been criticized for the excessive number of neo-
Gregorian chants composed by the editor and the ambitious repertory,
but every member of every Catholic choir in the United States should
have a copy of this publication as a source of an alternate repertory. In the
ideal world, Worship III would supply the core repertory for a church, but
the choir could frequently turn to Hymns, Psalms, and Spiritual Canticles
for a wide selection of first-class service music which the congregation
could easily pick up "by ear," without ever holding the book.

The four hymnals mentioned above are signs of an amazing vitality
in the American Catholic community. These publications belong in the
parishes not just because they are significant artistic accomplishments
but because the editors of these books understood exactly what kind
of "sound" creates and encourages good congregational singing. (There

are, I have to warn the reader, annoying imperfections in all of these hymnals.) The editors also shrewdly exploited the power of history and included some compositions from Catholicism's rich tradition of chant. This traditional music encourages that "pride of ownership" which is so important for a congregation's self-esteem.

The good advice could go on for pages but all of it comes down to the simple matter of respect for people — their intelligence, ability to learn, religious aspirations, limits of patience, and right to be left alone. The attempt to make Catholics loud and excited liturgical participants by means of loud and excited trendy music will work here and there, but for the most part it will always be a form of mental cruelty. The greatest and most successful results will occur whenever the music merely sounds like an inevitable and organic part of the ritual.

Good musical advice is one thing; implementing it in the Catholic church today is a little like trying to plant a simple but healthy crop in the middle of a hurricane. The winds seem to be coming from all directions: from the liturgical utopians, functionalists, and futurists, from the lovers of kitsch with convenience, from the cult of priestly personality, and above all from those pathetically insecure bullies behind a microphone, the loudmouthed songleaders. Musical "good advice" — the accumulated practical wisdom of the ages, the living traditions Roman Catholic, Orthodox, and Protestant Christianity — constantly reminds the congregation that the immortal God entered human history, in order to bring redemption and a message of love. But all the musical "good advice" in the world is wasted on a people who think of themselves as the most important aspect of worship. It may be impossible to have any productive dialog with people who can see nothing wrong with the vulgar pantheism of the "Voice of God" song and who constantly crave liturgical music which tells about how they are being absorbed into the very Godhead. It may also be impossible for musical "good advice" to get past the front door of the thousands of Catholic churches and chapels where the message of liturgy goes something like this: "I am here, God, and I am great. I have loved myself with an everlasting love. And all of us here are one big I, formed by rapport into a gathered community which offers itself to you. Now let us all share the whole-wheat bread."

Notes

3. The Irish Way

1. Letter to the author, December 20, 1973.

2. See Paul Hume, *Catholic Church Music* (New York: Dodd, Mead, 1956), p. 45. As part of his research for this book, Hume, a prominent music critic, asked 137 Catholic choir directors to list the composers in their current repertoire (mostly Latin Masses and motets). Yon's name was at the top of the list. No other composer came close to him in popularity.

3. Early examples of this repertory can be found in *Favorite Songs of the Nineties: Complete Original Sheet Music for 89 Songs*, ed. Robert A. Fremont (New York: Dover, 1973).

4. J. Vincent Higginson, *Handbook for American Catholic Hymnals: Survey* (Fort Worth, TX: Hymn Society of America, 1976); *History of American Catholic Hymnals: Survey and Background* (Springfield, OH: Hymn Society of America, 1982). See also Charles Hughes, Albert Christ-Janer, and Carlton Sprague Smith, *American Hymns Old and New* (New York: Columbia University Press, 1980).

5. On June 19, 1986, the daughter of President and Mrs. Kennedy, Caroline Kennedy, was married to Mr. Edwin Schlossberg. For this event the Chamber Singers from the New England Conservatory of Music sang classical choral selections.

6. At this funeral Mass a choir briefly sang the *Libera Me* by Lorenzo Perosi.

7. This Mass in Holy Cross Cathedral was recorded in its entirety: *A Solemn Pontifical Requiem Mass in Memory of John Fitzgerald Kennedy* (RCA Victor, LSC 7030).

In his diary, George Templeton Strong (1820-75) reported that Mozart's *Requiem* was sung, with orchestral accompaniment, at a liturgy in St. Peter's Roman Catholic church (New York City) in 1839. See Vera Brodsky Lawrence, *Strong on Music*, vol. 1, *Resonances (1836–1850)* (New York: Oxford University Press, 1988), p. 13. By 1963, however, nearly every American Catholic thought it was blasphemous even to suggest that Mozart's *Requiem* or anything like it could ever be used in an American Catholic church.

173

4. De-Ritualization

1. Jan (Johann, Johan) Huizinga, *Homo Ludens: A Study of the Play Element in Culture* (Boston: Beacon Press, 1964); quotations from pp. 17, 18, 19.

2. For more information about this colorful character, see his autobiography, *A Degree of Difference* (New York: Farrar, Straus & Giroux, 1969). Well before Vatican II even met, the congregation at Corpus Christi was energetically singing at the High Mass every Sunday — supposedly the only parish in the archdiocese where such things happened.

3. This essay is reprinted in *H. L. Mencken's Smart Set Criticism*, ed. William H. Nolte (Washington: Regnery/Gateway, 1987), pp. 88-94. Part of this essay is reprinted in *The Vintage Mencken*, ed. Alistair Cooke (New York: Vintage/Random House, 1955), pp. 137–40.

4. During televised Masses it is now *de rigueur* to have a commentator whispering explanations from beginning to end, even when the Mass is in the vernacular. Discreet explanations are, to be sure, always welcome, especially for something like a Latin Mass from the Vatican (with subtitles for translations), but most of these commentaries tend to be nervous left-brain apologies for the right-brain poetry of the Mass.

5. Ego Renewal

1. The originator of this expression is Robert J. Batastini.

2. For a description of Beethoven's efforts to make his *Missa Solemnis* conform to tradition, see Warren Kirkendale, "New Roads to Old Ideas in Beethoven's *Missa Solemnis*," *The Musical Quarterly*, vol. 56, no. 4 (October 1970): 665–701; reprinted in *The Creative World of Beethoven*, ed. Paul Henry Lang (New York: W. W. Norton, 1971).

3. For more information about the Medieval cantors who got carried away with their brilliant virtuosity, see William Dalglish, "The Origin of the Hocket," *Journal of the American Musicological Society*, vol. 31, no. 1 (Spring 1978): 3–20.

4. In the mid-1960s a distinguished German musicologist and an even more distinguished member of the Vatican's musical establishment toured the United States. At the end of their tour, during dinner with one of my teachers, they explained that, although they did not know what to make of this new folk music with guitars (downstairs), they could live with it. But what really appalled them was the pusillanimous noise that American Catholics at the time called "traditional" music for the church (upstairs).

5. Occasionally, an old hymn will contain divine words but they are set off by quotation marks. The newer "Voice of God" song does not make any typographical distinction between the human and the divine voice.

6. Later editions of this publication have been greatly improved.

7. The current theory is that, in the old days, the congregation was passively inspired by "escapist" choral music; nobody "participated." In reality, however, listening to a choir elegantly decorate each syllable of the Gloria from, let us say, Palestrina's *Missa Papae Marcelli*, sitting there and patiently waiting for each

word to unfold — that too was hard, sweat-making work. It was not all beauty and ecstasy.

6. The People

1. Mark Searle: "The Notre Dame Study of Catholic Parish Life," *Worship*, vol. 60, no. 4 (July 1986): 319, 322.

2. Council of Trent, Session 22, September 1562. My translation.

3. This distinction between an "actual church music" (the heritage of Christian art music, which the church no longer needs) and "utility music" was attacked by Joseph Cardinal Ratzinger, the Vatican's prefect of the Congregation for the Doctrine of the Faith and chief watchdog for doctrinal orthodoxy. See his essay "On the Theological Basis of Church Music," in *The Feast of Faith* (San Francisco: Ignatius Press, 1986), pp. 97–126; I have used this essay for translations of the controversial commentaries by Rahner and Vorgrimler. In an odd twist of fate, the arch-conservative Cardinal Ratzinger has become so identified with this issue that some people think he is the one who originally made this distinction between useless art music ("actual") and the music which Vatican II supposedly wanted ("utility").

4. Archabbott Rembert Weakland, O.S.B., "Music as Art in Liturgy," *Worship*, vol. 41, no. 1 (January 1967): 5–15.

5. Miriam Therese Winter, "Catholic Church Music: A Theological Perspective," *Pastoral Music*, vol. 7, no. 6 (June 1983): 26.

6. Edward Foley, "The Cantor in Historical Perspective," *Worship*, vol. 56, no. 3 (May 1982): 213.

7. See "Letters to the Editor," *The American Organist*, vol. 21, no. 2 (February 1987): 34.

8. Edwin O'Connor, *The Edge of Sadness* (Boston: Little Brown, 1961), p. 17.

7. The Stick and the Carrot

1. William M. C. Lam: *Perception and Lighting as Formgivers for Architecture* (New York: McGraw-Hill, 1977); *Sunlighting as Formgiver for Architecture* (New York: Von Nostrand Reinhold, 1986).

2. The credibility of the ICEL's translations was totally demolished in Richard Toporoski, "The Language of Worship," *Communio: International Catholic Review*, vol. 4, no. 3 (Fall 1977): 226–260; reprinted in *Worship*, vol. 52, no. 6 (November 1978): 489–508. Using scholarly and critical methods, Toporoski shows how the ICEL's translations, besides being inept, constantly garble the message of Catholic theology. In all fairness, it must be remembered that the ICEL was under pressure to put out its translations very quickly.

3. Kevin W. Irwin, "Method in Liturgical Theology: Context Is Text," unpublished article, footnote 25; scheduled to be published in *Église et Théologie* (Ottawa). I am very grateful to Father Irwin for granting me permission to quote from his paper.

4. For the best and most thorough analysis of the rock phenomenon, see Robert Pattison, *The Triumph of Vulgarity: Rock Music in the Mirror of Romanticism* (New York: Oxford University Press, 1987). Pattison's commentary on the passionate pantheism inherent in the whole rock phenomenon should be kept in mind when listening to the "Voice of God" folk songs for worship. I should confess that I like rock, but I despise it whenever it becomes totalitarian.

5. See John Bellairs, *St. Fidgeta and Other Parodies* (New York: Macmillan, 1966). The title story, "St. Fidgeta: Her Life and Amazing Times," originally appeared in *The Critic*, vol. 23, no. 6 (June-July 1965): 46–50.

6. Alec Guinness: *Blessings in Disguise* (New York: Knopf, 1985), p. 45.

7. Pat Conroy, "Confessions of an Ex-Catholic," reprinted in John P. Ferré and Steven E. Pauley, *Rhetorical Patterns: An Anthology of Contemporary Essays* (Columbus, OH: Charles E. Merrill, 1981), p. 41.

8. *U.S. Catholic*, vol. 52, no. 6 (June 1987): 8.

9. Greeley's comments on this study were given at a press conference; see the *New York Times*, Wednesday, June 10, 1987, A22.

8. Mr. Nice Guy

1. Robert J. Power, *Jesus Help Me: A New Prayer Book for a Very Young Child* (New York: Regina Press, 1939), p. 30.

2. M. Francis Mannion, "Concert Masses: A Reply," *Liturgy 80*, vol. 19, no. 6 (August-September 1988): 10–11. This journal is published by the archdiocese of Chicago.

3. For an appraisal of this lectionary see Robert L. Hurd, "Commentary: A Proposal for Liturgical Language," *Worship*, vol. 61, no. 5 (September 1987): 398–99.

4. Margaret R. Miles, *Image as Insight: Visual Understanding in Western Christianity and Secular Culture* (Boston: Beacon Press, 1985), pp. 25–26.

5. Victoria Sirota, in a study made for the American Guild of Organists in the New England area, gathered more details about this shortage. Her letter to AGO members (December 16, 1985), backed up by several local reports, tells about a grim situation: churches are having a hard time finding organists and very few students are being trained to take over in the next generation. In 1988, the Baptist Church Music Leadership Conference, meeting at the Glorieta (NM) Baptist Conference Center, discussed ways to cope with this shortage of church musicians — a situation described as having reached "crisis proportions." See *United Methodist Reporter*, vol. 135, no. 10 (August 5, 1988): 4.

6. The researchers who visited parishes for the *Notre Dame Study of Catholic Parish Life* observed that "when the organ is played throughout the liturgy, congregational singing is likely to be more wholehearted than when a guitarist played.... In our data, where a guitar is used, people at the front sing well, but people in the back sing less, if at all." *Notre Dame Study*, Report No. 5, p. 7.

9. The End

1. In the Episcopal *Hymnal 1982* there is a setting of "Lord, have mercy" by Schubert in a faultless arrangement by Richard Proulx. The same music appears in the Roman Catholic *Worship III*, except that the editors have snipped off the brief "tag" which Schubert wrote to end the piece. Episcopalians take pleasure in Schubert's five-second meditative cadence; Roman Catholics, however, have to forego such pleasures because it is presumed that some members of the congregation will be looking at their watches.

Index